HARRISON BIRTWISTLE: *THE MASK OF ORPHEUS*

Harrison Birtwistle:
The Mask of Orpheus

JONATHAN CROSS
Christ Church, University of Oxford, UK

ASHGATE

Published by
Ashgate Publishing Limited
Wey Court East
Union Road
Farnham
Surrey, GU9 7PT
England

Ashgate Publishing Company
Suite 420
101 Cherry Street
Burlington
VT 05401-4405
USA

www.ashgate.com

British Library Cataloguing in Publication Data
Cross, Jonathan, 1961–
    Harrison Birtwistle, The mask of Orpheus. – (Landmarks in music since 1950)
    1. Birtwistle, Harrison. Mask of Orpheus.
    I. Title II. Series
    782.1–dc22

Library of Congress Cataloging-in-Publication Data
Cross, Jonathan, 1961–
    Harrison Birtwistle: the Mask of Orpheus / Jonathan Cross.
        p. cm. – (Landmarks in music since 1950)
    Includes bibliographical references and index.
    ISBN 978-0-7546-5383-7 (hardcover: alk. paper) 1. Birtwistle, Harrison. Mask of Orpheus.
    I. Title.
    ML410.B605C77 2007
    780.92–dc22

2009016965

ISBN 9780754653837 (hbk)

Printed and bound in Great Britain by
MPG Books Group, UK

Frontispiece: Philip Langridge as Orpheus in the world premiere production of *The Mask of Orpheus*, English National Opera, London, May 1986 © Zoë Dominic

Note on the CD recording:

As a consequence of copyright restrictions, it has not been possible to include the three-disc recording of *The Mask of Orpheus* with this book. However, NMC Recordings Ltd is offering the CD boxed set to readers for £15.99 (plus postage and packing) instead of the recommended retail price of £25.99. An order form can be found at the back of this book if you would like to take up this offer.

Contents

List of Figures and Illustrations

Figures

Illustrations

List of Music Examples

List of Tables

General Editor's Preface

Since its inception (in 2004), Ashgate's 'Landmarks in Music' series has aimed to promote studies of compositions from a wide range of idioms, genres and countries. Although the choice of works has never been conditioned by popular taste alone, public esteem *has* been a guiding principle – as is the desire to draw on the very best research by younger as well as more established scholars. Indeed the five volumes already published are a testimony to these objectives, with individual books devoted to chamber music, song, and orchestral music (of varying types) by Russian, Hungarian, Dutch, French and British composers. In each case, the authors have refined appropriate analytical strategies and critical methods in order to reveal the cultural and technical significance of their chosen work. Interviews with performers and/or the composer serve to augment the discussions of reception, context and aesthetics within the main text.

In one sense, at least, the present volume represents a slight departure from the format of its predecessors because its subject is an opera – or, to be more precise, one of the most innovative operas written in the second half of the twentieth century. Dealing with visual and dramatic issues as well as with sonorous and motivic parameters poses a special challenge to the author – particularly since the reader may not have seen (or be able to recall details of) a staged production. For this reason, Jonathan Cross, by way of introduction, has provided a masterly account of the evolution of the Orpheus myth before dealing with Harrison Birtwistle's monumental reinterpretation of the subject. Analysis of each of the three acts is prefaced with an outline synopsis of the plot, followed by a chapter that assesses the significance of the work within the context of wider debates surrounding modernism. Interviews with the composer and his librettist further illuminate the nature of their cooperation and the genesis of this most remarkable stage work.

Professor Cross is the author of acclaimed books on Birtwistle and Stravinsky as well as numerous articles and research papers on twentieth-century music and musical analysis. He is uniquely well qualified to write about this opera, and he brings to this book (and the series) a blend of fascinating insights and communicative skills. By a fortunate coincidence, this volume will appear in time to help celebrate Birtwistle's 75th birthday year. His achievements are too many to be listed here but *The Mask of Orpheus* is clearly a landmark in his output – as it is in twentieth-century British music. His most recent works demonstrate that his creative urge is as strong as ever – long may it continue!

Wyndham Thomas
University of Bristol

Acknowledgements

I am deeply indebted to all those who have helped, advised, supported and encouraged me during the preparation of this book, which, like *The Mask of Orpheus*, had a long gestation with many interruptions. I am especially grateful to: Heidi Bishop, Rachel Lynch and colleagues at Ashgate; the series editor, Wyndham Thomas; Mark Gotham for his setting of the music examples; Johanna Blakst, Robert Piencikowski, Tina Kilvio Tüscher and colleagues at the Paul Sacher Stiftung, Basel; Tigger Burton, Peter Ward Jones, Stephen Jordan, Jenny McParland and colleagues at the Faculty of Music and Bodleian Libraries, Oxford; Clare Colvin at the English National Opera Archive; David Ogden at the Archive of the Royal Opera House, Covent Garden; the Glyndebourne Opera Archive; David Allenby and colleagues at Boosey and Hawkes; Rebecca Dawson and colleagues at Universal Edition; Hannah Vlček at NMC Recordings; Arnold Whittall for generously reading and commenting on a draft of the text; Robert Adlington; Craig Ayrey; David Beard; Emma, Alice and Rebecca Cross; Simon Emmerson; Julian Johnson; Christopher Pelling; Andrew Rosner; Jim Samson; Jenny Tamplin; Sir John Tooley; Sir Harrison Birtwistle and Peter Zinovieff.

Research for the book was funded by a Research Leave Award from the Arts and Humanities Research Council. An overseas conference grant from the British Academy enabled me to present some of my early ideas in the USA. The *Music Analysis* Development Fund generously supported the cost of reproduction of the facsimiles. The Faculty of Music at the University of Oxford and Christ Church, Oxford, also supported research and production costs.

Excerpts from *Nenia: the Death of Orpheus* are © Copyright 1974 by Universal Edition (London) Ltd, London/UE 15410. Reproduced by Permission. All rights reserved. International copyright secured.

Excerpts from *The Mask of Orpheus* are © Copyright 1986 by Universal Edition (London) Ltd, London. Reproduced by permission. All rights reserved. International copyright secured.

The excerpt from *26 Orpheus Elegies* is © Copyright 2003 by Boosey & Hawkes Music Publishers Ltd. Reproduced by permission of Boosey & Hawkes Music Publishers Ltd.

Facsimiles of the sketches of *The Mask of Orpheus* in the Harrison Birtwistle Collection are reproduced by permission of the Paul Sacher Stiftung, Basel.

A drawing and chart from the Libretto and Scenario of *The Mask of Orpheus* are reproduced by kind permission of Dr Peter Zinovieff.

Notes on References

References throughout the text to the 'libretto' refer to the published version of the 'Libretto and Scenario' to *The Mask of Orpheus* by Harrison Birtwistle and Peter Zinovieff, dated 'Isle of Raasay, 1978' and published by Universal Edition, London, in 1986. This is a substantially abridged and revised version of the four-volume typescript, entitled 'Explanatory Document (1974)', now housed as part of the Harrison Birtwistle Collection at the Paul Sacher Stiftung, Basel. It should be noted, however, that this 'Explanatory Document' makes the claim that 'There is no libretto as such. The words are a series of poems that fit together into a number of tight structures some of which are musical, some dramatic.' A slightly more extensive version of the 1986 libretto, containing more detailed introductory material and more elaborate stage directions, was published to accompany the release of the NMC CD recording of the work in 1997 (NMC D050). This is referred to in the text as 'libretto 1997'.

References to pages of the sketches and draft scores that are held as part of the Harrison Birtwistle Collection in the Paul Sacher Stiftung, Basel (abbreviated PSS), are identified, wherever possible, by the relevant microfilm spool and slide numbers, e.g., 0531-0215, where the figure before the hyphen refers to one of the three spools containing the material, and the figures after the hyphen identify the particular slide or slides. The original sketches and associated material are contained in some 15 folders plus four boxes of text typescript along with the first fair copy. Much crucial early work in identifying and organizing these materials was undertaken by Robert Piencikowski (Paul Sacher Stiftung) and Michael Taylor (Trinity College, Dublin).

References to the 'score' refer to the three volumes (one for each of the three acts) of full score made available by Universal Edition, London, in 1986. This score (and the associated set of parts) was prepared for the initial run of performances in that year. It was copied in a variety of hands. The score gives no indication of the cuts that have been incorporated into all performances of the work to date. (For details of these cuts, see Appendix B.)

The composer and librettist throughout use the Italian spelling of the name Eurydice as Euridice. I follow the former more common usage, except when quoting directly from the libretto.

Each of the 126 separate structural 'events' in the work (the equivalent of operatic 'numbers') is given a dual designation by the librettist to indicate both its main category (upper case) and its specific name (lower case). There are always three specific forms of each of the 42 categories. The libretto and score show, for example,

1ST DUET OF LOVE
Duet of Hope

which is indicated in the text as 'first Duet of Love (Duet of Hope)'. The appearance of the Duet in Act II is similarly 'second Duet of Love (Duet of Distance)', and so on. A full list of the events can be found in the libretto (pp. 66–7).

Where it is necessary to give the precise register of pitches, the following system of designations is used: c^1 = middle C, c = one octave below middle C, C = two octaves below, C^1 = three octaves below, and so on; c^2 = one octave above middle C, c^3 = two octaves above middle C, etc. Thus, for example, d^1 represents the pitch a tone above middle C, and b♭ represents the pitch a tone below middle C.

Introduction

The 1980s were extraordinary years for new and challenging opera. Adams's *Nixon in China*, Berio's *La vera storia*, Messiaen's *Saint François d'Assise* and Stockhausen's *Donnerstag aus Licht* all received their first performances during this decade, renewing a genre that had been out of favour with the post-war avant-garde since Boulez's battle-cry of 'blow up the opera houses'. Perhaps the most eagerly awaited premiere of all was that which took place at the London Coliseum on 21 May 1986. Harrison Birtwistle and Peter Zinovieff's *The Mask of Orpheus*, on which composer and librettist had been working since the late 1960s, was immediately hailed as the most important musical and theatrical event of its decade. Critics around the world proclaimed it 'the most important opera of the post-war years', 'one of the important works of contemporary music-theatre', a 'grandly scaled, world-defining modernist opera'.[1] Wilfrid Mellers went so far as to assert that '"Opera" will never be the same again'.[2] Eleven years after the premiere, reviewing the recording of the work, Andrew Clements still claimed it as 'not only one of the handful of operatic masterpieces composed in the last quarter century, but also unquestionably the greatest achievement by a British composer in our time'.[3] Now, more than 20 years since it was first heard, and despite (or perhaps because of) a paucity of performances and a complete absence of any further fully staged productions, its standing has grown all the greater. *The Mask of Orpheus* is undoubtedly a central work in Birtwistle's output, and all his subsequent pieces for stage and concert hall demand to be evaluated in its light. But also, increasingly, it has come to be recognized as a key work in the development of music since the Second World War, a work that, like no other, pushed at the boundaries of what was possible in lyrical theatre. In its imaginative fusion of music, song, drama, myth, mime and electronics, it has become a beacon for younger composers, and the object of wide critical and scholarly attention.

But there is more to *The Mask of Orpheus* than just its artistic achievements, remarkable though they are. The work's central themes of time, memory and identity

---

[1] Jorge Calado, *Expresso* (23 August 1986) ('está a ser apontada como a mais importante ópera do pós-guerra'); unattributed review, *Neue Zürcher Zeitung* (25 May 1986) ('eines der bedeutenden Werke des gegenwärtigen Musiktheaters'); John Rockwell, *New York Times* (22 May 1986).

[2] Mellers's review, published initially under the title 'Body music' in the *Times Literary Supplement*, is reworked in Wilfrid Mellers, *The Masks of Orpheus: Seven Stages in the Story of European Music* (Manchester: Manchester University Press, 1987), 170.

[3] Andrew Clements, 'Don't look back', *Guardian* (5 December 1997).

– explored through retellings of the myth of Orpheus – speak powerfully of the twentieth century. That century, the most violent known to human history, witnessed the most terrible losses and the collapse of civilized society, the collapse of the modern project of enlightenment. Birtwistle's modernist art attempts to articulate this failure through its fragmentation, its multiplicity, its melancholic laments. The alienated late-modern subject (represented by Orpheus himself) constantly yearns to be reconnected with a more complete past. Orpheus keeps turning back: 'I remember', he sings, continually. Yet a return to that past is impossible, and it is the recognition of this fact that imbues *The Mask of Orpheus* with a deep and powerful pessimism. The (unresolved) conflict in Birtwistle's music between the violent and the lyrical, the rational and the irrational, the ancient and the modern, speaks profoundly of the preoccupations and anxieties of late-modern culture. *The Mask of Orpheus* is thus a work both of its time and of ours. Its rich reinterpretation of the myth of Orpheus helps us to approach an understanding of who we are, and why we are the way we are now. This is, I argue, the principal triumph of this exceptional work.

Jonathan Cross
Oxford, December 2008

Chapter 1
The Myth of Orpheus

Men say that he by the music of his songs charmed the stubborn rocks upon the mountains and the course of rivers. (Apollonius Rhodius)[1]

There is something absolutely fundamental about Orpheus – the subject matter is music, it's about the birth of music. (Harrison Birtwistle)[2]

Orpheus through the Ages

Orpheus the musician has remained an icon down the ages. Orpheus, who charmed nature by his music. Orpheus, whose singing persuaded Hades to let him pass into the world of the dead. Orpheus, whose lamenting moved all those who heard him to tears. Orpheus, whose head though severed from his body continued to sing. It should hardly surprise us that Orpheus has long held a fascination for musicians. Since the birth of opera in the late sixteenth century, Orpheus' song has continually been adapted and reinterpreted on the musical stage, from Monteverdi's pleading 'Possente spirito' of 1607 to Birtwistle's singing Head of Orpheus in *The Second Mrs Kong* of 1993–94. But Orpheus has not been of interest solely to musicians.

Orpheus made his first appearance in history in the sixth century BC, and by then he was already a celebrity. ’Ονομακλυτὸν ’Ορφήν – 'famous Orpheus' – are the two words of the poet Ibycus. Further details about Orpheus in the earliest Greek literature and art are, however, fragmentary at best. Although he subsequently became known to many, his origins remain obscure. Was there a real Orpheus, a historical figure, or was he merely the product of ancient Greek imagination? These are unanswerable questions. 'As we try to trace him back through the ages he becomes more shadowy, more elusive, more Protean in his aptitude for slipping away from anyone who tries to lay actual hands on him and make him tell just what he is and what he stands for.'[3] Given the myriad ways in which Orpheus' story has been rewritten across the millennia, this would perhaps seem to be entirely appropriate. The 'original' Orpheus lives for us now in a world of shadows. What he is and what he stands for

---

[1]   *The Argonautica*, tr. R.C. Seaton (London: Heinemann, 1912), Book I, ll. 27–8 (p. 5).

[2]   'Birtwistle on Birtwistle', The Harrison Birtwistle Site, http://www.braunarts.com/birtwistle/harry2.html (accessed 30 September 2008).

[3]   W.K.C. Guthrie, *Orpheus and Greek Religion: a Study of the Orphic Movement* (Princeton: Princeton University Press, 1952), 1.

have been different for every generation. Each age has reclaimed Orpheus for itself; each age has remade Orpheus in its own image. The myth of Orpheus is really no longer a Greek myth because it has become a vehicle through which we all strive to find a deeper understanding of ourselves. From our postmodern perspective we might say that Orpheus has become pure representation.

What was known about Orpheus by the Greeks themselves?[4] It is clear that the story was not told in a single or consistent way, though there would appear to be essentially two different traditions depending on whether Orpheus was viewed as a religious figure (the founder of a cult that came to be known as Orphism) or as an artistic figure (the poet and musician). Nonetheless, a number of common key features emerge concerning: his lineage – his birth to the muse Calliope and the Thracian river-god Oeagrus, or sometimes of Apollo; his time spent with Jason as an Argonaut; his ability to charm nature through music; his religious aspects as a priest of Dionysus or as a follower of Apollo; his abilities as a poet and prophet; his journey to the underworld to retrieve Eurydice; his death at the hands of the Thracian women (the Furies or Bacchantes); and his destiny following his death as an oracle.[5] Details of Orpheus' lineage, life, death and cult are to be found in, among other ancient literary sources, Pindar's *Pythian Odes* (fifth century BC), the *Argonautica* of Apollonius Rhodius (third century BC), *The Library* of Apollodorus (second century BC, but probably compiled in the first or second century AD), Horace's *Odes* (first century BC) and various references across Plato's works. Vase paintings, sculptures and coins give representations of Orpheus as lyre player, as pursued by the Maenads or as a decapitated prophet.[6] And there are other surviving Orphic texts, claiming to be descended directly from the teachings of Orpheus, principally the *Orphic Hymns* – 87 short religious poems composed in either the late Hellenistic or the early Roman era – and the *Argonautica*, composed between the fourth and sixth centuries AD.

But the two narratives that have had the greatest impact on later interpretations of the Orpheus myth are, without doubt, those of the Latin poets Virgil, primarily in the *Georgics* (29 BC), and Ovid, in the *Metamorphoses* (*c*.1–8 AD). Ostensibly didactic texts on farming, the *Georgics* are in fact some of the most beautiful poems of the Roman era. The fourth book is about bees, and it is in this context that Virgil is the first writer to introduce the name of Aristaeus, shepherd and bee-keeper. From here he goes on to tell the story of Eurydice's death as a result of a snake-bite escaping Aristaeus' amorous pursuit, of Orpheus' quest to recover her from the underworld, of his losing her for a second time by turning back to look at her, of his grieving, of

---

[4]   For a full exploration of Orpheus and the Greeks, see J.B. Friedman, *Orpheus in the Middle Ages* (Cambridge, MA: Harvard University Press, 1970), 6 ff.; and Guthrie, *Orpheus and Greek Religion*.

[5]   After Friedman, *Orpheus in the Middle Ages*.

[6]   For a fuller summary, see 'What is meant by Orphism? The nature of the evidence', in Guthrie, *Orpheus and Greek Religion*, 6–24.

his death at the hands of the Thracian women and of his severed head still calling his lover's name as it was carried away by the river.

> And so it was
> That as the river of his fatherland,
> The Hebrus, bore in the middle of its current
> His head, now severed from his marble neck,
> 'Eurydice!' the voice and frozen tongue
> Still called aloud, 'Ah, poor Eurydice!'[7]

Ovid's motivation in the *Metamorphoses*, as his title tells us, is to weave together over 250 mythological stories interpreted as common tales of the transformation of people and objects from one state to another – Bacchus, for example, avenges the murder of Orpheus by turning the Thracian women into oak trees. In the tenth and eleventh books Ovid tells much the same tale of Orpheus as Virgil does, but in greater detail. (Aristaeus, however, is absent.) Most striking is the lengthy sung entreaty by Orpheus to the 'lord of the shades' at the gates of Hades to the accompaniment of his lyre:

> Now by these regions filled with fear,
> By this huge chaos, these vast silent realms,
> Reweave, I implore, the fate unwound too fast
> Of my Eurydice.[8]

By the sixth century AD the story of Orpheus was being interpreted as a fable, a moral tale, as can be seen in Boethius' *Consolation of Philosophy*, where the loss of Eurydice is being read as a consequence of Orpheus' inability to control his passions. This became one of the most popular texts of the Middle Ages, inspiring such romances as the anonymous *Sir Orfeo* (late thirteenth or early fourteenth century) and *Orpheus and Eurydice* by the Scottish poet Robert Henryson (*c.*1430–*c.*1506). For many medieval writers it was the relationship between the two as courtly lovers that was the most significant aspect of the story, and a number of versions even had happy endings, which became a regular feature of later operatic representations. *Sir Orfeo* is a tale set in medieval England, where Eurydice (Heurodis) is abducted by the fairy king, while Henryson's poem is a typical quest narrative in the romance tradition, 'the traitie of Orpheus kyng and how he yeid to hewyn & to hel to seik his quene'.[9]

---

[7] Virgil [Publius Virgilius Maro], *The Georgics*, tr. L.P. Wilkinson (London: Penguin, 1982), Book IV, ll. 523–8 (p. 142).

[8] Ovid [Ovidius Publius Naso], *Metamorphoses*, tr. A.D. Melville (Oxford: Oxford University Press, 1986), Book X, ll. 28–31 (pp. 225–6).

[9] See the website of the National Library of Scotland for a digital image of the opening page: http://www.nls.uk/firstscottishbooks/page.cfm?folio=149 (accessed 30 September 2008).

In both poems Orpheus' harp playing is central. The harp charms both nature and men; metaphorically it brings harmony to worldly affairs. Across the centuries the lyre has also been important in Orphic symbolism and iconography. There was understood to be a correspondence between the lyre and the harmony of the spheres, between the strings of the lyre and the patterns of the universe, where the seven strings related to the seven spheres. The lyre assisted in easing the soul's journey to the stars, and it was in the heavens that the lyre of Orpheus was said (by Hygenius in the *Astronomica*) to have been placed by Apollo after his death as the constellation Lyra. Friedman makes a helpful distinction between stringed instruments, which were believed to appeal to the rational part of the soul, and wind instruments such as the flute, which were 'characterised by their power over the irascible and concupiscent passions, which held the soul to the earth when the lyre could draw it to the heavens'.[10] This is embodied in the myth of the contest between Apollo, the lyre player, representative of the rational, and the Dionysian satyr Marsyas, the aulos player, representative of the instinctive. (Ovid tells this story in Book VI of the *Metamorphoses*.) Such instrumental associations echo down to the present day, and traces remain even in Birtwistle's thinking.

Early Christian artists frequently adapted pagan imagery and applied it to their own purposes. In Orpheus they found a saviour-like figure. He became a favourite subject of art, in which the pastoral Orpheus, taming the wild beasts through his music, was taken over to represent Christ the Good Shepherd. The famous painting from the Cemetery of the Two Laurels in fourth-century Rome depicts a central Orpheus-Christus figure, not with a multitude of animals, but with just two birds (dove and eagle) serving 'as an emblem for the Christian soul in this life and the next'.[11] Parallels were frequently made between Orpheus' ability to rescue Eurydice from the clutches of hell and Christ's ability to lead souls to the immortality of the afterlife. Even his lyre became an important symbol in allegorical representations: both Orpheus' lyre 'and the cross had magical power over the king of the underworld and both had been interpreted as manifestations or symbols of the Logos'.[12]

Later medieval reinterpretations of the Orpheus story as a Christian allegory followed Boethius' example in reading the story as a moral tale. The very title of the anonymous *Ovide moralisé* (*c.*1310) reveals its purpose. Here, Orpheus is explicitly conflated with Christ, Eurydice is Eve, and the seven strings of the lyre are the seven virtues. One of the most extraordinary examples of allegorical writing is to be found in the reading of Ovid by the fourteenth-century French monk Pierre Bersuire. In the *Reductorium morale* (*c.*1325–37), Orpheus is portrayed as 'the child of the sun', as 'Christ the son of God the Father, who from the beginning led Eurydice, that is the human soul to himself. And from the beginning Christ joined her to himself through his special prerogative.' Eurydice, like Eve, is tempted by the forbidden fruit but,

---

10   Friedman, *Orpheus in the Middle Ages*, 81.
11   Ibid., 49.
12   Ibid., 126.

unlike Eve, she is 'ripped from the hands of the rule of Hell' by Christ-Orpheus: as they make their way to the upper world, they chant a verse from the Canticles.[13] Thus, by the mid fourteenth century, Orpheus, through allegory, had been converted into a thoroughly Christian figure.

For the later medieval reader King Orpheus was principally a minstrel. Further, Orpheus represented wisdom and eloquence, *sapientia et eloquentia,* 'one of the most important educational topoi in the Middle Ages',[14] attributes embodied in Orpheus the musician and in Orpheus the poet and writer of songs. Resonances of this Orpheus can be heard in, for example, the French traditions of the *troubadours* and *trouvères* of the twelfth and thirteenth centuries. These poet-musicians – generally aristocratic and certainly well educated – sang and accompanied their own verses on the theme of courtly love. And by the late fourteenth century, with the rise of humanism in Renaissance Italy, Orpheus was being deployed to project the new significance of poetry and the artist. In this context, his severed head took on a new importance. In Boccaccio, for instance, the head that continued singing after the death of the poet was an allegory for the enduring influence and fame of the artist.

An important landmark in the secularization of religious drama is Angelo Poliziano's *La fabula d'Orfeo,* the first secular drama in vernacular Italian, written for a Gonzaga banquet at Mantua in 1480. Poliziano was a humanist, poet and classical scholar. The modernity of this work is striking: it was 'a highly musical play outside the Aristotelian genres ... that dealt with the power of music in a classical setting'.[15] None of the music now survives; nonetheless, this retelling of the tale through music was an important precursor of and influence on opera, which was to emerge a century later – the birth of opera out of the spirit of humanism, as Sternfeld memorably put it.[16] Here, Orpheus the musician stands as a representative of modernity.

From the Middle Ages onwards the Orpheus myth has been the paradigm for all manner of other symbolic and allegorical quest narratives. The journey of the poet through the darkness of the 'Inferno' to the brightness of 'Paradise' in Dante's *The Divine Comedy* (c.1308–21), Tamino's negotiation of the trials to reach Pamina (and enlightenment) in Mozart and Schikaneder's *The Magic Flute* (1791) and the life of the poet-musician Christian in Baz Luhrmann's *Moulin Rouge!* (2001) are all, in one way or another, reworkings of aspects of the Orpheus story. Its potency persists. And in each case the familiar story is refashioned in the image of its own age.

But it is perhaps in music, and in opera in particular, that the Orpheus story is today most familiar to us. The theories about the new music of the so-called second practice that emerged from the Florentine Camerata emphasized that music 'turns

---

[13]   See ibid., 127.

[14]   Ibid., 101.

[15]   Howard Mayer Brown, 'Opera (i), II: origins', *Grove Music Online,* http://www.oxfordmusiconline.com/subscriber/article/grove/music/40726pg2 (accessed 30 September 2008).

[16]   F.W. Sternfeld, *The Birth of Opera* (Oxford: Clarendon Press, 1993), vii.

on the perfection of the melody'.[17] Devoted to the values of humanism, these late-sixteenth-century intellectuals looked back to the humanist values of the Greeks, whose monodic music they saw as expressing sentiment simply and directly. Because he was a singer and poet who had the power to tame wild beasts and nature, Orpheus quickly became the vehicle for the expression of these new ideas. As Mladen Dolar writes, 'the Orpheus myth has a lot to recommend itself, because the music is not only there to illustrate the plot but is an immediate mover of the dramatic action'.[18] The conditions were right for the birth of opera. 'All opera is Orpheus', observed Adorno.[19]

Within two years of each other, Peri (1600) and Caccini (1602) had both set Rinuccini's *Eurydice*, thus creating the earliest surviving operas.[20] These paved the way for Striggio and Monteverdi's *La favola d'Orfeo* of 1607, in many ways the model for all subsequent operatic retellings of the tale, to which so many later composers have alluded. The (literally) central moment of *Orfeo*, Orpheus' strophic song 'Possente spirito', brings together the three key identities of Orpheus as lover, singer and hero. Distraught at the loss of his lover, Orpheus the musician makes the heroic choice to use his musical and expressive skill to try to persuade Charon, gatekeeper to the underworld, to allow him to enter Hades to retrieve Eurydice. (In actual fact he does not succeed in winning over Charon, who falls asleep, but the outcome for Orpheus is nonetheless what he desires!) Music succeeds where rhetoric alone would have failed: *prima la musica, dopo le parole.* The art of persuasion that Monteverdi's Orpheus shows – achieved by means of both craft and expression – is an extraordinary exemplar of the power of music that remains the model even today. 'The effect of music can be measured only by and through music; the equivalent of musical power can be given only in musical currency.'[21] *Orfeo*, it could well be argued, has echoed in various ways through all subsequent operatic versions of the tale, among the better-known of which are those of Rossi (1647), Matthew Locke (a 'masque' of 1673), Charpentier (1685), Lully (1690), Telemann (1726), Wagenseil (1750), Gluck (1762), Haydn (1791), Offenbach (1858), Milhaud (1925), Krenek (1925), Casella (1932) and, of course, Birtwistle (1986). Both Rameau and Debussy planned but did not complete versions. Other significant composers may not have placed Orpheus on the opera stage, but nonetheless proved that they could not resist his lure. In 1827, for example, Berlioz composed a 'monologue et bacchanale' on

---

[17]   Claudio Monteverdi, foreword to his fifth book of madrigals (1605, foreword 1607), in Oliver Strunck, *Source Readings in Music History* (New York: Norton, 1950), 409.

[18]   Mladen Dolar, 'If music be the food of love', in Slavoj Žižec and Mladen Dolar, *Opera's Second Death* (New York: Routledge, 2002), 8.

[19]   Theodor W. Adorno, *Quasi una fantasia: Essays on Modern Music*, tr. Rodney Livingstone (London: Verso, 1992), 30.

[20]   For a comprehensive account of the early history of opera as a response to the Orpheus myth, see Sternfeld, *The Birth of Opera*.

[21]   Dolar, 'If music be the food of love', 11.

the theme of *La mort d'Orphée*; Liszt's symphonic poem *Orpheus* of 1854 was written as a prelude to a performance of Gluck's opera; and in 1948 Stravinsky produced his ballet *Orpheus* with the close collaboration of the choreographer George Balanchine.

Orpheus for the Twentieth Century

The historian Eric Hobsbawm describes the decades from the outbreak of the First World War to the aftermath of the Second as 'an Age of Catastrophe'.[22] He prefaces his account with a 'bird's eye view', consisting of brief quotations from some of the century's influential thinkers and artists. Many of the chosen texts serve to emphasize the unprecedented horrors of the era: 'the most terrible century in Western history' (Isaiah Berlin), 'the most violent century in human history' (William Golding). Primo Levi, a holocaust survivor, turns to the most dreadful of all monsters from Greek mythology to make his point: he writes quietly but powerfully of those who 'touched bottom', those 'who have seen the face of the Gorgon, did not return, or returned wordless'.[23] The pointless slaughter of millions of Europe's youth in the killing fields of France; the unimaginable terrors of systematic genocide; the horrific consequences of the dropping of the atom bomb: the human losses to violent conflict in the twentieth century are counted in the hundreds of millions. The twentieth century is coloured and shamed by the most extreme inhumanity of man to man, by the most extreme challenges to the individual, to the very status of the subject. It should therefore not surprise us that so many artists (and psychologists, anthropologists and sociologists) were drawn again to myth as a way of coming to terms with contemporary events that were, literally, unspeakable. As in earlier times, retelling mythical stories could help to 'explain' difficult phenomena within a symbolic realm. The Orpheus story had particularly strong resonances with the twentieth century, and twentieth-century artists inevitably focused on the terrible and unnecessary deaths of the youthful Orpheus and Eurydice. The darkness of the underworld, it might be said, echoed the terrible chambers of Stalin's gulags and Hitler's death camps: abandon every hope, all you who enter. '[H]istory is understood under the sign of myth', writes Michael Bell, after Nietzsche.[24] Among other artists, Anouilh, Cocteau, Henze, Kokoshka, Krenek, Müller, Rilke and Stravinsky have reinvented Orpheus as a victim of their age. As Wilfrid Mellers has commented in relation to Stravinsky, but with possible application to many other creative figures of the age, 'in the Waste Land of the twentieth century and in the wake of two world

---

[22]   Eric Hobsbawm, *The Age of Extremes: the Short Twentieth Century, 1914–1991* (London: Abacus, 1995), 7.

[23]   All quotations from ibid., 1–2.

[24]   Michael Bell, 'The metaphysics of Modernism', in Michael Levinson (ed.), *The Cambridge Companion to Modernism* (Cambridge: Cambridge University Press, 1999), 14.

wars to destroy, not save, Civilisation, [Stravinsky] restated the pristine savagery of the original myth, allowing the Terrible Mothers to rend Orpheus to pieces in revenge on his patriarchal pride'.[25] Orpheus' melancholic songs of loss and lament came to speak painfully and eloquently for the century. Orpheus stands as a symbol for late-modern man. His primary mode is that of lament.

The artist, playwright and poet Oskar Kokoshka was seriously wounded on the Russian front in 1915 and, on his return to the front alongside war artists in 1916, suffered shell shock following a grenade attack. *Orpheus und Eurydike* is the name shared by both a drama and a picture that he conceived and sketched in various military hospitals and sanatoria during the years of the First World War. He was drawn to the Orpheus myth as a direct consequence of his terrible wartime experiences; indeed, one of the etchings that were to accompany a planned edition of the play is entitled 'Orpheus on the Battlefield (Memory of the Battlefield in Russia)',[26] and elsewhere it is clear that Kokoshka projects the deaths he had witnessed of Russian soldiers on to the death of Orpheus. (The myth also had a personal meaning for Kokoshka as, through it, he attempted to express his lost love for Alma Mahler, with whom a passionate relationship had just ended.) Decades later he wrote, in decidedly expressionist terms, of the drama that was 'with blood not written, but spoken, whispered in ecstasy, in delirium, cried, pleaded and howled in deathly fear and fever'.[27] In 1923 Ernst Krenek set the play to music.

Jean Cocteau, like so many twentieth-century French writers, was fascinated by ancient Greek mythology and the possibilities of its relevance to the contemporary world. His principal obsession, however, was with the Orpheus story. His 1925 stage play *Orphée* was later significantly reworked as the centrepiece of an 'Orphic trilogy' of films, beginning with *Le sang d'un poète* (1932) and ending with *Le testament d'Orphée* in 1960. In *Orphée* (1950) Cocteau transformed Orpheus into a famous left-bank poet in post-Second World War Paris. The film is a work of haunting images, not least in its use of mirrors as gateways to the other world. Especially striking are the vivid reminders of the French Occupation in the shape of the black-clad, helmeted, motorcycling messengers of death, the threatening tribunal of the Judges of the Dead and the stone-throwing mob of vengeful Bacchantes, menacingly accompanied by Dionysian drums. The stylized manner of acting only serves to reinforce the film's oppressive atmosphere of fear and uncertainty. (There are echoes

---

[25]   Wilfrid Mellers, *The Masks of Orpheus: Seven Stages in the Story of European Music* (Manchester: Manchester University Press, 1987), 166–7.

[26]   'Orpheus auf dem Schlachtfeld (Erinnerung an das Schlachtfeld in Rußland)'.

[27]   'mit Blut … nicht geschrieben, … sondern gesprochen, geflustert in Ekstase, im Delirium, geweint, gefleht und geheult in Angst und Fieber der Todesnahe'. In a letter from November 1955, in Oskar Kokoshka, *Schriften 1907–1955*, quoted in Claudia Maurer Zenck, 'Maler, Dichter, Komponist – *Orpheus und Eurydike* von Oskar Kokoshka und Ernst Krenek', in Claudia Maurer Zenck (ed.), *Der Orpheus-Mythos von der Antike bis zur Gegenwart* (Frankfurt am Main: Peter Lang, 2004), 250.

here of Stravinsky's *Oedipus rex*, on whose text Cocteau had collaborated with the composer in 1926–27.) Painful memories of recent events are mediated through an ancient story.

In the *Sonnets to Orpheus*, written at breakneck speed during February 1922, the poet Rainer Maria Rilke seems almost to identify with and speak through Orpheus. In part a memorial to the dead nineteen-year-old daughter of a friend (who becomes a kind of Eurydice) and in part a general elegy for dead youth, the work presents Orpheus the musician again as a poet for the new age. Of particular importance to Rilke was what he called the *Unsäglichen*, the unsayable: 'Most phenomena are *unsayable*, and have their being in a dimension which no word has ever entered; and works of art are the most unsayable of all – they are mysterious presences whose lives endure alongside our own perishable lives.'[28] In one of these sonnets he addresses the destructive threat of the machine age to the human life-force – as witnessed during the First World War – but then, by contrast, he turns to the endurance of human creativity and the ability of music, in particular, to express the unsayable. Words may fail, but Orpheus's song continues to resound.

> Alles Erworbne bedroht die Maschine, solange
> sie sich erdreistet, im Geist, statt im Gehorchen, zu sein.
> …
> Worte gehen noch zart am Unsäglichen aus …
> Und die Musik, immer neu, aus den bebendsten Steinen,
> baut im unbrauchbaren Raum ihr vergöttlichtes Haus.
>
> The machine will forever imperil all human creation
> while it presumes to direct us instead of to serve.
> …
> Words still continue to tiptoe past the Unsayable.
> Music, ever renewed in inviolable Space
> builds of precarious stones its celestial house.[29]

Elsewhere, we find Orpheus in, among other places, a drawing by Paul Klee (*Ein Garten für Orpheus*, 1926) and etchings by Pablo Picasso ('Mort d'Orphée', *Les métamorphoses d'Ovide*, published 1931), though for neither artist was Orpheus a central figure; in the dramas of Jean Anouilh (*Eurydice*, 1941) and Tennessee Williams (*Orpheus Descending*, 1957); in poems of Guillaume Apollinaire (*Le Bestiaire ou cortège d'Orphée*, 1911) and W.H. Auden (*Orpheus*, 1937); in a film of Marcel Camus (*Orfeu Negro*, 1959, after a play by Vinicius de Moraes); and in the

---

[28]   Rainer Maria Rilke, in his first letter to the young poet Franz Xaver Kappus (Paris, 17 February 1903), in *Sonnets to Orpheus with Letters to a Young Poet*, tr. Stephen Cohn (Manchester: Carcanet, 2000), 173.

[29]   Rilke, *Sonnets to Orpheus*, Part 2, poem 10, ll. 1–2, 12–14.

novels of Russell Hoban (especially *The Medusa Frequency*, 1987). For Hoban, the future librettist of Birtwistle's opera *The Second Mrs Kong*, Orpheus is an almost pathological obsession. Orpheus is brought into the contemporary world of Hoban's novels to articulate, as for Rilke, the ungraspability of reality, what Hoban calls 'the moment under the moment': 'The raging of the head of Orpheus is not to be understood. That is not the nature of it.'[30] Each artist finds something different in Orpheus. By no means all are drawn to the violence of his story. Many twentieth-century thinkers engaged with myth because it offered consolation in a troubled present or, particularly through Orpheus' civilizing song, it offered hope for the future. After two world wars and many other terrible conflicts, Orpheus' music suggested a way of beginning again.

Unsurprisingly, then, it was for musicians that Orpheus remained the most resonant figure throughout the twentieth century, drawn to him – among other reasons – through his power to make music against all odds. Between the wars a number of key musical representations of the myth were produced by Milhaud (*Les malheurs d'Orphée*, 1924), Krenek (*Orpheus und Eurydike*, premiered 1926), Paul Dessau (*Orpheus*, 1930–31) and Casella (*La favola d'Orfeo*, 1932). After the Second World War, retellings of the myth are to be found frequently in operas, ballets, concert works and tape pieces, including works by composers as diverse as Schaeffer and Henry (*Orphée 51*, musique concrete, reworked as *Orphée 53*, a 'spectacle lyrique'), Foss (*Orpheus*, 1972, an instrumental work in various versions), Andriessen (*Orpheus*, 1977, a music-theatre piece in three acts), Carter (*Syringa*, 1978, a setting of a poem by John Ashbery on Orpheus and the power of music, interspersed with fragments from ancient Greek texts), Glass (*Orphée*, 1993, an opera in two acts after the Cocteau film), Furrer (*Begehren*, 2001, a music-theatre piece in ten scenes with texts on Orpheus and Eurydice from Virgil, Ovid and others) and Neuwirth (*Eurydike*, 2004, a theatre piece).[31] In most cases, it is never merely a familiar and convenient story on which to hang music, but a powerful reinterpretation or recontextualization of the myth that attempts to articulate something of what it means to live in the late-modern era. For the most overtly political composers, Orpheus became a spokesman for the century's persecuted, tortured and murdered.

Although it is not ostensibly 'about' the Second World War, it is nonetheless telling that Stravinsky chose Orpheus as the subject for his ballet begun within a year of the end of that war. Never one to reveal his 'true' feelings about himself or his politics, Stravinsky was continually changing and hiding behind his masks; so it was thus, perhaps, behind the 'mask of Orpheus' that he was best able to come to

---

[30]   Russell Hoban, *The Moment under the Moment* (London: Picador, 1993), 239.

[31]   For an attempt at an ongoing complete chronological list of all manner of works on Orpheus and Eurydice, see Reinhard Kapp, 'Chronologisches Verzeichnis (in progress) der auf Orpheus (und/oder Eurydike) bezogenen oder zu beziehenden Opern, Kantaten, Instrumentalmusiken, literarischen Texte, Theaterstücke, Filme und historiographischen Arbeiten', www.musikgeschichte.at/kapp-orpheus.pdf (last updated 27 May 2007).

terms with both a series of tragic personal losses and the horrors of the world situation during the war years. *Orpheus* (following *Apollo* and *Persephone*) is the last of a trio of ballets on Greek myths written over a period of 20 years, and is the most stylized of the three. Exiled for a second time in the USA, Stravinsky experienced the terrors and privations of war only at a distance; indeed, it is a sense of distance – from the story's violence, from overt emotion – that in general characterizes this work. With the close collaboration of the choreographer George Balanchine, whose initial idea it was to use Orpheus as subject, Stravinsky worked out a scenario that starts with Orpheus weeping at Eurydice's funeral and ends with his apotheosis, where Apollo appears, 'wrests the lyre from Orpheus and raises his son heavenwards'. The music throughout is restrained, distanced. The sense of formality is reinforced by, among other things, the chorale-like frame of prologue and epilogue, and the importance throughout of counterpoint. The designer chosen for the premiere production was Isamu Noguchi, a sculptor whose abstract geometric sets, costumes and masks perfectly matched the distilled purity of Stravinsky's music and Balanchine's dances.

The apparent turning away from violence in *Orpheus* is not a sign of retreat from the horror of the war. In the face of such slaughter, not least in the far-away country of Stravinsky's birth, another barbaric *Rite of Spring* would hardly have been possible. Like other archetypical neoclassical works of the war years, such as the Symphony in C and the Symphony in Three Movements, *Orpheus* offers 'timely reflections on war and death', to appropriate Freud's phrase of 1915, but with a sense of detachment. One key aspect of modernism, as understood by Adorno among others, was a profound nostalgia for what had been lost in the brutal twentieth century. The modernist dwells on this loss, on the impossibility of retrieving what has been lost. Edward Said has written compellingly of the 'return to the eighteenth century' in the work of such (neoclassical) figures as Stravinsky, Britten and Strauss.[32] By adopting 'old' manners and techniques these composers were, Said argues, highlighting their alienation from the horrors with which they had been confronted.[33] Stravinsky's *Orpheus* seems to offer a prime illustration of this idea: it is imbued with a melancholic world-weariness. Alienation, memory and mourning become the defining features, not just of this work, but of modernist music generally. This is captured poignantly in the ballet's opening. 'Orpheus weeps for Eurydice. He stands motionless, with his back to the audience.' The falling, lamenting Phrygian lines of Orpheus' lyre are both ancient and modern; they speak directly of loss.

Stravinsky is everywhere in Michael Tippett's music: in his forms, harmonies, rhythms and instrumentation. And Tippett makes good use of Orpheus in *The Mask of Time* (1980–82), 'fragments or scenes from a possible "epiphany" for today'.[34] The second movement, 'Creation of the World by Music', refers to 'Orpheus plucking

---

[32] Edward W. Said, *On Late Style: Music and Literature against the Grain* (London: Bloomsbury, 2006), chap. 2.

[33] Ibid., 16, 17.

[34] Composer's preface (1983).

from the lyre / power to move stone'; the cosmic creative force operates through music which can bring order. A sustained low (Phrygian) E♮ seems to represent the beginning of the world; ceremonial brass instruments call events to order, while Orpheus' lyre is a Stravinskian combination of harp and piano playing a chorale-like idea. Later, Orpheus is portrayed as that 'person who has known and suffered the dark side of the world' and therefore is the only one who can 'truly praise'. In 'The Severed Head', the baritone soloist plays the role of Orpheus, singing an excerpt from Rilke:

> Who alone already lifted
> the lyre among the dead
> dare, divining, sound
> the infinite praise.[35]

but not before he has intoned the opening of Dowland's *I Saw my Lady Weep*, alluding directly to the Elizabethan melancholic tradition. Orpheus' violent death stands for the deaths of so many others in 'our violent and turbulent times', but what is important to Tippett is the fact that the severed head continues to sing. The final, transcendent movement is thus called, simply, 'The Singing will Never be Done'. Fascinating in the context of the present study is just how many themes and musical ideas in Tippett's *Mask* parallel those of Birtwistle's *The Mask of Orpheus*, which was being written at exactly the same time but entirely independently. Attending the premiere of Birtwistle's *Mask* just two years after the first performance of his own, Tippett recalled being 'totally shattered by this tremendous work'.[36]

Hans Werner Henze claims that his first encounter with the subject of Orpheus was via Stravinsky's *Orpheus*, which he heard in 1949. He clearly alludes to Stravinsky's work in his own ballet *Orpheus* (1978) through, for example, the use of falling 'white-note' modal lines for harp (and guitar) and strings at the start of the Act I 'Danza generale'. Unlike Stravinsky's, however, Henze's motivations were unambiguously political, born of his childhood and youth in Nazi Germany, his espousal of a utopian kind of communism and his belief in 'music as a means of resistance'.[37] He later commented that he 'felt weak and naked in the face of the

---

[35] Quoted from the score. The text is a translation of the opening of *Sonnets to Orpheus*, Part 1, poem 9.

[36] Michael Tippett, *Those Twentieth Century Blues: an Autobiography* (London: Hutchinson, 1991), 225.

[37] 'Musik als Resistenzverhalten', lecture given in 1963, in Hans Werner Henze, *Music and Politics: Collected Writings 1953–81*, tr. Peter Labanyi (London: Faber and Faber, 1982), 122–9.

music for [his own] *Orpheus*. There was such sadness in the world, I could not even express it in words, it seemed to me, let alone in musical sounds.'[38]

The late 1970s and early 1980s represented for Henze (as for Birtwistle) a period of obsession with the Orphic myth, during which time he wrote a number of Orpheus-related works. Alongside *Orpheus* we find a triptych of portraits of the shepherds Tirsi, Mopso and Aristeo in the guise of a solo violin sonata (1977), the orchestral *Barcarola* (1979), a cycle of choruses to poems by Edward Bond called *Orpheus Behind the Wire* (1983) and various reworked scenes and arias extracted from the ballet, as well as an integration of these Orpheus pieces with newly composed numbers and spoken texts to form *Aristaeus* (2004). In 1976 Henze had presided over the first annual festival (*cantiere d'arte*) in the medieval Tuscan hilltop town of Montepulciano, birthplace of Il Poliziano. The *cantiere* was conceived by the town's communist council as a festival for all its population, one in which the townsfolk were to play an active role. Henze was 'motivated by the idea that as an artist I should make myself socially useful',[39] that 'it might be possible in Montepulciano to prove that music is not abstract and useless, not a mere pastime, and that it could do even more than improve the moral climate, as Stravinsky had hoped. I believed that it could raise the economic and social standards of the community'.[40] Orpheus was the inevitable focus. It was in Montepulciano, in the context of performances of a plethora of Orpheus-inspired works, that Henze began to conceive his own *Orpheus*, with its central theme of freedom through art. This idea is revealed most explicitly at the end of *Orpheus Behind the Wire*, a protest piece in defence of persecuted artists, victims of 'the Argentine military government, which sanctioned kidnapping, torture and murder'.[41] The chorus closes with a transcendent B major triad, disturbed only by a lone tenor singing a C♮ as a quiet reminder of the price paid in order to win freedom.

> Then we hear music of Orpheus
> Of triumph
> Of freedom.

The ancient tale of Orpheus and Eurydice is once again retold with powerful relevance to the late twentieth century.

---

[38] Hans Werner Henze, *Bohemian Fifiths: an Autobiography*, tr. Stewart Spencer (London: Faber, 1998), 376.

[39] Ibid., 342.

[40] Henze, 'The Montepulciano Cantieri, 1976–80', in *Music and Politics*, 263.

[41] Henze, quoted in Steffen Georgi, 'Orpheus takes a stand', liner note for CD (Mainz: Wergo, 2006), 13.

Birtwistle and Orpheus

Orpheus has, of course, been a bit of an obsession for me.[42]

Representing musically the death of Orpheus was an idea that had, apparently, been suggested to Harrison Birtwistle by girls at Cranborne Chase School, Dorset, where he had been a teacher in the early 1960s.[43] However, his first explicit presentation of aspects of the Orpheus story, *Nenia: the Death of Orpheus*, dates from 1970, and announces what was to become an enduring relationship with the myth. The composer had already been exploring a variety of related ancient Greek worlds for some years: the abstract formal concerns of *Tragoedia* (1965), whose structure is modelled on that of an archetypal Attic tragedy; the Choregos (chorus) figure present in *Monodrama* and *Punch and Judy* (both 1967); the melancholic *Linoi* (1968), a lament for the musician Linus, brother of Orpheus; the mythical subject matter of *Medusa* (1969); and the setting of fragments of Sappho from the sixth century BC in *Entr'actes and Sappho Fragments* (1964) and *Cantata* (1969). All of these works, it can be said, along with the melancholic *The Fields of Sorrow*, which followed a year after *Nenia*, acted as studies for the major Orpheus project that was to dominate the next decade of Birtwistle's creative life. Even during the hiatus in composition between Acts II and III of *The Mask of Orpheus* the composer was still trying out key ideas in the shape of the 'madrigal' *On the Sheer Threshold of the Night* (1980), which dramatizes Boethius's account of the central moment of the Orpheus story. And it was also during this period that he worked as composer at the National Theatre in London, most notably on Peter Hall's production of Tony Harrison's English version of Aeschylus' *Oresteia* (1981). Subsequently Birtwistle returned to Orpheus on a number of occasions. Head of Orpheus leads Kong on a quest after the object of his desire, the Girl with the Pearl Earring, in *The Second Mrs Kong*; the *26 Orpheus Elegies* (2003–04) are poignant settings of selected sonnets by Rilke; and *The Corridor* (premiered at Aldeburgh in 2009) has Eurydice as the central character.[44] He has even described his most recent opera *The Minotaur* (premiered 2008) as 'a genuine extension of the Orpheus idea'.[45] It is clear, then, that the Orpheus myth is more than just casual subject matter for Birtwistle; it appears to have prompted, in one form or another, a major part of his output, and remains at the very heart of his creative process.

---

[42]   Harrison Birtwistle in conversation with Gillian Moore, *Birtwistle Games* programme book (South Bank Centre, London, October–November 2004), 10.

[43]   This story is narrated by Michael Hall, *Harrison Birtwistle* (London: Robson, 1984), 69.

[44]   See Chapter 6.

[45]   Quoted in Michael Hall, *Harrison Birtwistle in Recent Years* (London: Robson, 1998), 153. It is not hard to understand why Birtwistle thought of this work in 'Orphic' terms, with its representation of the violent deaths of innocent youths and its central journey by a heroic figure to a place from which there was conventionally no return.

But why this fixation with Greek material and with the Orpheus story in particular? It seems to offer a striking contrast to the self-image that Birtwistle has consistently striven to present of the brusque, working-class Lancastrian, with his roots firmly planted in English cultural soil, who has never – it would seem – been able to read the sources of his ideas and works in their original language. While in the past the libraries of upper-middle-class and aristocratic composers would have been lined with copies of the classics, which formed the backbone of every English public schoolboy's daily educational routine, Birtwistle came from different stock. His father was a smallholder. He attended Accrington Grammar School (a successful, state-funded, selective day school for boys).[46] His musical education was received at the hands of the director of the military band in Accrington, and via recordings of the music of Vaughan Williams, Debussy, Ravel and Stravinsky borrowed from Burnley Public Library.

Birtwistle's earliest extant composition, a little piano piece called the *Oockooing Bird* composed when he was about 15 years old, is a prophetically melancholic study which betrays an early fascination with a mythical creature, in this case a bird of his own invention. In this light, it is perhaps fair to suggest that the composer's lifelong fascination with aspects of Greek and Roman literature has less to do with an espousal of the values of the classically educated middle classes (however much his works may speak to precisely such a bourgeois audience) than it does with a wider interest in the way in which certain kinds of mythical stories are able to touch deep ideas and feelings. *Down by the Greenwood Side* (1968–69), after an English mummers' play, *Bow Down* (1977), derived from versions of the ballad of the Two Sisters, and *Yan Tan Tethera* (1983–84), based on a northern folk tale, are examples of his works built from an interest in what one might loosely term British mythical material, while archetypal characters such as Mr Punch, the Green Knight and King Kong are taken from sources as diverse as a seaside entertainment, a medieval English romance and a Hollywood film. A sense of place and a sense of landscape (real or imaginary) are fundamental to Birtwistle's work. The pastoral is an enduring aspect of English art, and it is one with which Birtwistle identifies profoundly through a collective sense of 'folk' (even in individual characters, such as those named above, who represent a collective voice). This leads directly to the pastoral world of the Orpheus myth. As the quotation that heads this chapter reveals, there is something fundamental for Birtwistle about Orpheus. And the Orpheuses that stalk their way through his works really have very little to do with a distant character from the Greece of Antiquity.

---

[46] As the name 'grammar school' indicates, the teaching of Latin grammar was (in medieval times) a central part of the curriculum in such schools, and it remained in place even after the major educational reforms of 1944. However, a fluent understanding of this ancient language was not a skill Birtwistle appears to have acquired during his time at school. For a more polemical reading of Birtwistle's modernism in this context, see Dai Griffiths, 'On grammar schoolboy music', in Derek B. Scott (ed.), *Music, Culture, and Society: a Reader* (Oxford: Oxford University Press, 2000), 143–5.

Birtwistle's Orpheus is a figure who exists within an English landscape of the late twentieth century.

While in some of his earliest pieces – as we have seen – Birtwistle had engaged with Greek and Roman texts, it was apparently only after he had met Peter Zinovieff that his works began to reflect a deeper engagement with ancient, mythological subject matter. Birtwistle was clearly inspired in many ways by Zinovieff, a man who was born only a year before him, yet whom he has more recently described in adulatory terms as his 'male muse'.[47] Zinovieff had studied geology at Oxford in the early 1950s but carved his reputation as an early British pioneer of electronic music, especially in the musical application of mini-computers. He set up his own private studio in Putney, south-west London, in the mid 1960s, and in 1969 established Electronic Music Studios Ltd (EMS) in order to market his ideas. In late 1969 Birtwistle returned to England after a period in the USA at Princeton University and the University of Colorado at Boulder, and settled eventually in Twickenham, also south-west of London. He and Zinovieff began to work together in the Putney studio. When a fire destroyed much of Birtwistle's Twickenham house, he and his family moved in with the Zinovieffs for a stay of many months.

Their earliest collaborations were first aired publicly in 1969. *Four Interludes for a Tragedy* for basset clarinet and tape – a reworking of solo instrumental interstices from an earlier theatre piece, *Monodrama* (1967) – was premiered in its full version in London in February 1969. A new version of *Nomos* (1967–68) for clarinet, piano, tape and dancer was heard in London in April that same year. Their first extended collaboration was based partly on Greek mythology: *Medusa* (1969). It was an experimental work for Birtwistle, existing in a sound-world and playing with ideas in ways very different from any of his other music. Some instruments are amplified, and there are two tapes, as well as a contribution from the *shozyg*, which produces strange electro-acoustic sounds.[48] But their most successful work together in the EMS studio came a few years later and resulted in Birtwistle's only exclusively electronic piece, *Chronometer* (1971–72). Already at work planning *The Mask of Orpheus*, Birtwistle made this piece for two four-track tapes concurrently with his orchestral work *The Triumph of Time* (also 1971–72), and the shared exploration of time and temporality of these two works echoes one of the central concerns of *Orpheus*. 'In *The Mask of Orpheus*', writes Zinovieff (libretto, p. 2), 'time is expressed, through memory, as echoes and distortions.' In *Chronometer*, sounds of various clocks and

---

[47]   Birtwistle, interviewed as part of a BBC radio documentary on Zinovieff, first broadcast on BBC Radio 4 (14 June 2004), presented by the poet Katrina Porteous and produced by Adam Fowler.

[48]   The shozyg is an 'instrument' built by the composer Hugh Davies in 1969 inside the cover of the final volume of an old encyclopaedia (SHO–ZYG, hence the name). It contains various objects that are touched, rubbed or struck and the resultant sounds are amplified by contact microphones. In the revised version of *Medusa* the shozyg was replaced by a synthesizer.

chimes are analysed and transformed (by means of the *MUSYS* computer control language devised at EMS by Peter Grogono) and layered in a rich, contrapuntal texture. The opera's 'Time Shifts' are already prefigured in this work, as indeed are a number of its sonic and structural concerns.

That electronic music was ultimately to play a key role in *The Mask of Orpheus* evidently sprang from Zinovieff's expertise and enthusiasm. Birtwistle was fascinated by the sonic possibilities it offered while having little interest in the technology itself. Although the opera's tape components were eventually made in Paris rather than Putney, much to Zinovieff's regret,[49] early thinking on the project was driven by both Zinovieff's experimental zeal and his knowledge of classical literature. A 'diary', written in the summer of 1976, captures something of Zinovieff's excitement and reveals just how the electronic sounds were central to his concept of how to realize the Orpheus story.

> Suddenly the most marvellously rich, varied and amazing sounds come pouring out of the speakers. They ripple and change. They are the first absolutely fantastic sounds that the oscillator bank has made. Everyone is moved. At first no-one believes that they are not precomposed …
>
> I must keep this a secret. I shall give it to Harry [Birtwistle] for Orpheus. We must not allow these marvellous things to be heard for a year or two. Apollo's gift to Orpheus was music. I wonder where these sounds come from. Perhaps it's not fluke that we have been working on Orpheus for 3 years. This is our reward.[50]

One can only speculate about how this might have sounded. But we do have one piece of evidence from this time of their close collaboration on music written for a dramatic context. The sound track for Sidney Lumet's *The Offence* (1972) is Birtwistle's only film score; Zinovieff, once again, made the electronic realization. A disturbing picture of police brutality, it contains many themes that Birtwistle and Zinovieff had already been discussing in relation to the Orpheus project. 'The time (probably winter) and the place perfectly reflect the unacknowledged despair contained in almost every frame of this harrowing story', wrote the *New York Times* reviewer,[51] 'highly theatrical for the more or less realistic context'. One of the most striking and stylized scenes is the 'memory montage', supported by the sorts of Birtwistlian sounds that were later to be heard in *Orpheus*: slow, sustained clarinet

---

[49]   Having incurred increasingly burdensome debts, EMS Ltd folded in 1979.

[50]   Peter Zinovieff, 'Electronic music diary summer 1976', *Bulletin of the Computer Arts Society* (May 1977), reproduced at http://members.tripod.com/werdav/vocpzino.htm (accessed 30 September 2008).

[51]   Vincent Canby, reviewing the American release of the film, a year after the British release, in the *New York Times*, 12 May 1973. He makes no mention of the music.

lines at registral extremes, punctuated by brass chords, with violent percussion and electronic interjections. This is unequivocally the music of Hades.

The Death of Orpheus

A 'dramatic scene' for soprano, three bass clarinets, piano and crotales with a text by Zinovieff, *Nenia: the Death of Orpheus* was Birtwistle and Zinovieff's first extended collaboration on a conventional composition. It marked publicly the beginning of a long, Orphic journey they were to take together, which would culminate in the 1986 premiere of *The Mask of Orpheus*. *Nenia* represented the initial fruits of the close collaboration between two people who, from very different creative perspectives, recognized the primeval power of certain aspects of the Orpheus story. It also presented in microcosm many of the concerns that they were to explore on a much larger canvas in the opera. For this reason it makes a fascinating study for *The Mask of Orpheus*.

Nenia is, in Latin, a funeral song or dirge – here, a lament sung at Orpheus' funeral. Much of the work is in fact spoken, a consequence perhaps of its central concern with narration, with the retelling of a familiar tale. But this narrative is never presented as an uninterrupted line. There is one singer but she takes on the three roles of narrator, Orpheus and Eurydice (see Example 1.1). From the very start the narrative is broken up, words are fragmented, so that both Orpheus and Eurydice are present (in Virgilian style only through the singing of their names) within the narration; but the protagonists' names are torn apart so that often we are left with just isolated syllables. Sound becomes more important than sense. At key moments the crotales (the so-called 'antique cymbals') suggest something ancient, primitive, while their bell-like ringing reinforces the ritual dimension of this funeral ceremony. The plucked strings of the piano are clearly a stylized echo of Orpheus' lyre. Michael Hall has suggested that the three bass clarinets represent the chorus of Maenads,[52] the Dionysian women who ripped Orpheus apart and threw his head, torso and lyre into the river Hebrus.

As a 'dramatic scene' the work has a number of features from conventional opera: in particular, both recitative (narration) and aria (song) are present. However, the arias do not behave in the way one might expect, say, of a Baroque aria in revealing aspects of the inner feelings of the protagonists. As listeners we are not drawn into a character's world in order to understand his or her 'true' emotions. Orpheus's aria feels more like a song at arm's length, an aria in quotation marks. Although the incantatory character of the singing of the names is imbued with the power of the griever, who, at the loss of a loved one, tries to cling to the departed by repeating the name incessantly (with subtle echoes here of Monteverdi, Purcell and Gluck), the extreme stylization and fragmentation militate against our identifying with the

---

[52] Hall, *Harrison Birtwistle*, 77.

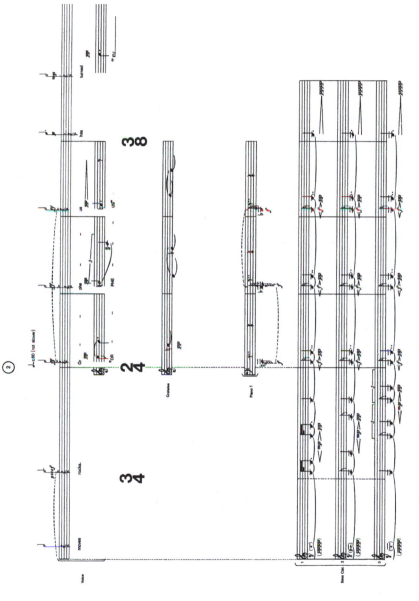

Example 1.1 *Nenia: the Death of Orpheus*, near opening

character. The music takes on an almost expressionistic dimension, especially where the most violent aspects of the story are related, when even pitches seem to dissolve into noise.[53] The narrative falls apart; it can no longer hold things together. Our attention is directed away from the story and its characters and towards the work's materials, that is, the sonic aspects both of the text and of the music.

The story, in so far as a story *is* told, is about Orpheus' *dis*-membering. Like Orpheus, Zinovieff's text, too, is torn apart by Birtwistle, limb from torso, bones from flesh. And yet we hear from the narrator:

> Singing and dreaming of Euridice,
> Whom he sees as a shadow,
> And questions to himself her existence.
> He turns again and again,
> Re-enacting the moment when he last saw her.

Orpheus' actions are thus concerned with *re*-membering – not just in the common sense of this word, as the *Oxford English Dictionary* defines it, of 'recalling the memory of (a person) with some kind of feeling or intention' but also in the sense of 'putting together again', that is, attempting to recapture his lost lover through memory. But he is doomed to failure, yearning for what cannot be. 'Hoping to catch Euridice in time', as the narrator sings, Orpheus is in fact the one who is caught. By the end of the work, the music too is caught in endlessly repeating mobiles (see Example 1.2). Its only option is to fade away *al niente*. We are left with just the name of Orpheus. But who is singing it? Zinovieff's text suggests it is Eurydice. But, intriguingly, the published score omits the quotation marks around Orpheus's name. It cannot be the narrator singing, because she can only speak. Could it, then, be the singer herself who is singing his name?

Although *Nenia*'s central concern is with narration, for much of the work the story itself gets lost. What Birtwistle seems to be interested in here is more the telling (and retelling) than the tale. The lament becomes a performance. Our attention is drawn not only towards the materials but towards the way in which those materials are presented. Arnold Whittall has written of what he calls the 'generic prototype' of lament in much twentieth-century music – what we might, indeed, describe as a general Orphic tendency. It is out of Birtwistle's 'frozen music' of 'exposition, not development' that emerges what Whittall describes as the 'ritual of lament'.[54] This is clear in the ending of *Nenia*. The lament here is not personalized, but ritualized: it becomes frozen in the music's repetitions. And because the singer adopts a number of different subject positions (including, as I have suggested, that of 'singer'), it has

---

53   See the discussion in Robert Adlington, *The Music of Harrison Birtwistle* (Cambridge: Cambridge University Press, 2000), 70.

54   Arnold Whittall, *Exploring Twentieth-Century Music: Tradition and Innovation* (Cambridge: Cambridge University Press, 2003), 161, 160.

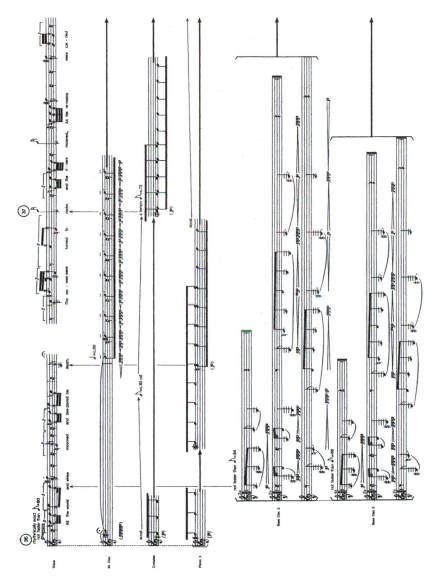

Example 1.2 *Nenia: the Death of Orpheus*, closing mobiles

the effect of alienating, of making strange, of distancing us as listeners. As audience we do not identify with Orpheus: we are not moved to tears by the loss of his lover, and we do not mourn his violent death. Because the narrative is fragmented, because the work's artifice is made visible, because the music becomes frozen, we are kept at a critical distance. We are merely spectators, not participants. In some senses, the work becomes about itself, that is, it is about lament, about the materials of lament, about *performing* lament, and not so much about the death of Orpheus.

These became central concerns for *The Mask of Orpheus*. In very general terms, the three acts of the opera follow a similar trajectory to *Nenia*, from the presentation of characters and situations in a pastoral landscape (Act I), through the violent death of Orpheus (Act II), to a ritualised lament in which the identity of Orpheus is subsumed back into the landscape (Act III). Time, memory and identity are key issues in the ways in which Zinovieff and Birtwistle represent the Orpheus myth. The (modernist) fracturing not just of musical and textual material but of the identities of the protagonists – there are three Orpheuses, Eurydices and Aristaeuses – is a fundamental aspect of the work's aesthetic. A fragile tension exists between past and present, between order and disorder, where the violence both to narrative continuity and to the stability of the subject is played out in the context of highly structural(ist) schemes and a dramaturgical formality represented in its recitatives, arias and choruses. The retelling of the Orpheus myth becomes a vehicle for engaging with the wider issues and crises of late-modern culture. In the violent twentieth century, when the threat to the subject has been at its greatest, perhaps the only legitimate response can be found in the performance of lament. As at the end of *Nenia*, all that is left at the close of *The Mask of Orpheus* is the ability to repeat endlessly, lamentingly, tragically. Identity is atomized and fades into a landscape of eternal nothingness. It offers a deeply pessimistic world view.

Orpheus Elegies

Birtwistle was in his mid thirties when he wrote *Nenia* and was beginning work on the Orpheus project. By the time he had completed the *26 Orpheus Elegies*, he was very nearly 70 years old. This return to Orpheus in maturity prompted a more reflective response in melancholic mode. Narration has now disappeared. Instead, in the manner of a Baroque aria, each short movement is concerned with just one musical or expressive idea. Described by the composer as postcards, the elegies take the form of 'settings' of some of Rilke's *Sonnets to Orpheus* for counter-tenor, oboe and harp, though in fact only six of them are sung. When the singer does sing, he does not play the part of Orpheus but offers a commentary on the text; it is more often the oboe's line that seems to represent the voice of Orpheus. In the instrumental elegies, short fragments of Rilke's text are placed after the music to suggest or intensify the mood, in the manner of Debussy's *Préludes*. There are occasional enraged outbursts, but for the most part the movements are, as the 'elegies' of the title suggests, songs of mourning and lamentation.

One of the simplest and most touching movements (No. 5; see Example 1.3) has the following excerpt from Rilke appended in German:

> Und mit kleinen Schritten gehn die Uhren
> neben unserm eigentlichen Tag.
>
> and the ticking footsteps of our watches
> walk beside our individual days.[55]

The harp stands for the lyre, a recurrent presence in Rilke's sonnets. The oboe carries conventional associations of both melancholy and the pastoral reed pipes (the ancient aulos). The singer is silent. But there is an additional presence here, a metronome ticking at ♩ = 84 'inside a box so as not to be seen and also to mute it'. Birtwistle has clearly been prompted by the 'ticking footsteps' of Stephen Cohn's translation,[56] and the mechanistic pulse is a very direct instance of the representation of ontological time that has sounded across Birtwistle's works from *Chronometer* via *Pulse Sampler* (1981) to *Harrison's Clocks* (1997–98).

We have already encountered Rilke's antagonism towards the machine, which symbolizes for him the dehumanizing aspects of modernity. In this movement we hear the incessant, unchanging, non-human ticks of the metronome as threatening, not least because the source (and the threat) remains hidden. The metronome (in Greek, *metro* + *nomos* = measure + law) might be understood to represent the absolutely rational law of Apollo. These mechanical sounds impinge upon the human, as can be heard in the harp, which, though less predictable, nonetheless remains under the control of the machine, that is, within its pulse frame. The harp part consists mainly of isolated, quasi-mechanical quavers, but intermittent pairings take on the character of a heartbeat. The highly constricted pitch material sets an atmosphere of unease. The oboe opposes this with a music that appears entirely irregular. Written exclusively in multiples of triplet quavers, it has a fluid melody which never coincides with the metronome's pulse, most notes in each phrase are of a different length, and most notes in each phrase start on a different part of the bar. This might be understood to represent the satyric realm of Dionysus. The conflict between the two is perhaps another version of the contest between Apollo

---

[55] Rilke, *Sonnets to Orpheus*, Part 1, poem 12, ll. 3–4.

[56] A transcription error ('eigenlichen' instead of 'eigentlichen') in Birtwistle's fair copy of the score (made available by Boosey & Hawkes before the definitive published version) suggests that he did not fully understand the German. Certainly the ticking metronome appears to have been prompted more by the translation than by Rilke's original. In any case, Birtwistle's typical response here is to the general mood and idea of the text rather than to its detail.

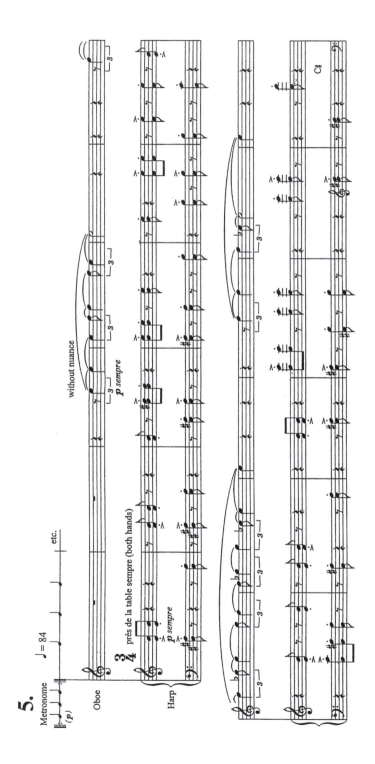

Example 1.3 *26 Orpheus Elegies*, No. 5, opening

and Marsyas, and forms the basis for the movement's sense of melancholy. (We should recall that the violent consequence of Apollo's victory in the contest was that Marsyas was flayed alive for his hubris.) More generally, as Hall first observed in the 1980s, the opposition between the regular and the irregular has been the 'central organizing principle' of all Birtwistle's music.[57]

But the oboe is also the elegiac voice of Orpheus, mourning – one might argue – the losses of modernity. Contained entirely within an eight-note chromatic set (from $d\flat^2$ to $a\flat^2$) and moving generally stepwise, it adopts the conventional characteristics of the lament. The falling semitone as a topic of sighing, weeping and lamenting, the so-called *pianto*, goes back (appropriately) at least as far as the late-sixteenth-century Italian madrigals and Elizabethan lute songs, and even today can still be taken to symbolize grief. The opening semitonal rising and falling figure of the oboe's melody has become a familiar sign of the lament in Birtwistle, most recently in his exploration of the world of Elizabethan melancholy. Close to the start of *The Shadow of Night* (2001) this same figure, transposed, is heard on a piccolo, which the composer asserts is a quotation of the opening three notes of Dowland's *In Darkness Let Me Dwell* (1610), an idea continued into the companion piece *Night's Black Bird* (2004). Whatever its origins, the implications of the idea, not just here but in Birtwistle's music in general, should be clear. This motif and variants on it signify the melancholic; it is to be found everywhere in *The Mask of Orpheus*.

Striking, too, is the emphasis in this movement (and more generally in many of the *26 Orpheus Elegies*) on the pitch class E. It is the first and final note of the oboe's melody; the harp's pitch material is formed entirely of semitonal clusters about E and its fifth, B. In nearly all Birtwistle's music, from his 'opus 1' *Refrains and Choruses* (1957) to his latest works, the note E forms a crucial and recurrent point of reference. It is another of his obsessions. However, he has never given a reason why, other than casually to suggest that it is his 'favourite' note. E often occurs, as here, at moments of beginning, beginning again, or ending, and it is associated with melancholy. That it is the lowest notated pitch of the composer's own lugubrious instrument, the clarinet, may have had a certain resonance for him. That it is also, in the diatonic modal tradition, the 'final' of the Phrygian mode, is perhaps more significant. (These two aspects conveniently coincide in Marsyas, the reed instrument player of Phrygian origin.) The Phrygian is the only mode characterized by a semitone above the final, which gives its cadence a peculiarly melancholic affect. Further, the movement either side of the final in this mode generates a version of Birtwistle's 'signature' motif (discussed more fully in Chapter 2), which moves a semitone in one direction, a whole tone in the other (E–F–D in its 'prime' form).

Plato writes about the character and ethics of the Phrygian mode in the *Republic*. One of only two modes appropriate to the education of guardians, it represents the 'voice and accent of a brave man … in the voluntary non-violent occupations of peace-time … and in all showing no conceit, but moderation and common sense

---

[57] Hall, *Harrison Birtwistle*, 13.

and willingness to accept the outcome'.[58] At the end of the fifth of the instrumental elegies, Orpheus, the heroic man of peace, acquiesces to the law of Apollo. His reed pipe is silenced as the machine ticks on. Does the presence of the Phrygian E symbolize his melancholic acceptance of the inevitable? It certainly seems to carry many parallels with the Es that dominate the final act of *The Mask of Orpheus*. The 'plaintive quality' of the music and the 'bleakly attractive landscaping' of the stage were noted by Stravinsky in relation to his own *Orpheus*.[59] Is this subtly echoed here too? After all, in that work it is the falling Phrygian lines of Orpheus' lyre that provide the context for his weeping for Eurydice.

Other Orphic Landscapes

One of Birtwistle's most striking Orphic landscapes is also built around this Phrygian E: *The Fields of Sorrow* (1971) captures eloquently the pastoral lament. It takes the form of a setting of an excerpt from the fourth-century Latin poet Ausonius, beginning:

> Errantes silve in magna et sub luce maligna
> Inter harundineasque comas gravidumque papaver
>
> They wander in deep woods, in mournful light,
> Amid long reeds and drowsy-headed poppies[60]

Who are 'they'? The souls of unnamed lovers from Virigil's *Aeneid* wandering eternally through the forests of the underworld. Orpheus and Eurydice never seem far away.

The E♮s sound on the piano in bell-like octaves from the very start, coloured with notes a semitone either side. These E♮s are then picked up by the chorus. At the back of the performing space stand two soprano soloists, calling to each other like ritual mourners, the first of whom begins with the familiar E–F–E lamenting motif. This melancholic landscape is slowly filled out while, in the foreground, woodwind soloists articulate short, soft motifs, beginning with the dark cor anglais (aulos). A new section is marked by a return to the piano octave Es as the landscape shifts, the chorus opens out to a music centred on the interval of a third (E–G♯), and in the

---

[58]   Plato, *The Republic*, tr. Desmond Lee (Harmondsworth: Penguin, rev. ed. 1974), 399b (p. 159).

[59]   Igor Stravinsky and Robert Craft, *Themes and Conclusions* (London: Faber and Faber, 1972), 53.

[60]   Reproduced in the front of the score. The English translation is by Helen Waddell, whose *Mediaeval Latin Lyrics* (London: Constable, 1929) was a favourite source for Birtwistle at this time.

foreground is heard a mournful horn melody, doubled in quasi-medieval organum at the fourth or fifth by the vibraphone. In the final section of the piece, the landscape changes again as first the chorus and sopranos, and later the horn and vibraphone, land on a new centre of D, on the 'other side' of the Phrygian final. By the end, with the return of the woodwind motifs played as mobiles, all the music can do is repeat. It is a strikingly similar situation to the end of *Nenia: the Death of Orpheus*. Tolling bells, lamenting voices, perpetual repetitions: all contribute to the representation of a landscape that is hauntingly beautiful in its melancholic desolation.

Birtwistle has created many other landscapes, none of which is explicitly Orphic, but all of which are satellites to the larger Orpheus project. *The Triumph of Time* is fascinating because of the striking reappearance at its climactic moment of the opening of *The Fields of Sorrow*, rescored to bring out its bell-like associations. Robert Adlington comments that whereas *Chronometer* had dealt with the 'quantitative' aspects of time, *The Triumph of Time* concerns itself with the 'qualitative'. It 'involves itself not so much with time's extent and length as with the form of its *motion*';[61] this is a primary concern also of *The Mask of Orpheus*, whose ending, I shall argue later, represents an allegorical transcendence of time. In *The Triumph of Time* the composer plays with the image of the motion of a procession across a landscape. *An Imaginary Landscape* (also 1971) is a personal lament to the memory of the composer's mother and is a landscape built from five recurring chorales. *Silbury Air* (1977) – another 'imaginary landscape' – shows a preoccupation with pulse and the focal note E to evoke, ritually, an ancient sense of place. The (Orphic) aria of the second half of the piece is called to a halt by a distinctive (Apollonian) four-chord harp cadence, identical to that which appeared twice in *Tragoedia* and which also cut short the solo clarinet's final stumbling ostinato in *Melencolia I* (1976). *Grimethorpe Aria* (1973), for brass band, stands at the intersection between the rural and urban landscapes of Birtwistle's youth.

Two other Arcadian landscapes merit attention here. According to certain accounts of their lineage, both Linus and Orpheus were the sons of Apollo by the muse Calliope. *Linoi* represents Orpheus's brother through the musical line of the basset clarinet, while, as in *Nenia*, Apollo's lyre is portrayed by the sound of plucked piano strings. Linus' melancholy song never fully flowers and he is ultimately silenced, violently, by Apollo. Linus, like Orpheus and Marsyas, committed the hubris of rivalling Apollo in his musical skills; he, too, paid the ultimate price. In *On the Sheer Threshold of the Night* the landscape is set out for us on the concert platform, with Hades (bass) and Eurydice (soprano) to the far left and right respectively, and the chorus ranged in between. In the centre stand tenor and counter-tenor, who, together, in rhythmic unison, represent two aspects of Orpheus: the rational and the instinctive. The work's text is drawn from Boethius' *De consolatione philosophiae* and is sung principally in Latin. As we have come to expect, Orpheus and Eurydice can only intone one another's names. But at the work's dénouement the chorus sings

---

[61] Adlington, *The Music of Harrison Birtwistle*, 100.

in English of Orpheus' inability to conquer his instincts, with terrible consequences: 'On the sheer threshold of the night Orpheus saw Eurydice, looked, and destroyed her.' Hades points home Boethius' moral: 'Ye who read, look up: the gods in daylight dwell. All that you hold of loveliness sinks from you, looking down at Hell.'[62] The work ends, again, in fragmentation and repetitions. The dark and strange landscape across which Orpheus and Eurydice call to each other is another field full of sorrows.

* * *

The composer's obsession with Orpheus, then, is not in doubt. But beyond acknowledgement of this fixation, he has been reluctant to address the reasons why he is so possessed by the myth. He has sometimes suggested that the subject matter is, to an extent, irrelevant, and it is true that he will often conceive a theatre piece initially independently of its subject or characters. He is fond of reminding his audiences that *The Mask of Orpheus* began life as a retelling of the Faust legend, but that he switched to the Greek myth because, as for so many opera composers, it meant he could deal musically with music and musicians. Faust was 'too psychological'.[63] 'I couldn't possibly write an opera with a direct psychology, with people in suits.'[64] But there has to be more to it than this. He would not have kept returning to Orpheus for over 40 years if he were not deeply engaged by the subject matter.

The fact is that the Orpheus story is the ideal medium through which Birtwistle is able to explore his wider musical and aesthetic preoccupations with myth and memory, melancholy and lament, time, and the nature of music itself. Birtwistle's work has always attempted to express the deep conflict between the violent and the lyrical, the rational and the irrational, the ancient and the modern. For a modernist any agreement between these extremes is ultimately unachievable, but it is also symptomatic of a modernist to be questing continually after such an accommodation, even in the knowledge that he is destined to fail. *The Mask of Orpheus* is a work concerned with failure. The consequences, as we have seen, are melancholic and pessimistic. Yet Orpheus continued to sing, even though his head had been severed from his body. An Orphic lyrical conviction underlies all Birtwistle's art. Birtwistle has reinvented the myth for the late twentieth century: Birtwistle's lamenting Orpheus stands as a symbol for late-modern man.

---

[62]   The translation is again by Helen Waddell.

[63]   Birtwistle, quoted in Christopher Wintle, 'A fine & private place', *Musical Times*, 1845 (November 1996), 6.

[64]   Birtwistle in interview with David Beard, 'Beauty and the beast: a conversation with Sir Harrison Birtwistle', *Musical Times*, 1902 (Spring 2008), 17.

Composing Orpheus

The Mask of Orpheus had a long and troubled gestation period. We have already seen how the seed for the work was planted early and how, in many different ways during the 1960s and early 1970s, Birtwistle was exploring those aspects of the Orpheus story that mattered to him most. Cyril Bennett, controller of London Weekend Television, had approached Birtwistle to write a television opera, to be directed by Peter Hall, for the opening of the station in 1968, and Orpheus was soon agreed upon as the subject matter, but the project fell through. Following the success of *Punch and Judy* at Aldeburgh in 1968, which had been commissioned by the English Opera Group (under the management of the Royal Opera House, Covent Garden), John Tooley, general director of the Royal Opera, approached Birtwistle to commission a new work for the Royal Opera House. Peter Hall was again central to the project, being a frequent director of productions at Covent Garden. In 1970 Hall, along with the conductor Colin Davis, was appointed a co-director of the Royal Opera; he was due to take up his appointment in September 1971.

Tooley recalls that the Orpheus myth was the eventual agreed subject for the Covent Garden commission.[65] Birtwistle claims that his first idea had been an opera based on the Faust legend, but the minutes of the opera sub-committee of the Royal Opera House reveal a more complex story. Birtwistle first submitted a synopsis for a libretto with a Greek librettist (the name of the librettist and the subject are not specified) to the sub-committee in December 1969, but this failed to impress the Opera House Board, even while it remained committed to working with the composer. In October 1970 a new subject was revealed: a retelling of the Chronos myth. The poet Ted Hughes had been approached, but he declared himself too busy to write the libretto. A year later Birtwistle was still planning an opera called *Kronia*, but by November 1971 he had appeared to drop the idea in favour of a work about Faust after Michel de Ghelderode's play *La mort du Docteur Faust* (*The Death of Dr Faust*, 1925).[66]

Birtwistle's first idea for a collaboration with Peter Zinovieff had been a 'grand opera' called *Ye Olde Faust*, for which Zinovieff prepared a complete libretto.[67] This shared many characteristics with the later Orpheus work. As its preface states:

---

[65] John Tooley, *In House: Covent Garden. 50 Years of Opera and Ballet* (London: Faber & Faber, 1999), 79.

[66] The work of Ghelderode (1898–1962) must have been in the air at the time. At the end of 1972 Ligeti first began thinking about *Le grand macabre*, which was based on one of the plays of the Belgian writer. The opera was premiered in Stockholm in 1978, conducted by Elgar Howarth, who also conducted the London production at ENO in 1982.

[67] I am very grateful to Peter Zinovieff for showing me the original typescript of *Ye Olde Faust*, a *c.*80-page document.

It is especially concerned with the death of Faust. The story is not an interpretation of the legends but is a fantasy based on them. The main novelty (and difficulty) in reading the text lies in its division into three completely separate plays (operas). Only rarely are these three actions synchronous but they usually relate in some way to each other. There are three acts with three scenes and each with three levels of action.

Even the progress of the work is similar to that of *The Mask of Orpheus*. Act I is concerned with the evolution and enactment of myth; Act II is Faust's nightmare of his own death; Act III takes place in an elevated puppet theatre. Like *Orpheus* the work explores ideas of myth, shadow, dream, sacrifice and suicide. In Act III Faust even plays at being Orpheus. Like *Orpheus* the work is highly complex and stylized; unlike *Orpheus* it places the retelling of the legend in a contemporary setting. The subject was eventually switched to Orpheus because both composer and librettist wanted to produce something more mythological, but this did not fundamentally alter their conception of the work.

Peter Hall never took up his contract at the Royal Opera. Despite Hall's protestations to the contrary, Tooley sensed that he 'wanted to be seen to be free in the event of the National Theatre considering him to be its director',[68] and he did indeed take up that post in 1973. On leaving Covent Garden, Hall transferred his loyalties to Glyndebourne Opera, taking with him the idea of a work by Birtwistle. The composer had, in any case, begun to rethink the Orpheus project on a smaller scale more appropriate to Glyndebourne,[69] and by 1972 he was engaged in negotiations with the Sussex-based company. In May 1973 Glyndebourne reached an agreement with Birtwistle and Zinovieff to write an opera based on the Orpheus legend, and the commission was bought from the Royal Opera, with a view to mounting the work

---

[68]   Tooley, *In House*, 36.

[69]   During 1971 Zinovieff prepared a full-length (unset) libretto for *Orpheus 1*, a small-scale 'Opera for the Village Hall', completed at 'Fearns, Isle of Raasay. New Year, 1972'. (The date is fascinating, given that in the autumn and winter of 1971 Birtwistle was still discussing *Kronia* and *Dr Faust* with Covent Garden.) It appears to represent ideas in an earlier stage of development, a shorter and less complex work than *The Mask of Orpheus* was to become. For example, the idea of multiple characters is present but explored more conventionally: each character has three versions representing mortals, gods and heroes, e.g., the tenor plays Orpheus, Hades and a Farmer. (It is noteworthy that Orpheus started life as a tenor, later becoming a baritone, before much later reverting to a tenor again.) Electronic music is, unsurprisingly, considered fundamental but the tapes seem to have been conceived mainly to provide effects. The six 'passing clouds or allegorical interludes' are accompanied merely by pipes playing in unison. One striking feature, absent in the final version, is the presence throughout of the Announcer, who 'speaks pompously and with reserve. A mixture of an oracle, an announcer at the Lord Mayor's Banquet and a newscaster on TV'. The Announcer explains the plot to the audience. I am again grateful to Peter Zinovieff for showing me the original typescript, a *c.*60-page document.

under Hall's direction in 1975. Thus by the spring of 1973 Birtwistle felt confident enough in the future of *Orpheus* to begin composing.

The precise chronology of the composition of the work is difficult to pin down. Very few of the more than 1,000 pages of sketches, drafts and other materials now held in the Harrison Birtwistle Collection of the Paul Sacher Stiftung in Basel are dated. One important document is the first complete libretto, four volumes of typescript totalling more than 600 pages. It is titled an 'Explanatory Document' and is dated 1974 (i.e., it was prepared once the composition of the first two acts was well under way), but it helpfully contains the following inventory under the sub-heading 'The Documentation [1.2]':

1. An Introductory Document (1973). This was designed to show the main structures and tensions in the Opera but is superseded by the present document and the final libretto for each act.[70]

2. The finished libretto for Acts 1 and 2 (each one volume). Act 3 will be ready in January 1975. These documents can only be completed once the musical timings have been established by the composer.

3. The full orchestral score for Act 1. Act 2 follows in December 1974 and Act 3 in June 1975.

4. A 'shout-through' [a term Birtwistle liked to use, taken from Peter Hall] using limited instruments for Act 1.

5. A piano reduction for Act 1 (November 1975). The succeeding acts follow about six weeks after the finished orchestral score.

6. This document.

As we shall see, this was an entirely unfeasible timetable.

At this stage in the work's genesis it was still called simply *Orpheus*. The principal role was a high baritone, not a tenor, while Aristaeus was called 'The Shadow', a tenor role. It is interesting, in the context of the then recent collaboration of librettist and composer on *The Offence*, that the introduction to this document declares that '"Orpheus" should be presented more like a film than an Opera and more like a thriller than a philosophical statement'. It continues:

> The plot, which is often separate from the words and music, allows and encourages such a presentation and it is in the plot that the form of the Opera that is seen is to be found. The music and words as well as the thoughts and structures in them are, to a large extent, the composer's and librettist's own concern. It is the producer

---

[70] I am grateful to Peter Zinovieff for showing me a copy of this 'Introductory Document', complete with colour illustrations by his young daughter Sofka, some of which were reproduced as the covers of the 1997 CD. The title page, drawn by Sofka, clearly reveals that this 120-page document was prepared as a prospectus for 'an opera in three acts for Covent Garden'.

who must make 'Orpheus' a living and exciting work. He has, it is true, some direct help from the music, a little less from the words, but much less in either case than is habitually the case.

On the other hand the producer has a carefully worked out scenario – more like a film scenario than a conventional libretto – and this new type of opera-document contains salient features from both the orchestral score and the words. ...

This declaration of intention is important because it helps us understand just how radical Birtwistle and Zinovieff's ambitions were. The public version of the libretto, a relatively slim 68-page volume dated 'Isle of Raasay, 1978' but not published by Universal Edition until 1986, is a shadow of the original document. It had to be presented in such a compressed format that it is, in places, very difficult to follow and to relate to the music. It is not a conventional text 'to be set', and this was clearly an important part of the creators' original thinking. There are moments in the work when music, text and drama all seem to be working independently; as Birtwistle later declared to Michael Hall: 'There's a musical level and a dramatic level and they don't start coming together until the last act.'[71]

The earliest datable evidence that exists of Birtwistle's first thoughts are scribbled jottings on a scrap of paper in the Harrison Birtwistle Collection headed 'Orpheus 21.–3–73.' which show how, for him, musical and dramatic concepts were inseparable from the start, and that he needed some sense of the overall structure before he could start composing in earnest (see Figure 1.1).

Figure 1.1   Birtwistle's early sketched plan for Act I
(transcribed from PSS 0530-0945)

1   notation   instrumental
2   musical ideas. – gestural ideas ~~(musical)~~
3   character principles
4   overall musical concept
5   ~~get Peter draw general plan :~~ parados | act I | II | III | exodos

He uses a <u>lute</u>? only to sing songs of magic? other wise he is carrying the wretched thing everywhere.
Actor Orpheus only mimes playing

---

[71]   Hall, *Harrison Birtwistle*, 145.

Other (undated) papers include phonemes of the opening text with unpitched gestures marked above them and a graphic representation of 'elements of the 1st part of Orpheus'. Some early pages of numbers and rhythms appear in an unlined notebook from Swarthmore College, a small liberal arts institution near Philadelphia to which Birtwistle had been appointed Visiting Professor for the academic year 1973–74. (At the invitation of Morton Feldman, he took up a similar position in 1974–75 at SUNY at Buffalo.) Sketches and a graphic plan of most of Act I, scene 3 can also be found on headed paper from Swarthmore; elsewhere sketches for the Act I Ceremony are dated '17.4.74'. It is clear from this and other evidence that much of the first two acts of the opera were drafted while the composer was in the USA.

On his return to Britain Birtwistle decided to live on the remote island of Raasay in the Inner Hebrides, in a house bought from Zinovieff. The two spent extended periods there working on *Orpheus*. But by early 1974 it had already emerged that complications with the construction of the new National Theatre buildings on London's South Bank meant that Peter Hall would not be available at Glyndebourne in 1975, and the production of *Orpheus* would have to be postponed by a year or two. Hall eventually dropped out, and Terry Hands of the Royal Shakespeare Company agreed in principle to take over as director. However, the work had grown in size to such an extent that Glyndebourne was beginning to express concerns. (Andrew Rosner, Birtwistle's agent at Allied Artists London, considered that it was Hall who was principally responsible for the reputation *Orpheus* had earned as being extremely expensive to produce – Hall's conception of the piece was highly elaborate.[72]) In February 1975 the Glyndebourne Board resolved that it was not prepared to incur any financial loss in mounting *Orpheus*; unless the Arts Council of Great Britain (which had funded the commission) could cover the costs of production and rehearsal time, the performances would have to be abandoned. By the end of June it was clear to the board that the Arts Council was facing problems in making such a financial commitment.[73]

Fearful that the production would be lost, and rejecting the possibility of a staging by Glyndebourne Touring Opera, Birtwistle started to cast around for another organization that might be interested in taking over the project. Lord Harewood, managing director of English National Opera (ENO), reported to his music director that 'Harry came to see me on Thursday July 18 [1975] to tell me about his opera ORPHEUS.'[74] ENO received the idea with interest. Andrew Rosner approached George Christie, chairman of Glyndebourne Productions, to explain that Birtwistle was now determined that his opera should be produced at the Coliseum. In November

---

[72] Documented in an ENO memorandum of 25 September 1975 to Lord Harewood from his personal assistant; ENO Archive, London.

[73] Notes from the minutes of Glyndebourne Productions Ltd, provided courtesy of Glyndebourne Archive.

[74] ENO memorandum of 21 July 1975 from Lord Harewood to Charles Mackerras; ENO Archive.

Rosner wrote to ENO to confirm his understanding that Glyndebourne would co-operate in the transfer of the commission and that the work would be produced in London in September and October 1978 in a co-production with Frankfurt Opera, where it would be seen in March and April the following year. By August 1976 Rosner was able to verify in a letter to ENO that the first two acts were complete and that Birtwistle intended to finish the remainder of the opera by May 1977. But, in fact, composition had already ground to a halt and Birtwistle would only resume work on Act III once a realistic performance date had been settled. In 1975 Birtwistle had followed Hall to the National Theatre, where he was appointed music director. This job, along with the acceptance of other commissions, resulted in a long hiatus in the composition of *Orpheus*, and so to a prolonged series of postponements to the London production.

Birtwistle regards the period he spent at the National Theatre as one of the most fulfilling of his compositional career. He remained there until 1983, after which he became an associate director, and worked closely with playwrights, directors and actors on productions as varied as *Hamlet* and *Amadeus*. This demanded a rethinking of his compositional priorities and resulted in a codification, simplification and reorientation of his music. His work on the celebrated *Oresteia* production was central for him in many ways, not least in enabling him to work with the designer Jocelyn Herbert, who would go on to make the sets, costumes and masks for *The Mask of Orpheus*. Herbert understood perfectly the significance of the masks in *Orpheus*, not only in underlining the formal nature of the piece, but also in dealing with the difficulty of how to represent on stage the three forms of each of the principal characters. 'Harry wanted masks from the beginning', she writes.[75] They were fundamental to the idea of the work, as its later change in title made transparent.

In February 1980 the Arts Council stepped in to offer an additional sum to Birtwistle to complete the opera, and so in the autumn of 1981 he resumed composition. Michael Taylor has identified elements of the sketch material which indicate that some work on Act II was completed after the break, but the bulk of activity at this stage involved writing all of the music for Act III plus the preparation of the electronic components. New ways of working are in evidence, as will be discussed in Chapter 4.

With the collapse of Zinovieff's EMS company in 1979, the composer turned to IRCAM, the computer music research institute housed beneath the Centre Pompidou in Paris, in order to realize the tape materials. The director of IRCAM, Nicholas Snowman, suggested the New Zealand-born composer Barry Anderson (1935–87) to collaborate with Birtwistle. Anderson had been an influential figure in the 1970s in establishing a number of key British electronic music organizations. In particular, a piece composed in 1976 (revised 1985) for speaker, flute, percussion, tape and electronics, called *Mask*, suggested crucial aesthetic affinities between the

---

    75   Herbert, in Cathy Courtney (ed.), *Jocelyn Herbert: a Theatre Workbook* (London: Art Books International, 1993), 200.

two composers. Anderson was engaged jointly by ENO and IRCAM, and the two composers spent six months together in Paris in February–July 1982 developing the exciting sounds that would play such an important and integral part in the final production. The first informal airing of their collaboration took place at IRCAM in 1983; Anderson continued to work on the materials right up to the premiere (with occasional visits from Birtwistle), and he was also responsible for co-ordinating the complex sound diffusion during the performances. Ian Dearden, his assistant at the premiere performances, observes that Anderson's

> generosity of spirit marked him out as one of only a handful of people capable of entering into another composer's creative universe, absorbing it and responding to it with fidelity and freshness. As a result he was able to meet Harrison Birtwistle's ingenious strategies and schemes head on and, whilst others may have been lured into an exploration on their own terms, he managed to conjure a sound world for the opera that is at once original yet ingrained with Birtwistle's own voice.[76]

Indeed one of the most striking aspects about the creation of *The Mask of Orpheus* is just how much it was the product of a collaboration of creative partners. As a concept, as a response to ancient myths and texts, as a structure, and as a piece of theatre, *Orpheus* clearly took its impetus from Zinovieff, whose influence was far in excess of the 'conventional' role of a librettist; the innovative sonic world of the electronics belonged as much to Anderson as it did to Birtwistle – and, in turn, to the team of programmers and technicians at IRCAM, especially the head of musical research, Jean-Baptiste Barrière, who undertook most of the computing on the CHANT program for the voice of Apollo. And the role of the producer-director was going to be crucial in bringing to the stage a work where neither music nor text directly suggested an obvious narrative realization. The analogy with film again comes to mind: Birtwistle's role here might be thought of as that of a kind of *auteur*, drawing together the individual talents of many artists to serve his artistic vision through his recurrent musico-dramatic obsessions. However, notwithstanding the decisive impact of Anderson, Zinovieff and others on the final product, it remains pre-eminently *Birtwistle's* work, in that throughout it carries his imaginative and controlling imprint.

The work was essentially finished in 1983, at the same time as the composer moved house from Scotland to the Lot region of France. He also moved on to new compositional projects, echoing out beyond *The Mask of Orpheus*, including the stage work *Yan Tan Tethera* (a 'mechanical pastoral', premiered in London just six weeks after *Orpheus*) and a landmark ensemble piece, *Secret Theatre* (1984), which might well be understood as the imaginary love dance of Orpheus and Eurydice. A letter from ENO to the Arts Council dated 27 March 1984 confirmed that, more

---

[76]   Ian Dearden, 'The electronic music of *The Mask of Orpheus*', liner note for *The Mask of Orpheus* (London: NMC Recordings 1997, NMC D050), 15.

than a decade after composition had first begun, *The Mask of Orpheus* had been completed and the full score was now in the possession of Universal Edition. But even with the completion of the score, there remained much work to be done to prepare it for performance. Revisions were undertaken, though the location of the revised version of the score is unknown. Michael Taylor has made certain deductions from the surviving evidence:

> As the score issued by Universal Edition is a photocopy of the work of a copyist [more than one, in fact], it may be surmised that Birtwistle amended a copy of the original score [a fair copy of which is in the Harrison Birtwistle Collection], rewriting Orpheus' music for tenor and 'overhauling' ... the parts of the opera that were almost ten years old in the light of the recently completed third act.[77]

At last a production was on the cards, though ENO still had many anxieties about mounting the work. Preliminary costings indicated that a budget of £250,000 was needed, and serious attempts were made both to secure commercial sponsorship and to find a co-production partner. (Collaborations were discussed with opera houses in Berlin, Cologne, Frankfurt, Hamburg, New York, Stockholm and Vienna, and with festivals in Amsterdam and Florence, but all foundered.) Were it not for the donation of £150,000 from an anonymous American admirer, the production plans could still have come to nothing.

Retelling Orpheus

And so there remains the final story to be told: that of Orpheus himself. This is no simple task because Birtwistle and Zinovieff are not interested in a simple retelling. As the original libretto states, echoing the earlier *Faust* text, the 'story taken in this opera is largely a fantasy based on the legend'. And because Zinovieff takes the view that Orpheus never existed as an individual, it is the collective inheritance that interests librettist and composer. Thus, we are presented with multiple versions of the Orpheus legend. There are three Orpheuses, as there are three Eurydices and three Aristaeuses: each of these characters exists in the forms of the Man or Woman (a Singer), the Hero or Heroine (a silent Mime), and the Myth (a Puppet, who also sings). More than one of these versions of a character can (and do) appear on the stage at the same time. Orpheus dies on many occasions during the course of the work and four versions of his death are represented. Even Orpheus' journey to and from the underworld is presented only as a dream. Key events occur more than once, either simultaneously (for example, the death of Eurydice) or successively (for

---

[77]   Michael Taylor, 'Narrative and musical structures in Harrison Birtwistle's *The Mask of Orpheus* and *Yan Tan Tethera*', in Hermann Danuser and Matthias Kassel (eds), *Musiktheater heute* (Mainz: Schott, 2003), 177, n. 7.

example, in the 'Time Shifts'). Other stories – allegories within the larger allegory – interrupt the main action from time to time (the 'Passing Clouds' and 'Allegorical Flowers') to throw new light on the violence of Orpheus' death and the lyricism of his love for Eurydice. Figure 1.2 gives Zinovieff's graphic overview of the opera, as it appears in the various versions of the libretti.

Figure 1.2   Dramatic structure of *The Mask of Orpheus* (libretto, p. 6)

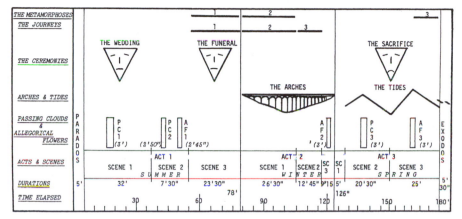

The Mask of Orpheus is a highly formal work. 'I wanted to create a formal world that was utterly new', says Birtwistle. The libretto reveals 126 separate structural 'events', the majority of which bear a designation as recitative or aria, but these are not necessarily recognizable to an audience as they might be in a Baroque opera or even in the boldly juxtaposed numbers of *Punch and Judy*. The complexity of the presentation of these events matches the complexity of the presentation of the allegory. The work is not concerned with a singular, linear narrative. Rather, as the original libretto proposes:

> ORPHEUS is an Opera or, rather, a Lyric Tragedy, in which the myth of the life and death of Orpheus is used as a carrier to otherwise express the transitions from chaos to order and back again of music, words and thought. At the highest level, it is with the evolution and degradation of civilised man that 'Orpheus' is concerned. On the visual and dramatic level these ideas are expressed primarily through showing the forms, fears and power of Death through the evolution of the Orphic myth. The story of Orpheus is used to hang on various structures and devices as well as to provide symbols.

The central themes of *The Mask of Orpheus*, then, are time, memory and identity.

* * *

The premiere of *The Mask of Orpheus* took place on 21 May 1986 at the London Coliseum, and seven further performances followed, one of which was recorded for broadcast by BBC Radio 3.[78] The impact and originality of its achievement were recognized instantly. 'The world afterwards is different', wrote Paul Griffiths in *The Times*.[79] A concert performance of Act II, dedicated to the memory of Barry Anderson, was given on 10 January 1988 at the Barbican Centre, London, as part of the BBC Birtwistle celebration 'Endless Parade', and was broadcast live on BBC Radio 3. For this performance Birtwistle included Orpheus' solo from the end of Act I ('First Shout of Gratitude') and linked the close of Act II to a short passage from Act III, scene 2. Ten years after the premiere, two performances of a new semi-staged production were presented on 11 and 12 April 1996 at the Royal Festival Hall, London, by the BBC Symphony Orchestra as part of the 'Secret Theatres' Festival, again broadcast by BBC Radio 3. A remixed and edited version of this transmission was released the following year as a CD by NMC Recordings. And, 13 years after it was last heard live, a Birtwistle 75th birthday performance of Act II took place on 14 August 2009 at the BBC Proms. One fully staged run of eight performances, two semi-staged concert performances and two performances of Act II: this is the entire performance history of *The Mask of Orpheus*. *Orpheus* remains, to date, an infrequently performed opera that has never been seen outside London.

Yet, from its premiere up to the present, *The Mask of Orpheus* has continued to garner plaudits from a diverse community of scholars, critics and composers. It is spoken of as a post-war landmark in music and music-theatre even by those who have not witnessed it on the stage. The work's impact has been far wider than its slender number of performances would suggest. Musicologists write about its influence; critics use it as a yardstick by which to judge other new operas; composers cite it as a crucial model. This is an extraordinary phenomenon. Why does this work address such a wide audience? In part, it is its single-minded musical originality. In part, it is its audacious combination of music, song, drama, myth, mime, dance and electronics – a work of total theatre. And in part, it is its treatment of the Orphic legacy that, in the hands of Birtwistle and Zinovieff, touches a deep sensibility in late-modern society. It is the aim of this book to explore something of its meanings and expressive power, to explore something of how and why it speaks in the ways it does.

---

[78]   The recording was made on 12 June 1986 and was scheduled for broadcast on 17 June (as advertised in the *Radio Times*). However, a fault with a microphone meant that Act II had to be re-recorded on 26 June and the broadcast was delayed until 1 April 1987.

[79]   23 May 1986; repr. in Paul Griffiths, *The Substance of Things Heard: Writings about Music* (Rochester, NY: University of Rochester Press, 2005), 325.

Chapter 2
The Mask of Orpheus: Act I

Synopsis

The opening Parados[1] (in Greek tragedy, the song sung by the chorus as it enters) represents Apollo presiding over the birth of Orpheus, teaching him to sing. The work begins from nothing, like the first sunrise, and the slow pace of change prepares us for the enormity of the epic drama that is to unfold.

Scene 1 begins with Orpheus' first Poem of Reminiscence, fragments of his memory of his journey with Jason and the Argonauts: 'the King stands highest over fifty men'. Orpheus falls in love with Eurydice, and they sing their first quietly ecstatic Duet of Love. Hymen is invoked by the priests for the wedding of Orpheus and Eurydice, punctuated by extensions of their first Love Duet. There are a number of bad omens. The couple dance to Orpheus' first Song of Magic.

Scene 2 opens with Eurydice's first Cry of Memory, sung standing by the river. Two versions of her death take place simultaneously (involving singers and mimes). In both, Aristaeus attempts to seduce Eurydice. In one case, she resists; in the other, she does not. She runs, followed by Aristaeus, and is killed by the bite of a water-snake. Aristaeus relates Eurydice's death to Orpheus.

The first Time Shift occurs at the beginning of scene 3 – a distortion of the events of scene 2. Now, it is Orpheus (Mime) who witnesses the death of Eurydice. Eurydice's Funeral Ceremony takes place, echoing the Wedding Ceremony. Orpheus consults the Oracle of the Dead, the verses of whose Hysterical Aria punctuate the remainder of Act I. In response to the Oracle's request for a secret, Orpheus exchanges his magical power of song for three rules he must follow in the underworld. But the Oracle has been tricked and she still cannot sing. Her terrible screeches close the act while Orpheus dreams of the 17 Arches and his journey to the underworld.

Parados

Act I begins with the presentation of a myth; indeed, it begins with the presentation of one of the most tenacious of all explanatory myths, namely the story of creation. The familiar narration from Genesis tells us that, in the beginning, 'darkness was upon the face of the deep'. Ovid's version at the start of the *Metamorphoses* recounts

---

[1]   Birtwistle and Zinovieff consistently misspell this word, which should be *parodos*, after Aristotle. To avoid confusion I have retained their spelling throughout.

that, in the time of Chaos, 'No sun as yet poured light upon the world'.[2] Robert Graves reminds us that

> the Orphics say that black-winged Night, a goddess of whom even Zeus stands in awe, was courted by the Wind and laid a silver egg [the moon] in the womb of Darkness; and that Eros, whom some call Phanes [the love-god; also the sun], was hatched from this egg and set the Universe in motion.[3]

The Mask of Orpheus commences with the rising of the sun.

> The Parados opens in absolute darkness. Gradually the sound of a bee is heard. The sun very slowly brightens. It becomes hot midsummer. A gradual exchange of sounds. In the end a true note. Orpheus has learnt to sing magic.

> The sunrise symbolises the birth of words, pitch and song. (Libretto, p. 10)

This Parados stands outside the main structure of the work and takes place in the time of 'before' (see Figure 1.2). In this sense it has more in common with the prologue of Greek tragedy, in which the dramatic situation is set out.

The Parados, which lasts under two minutes, presents both the first Orphic Hymn (Hymn of Ecstasy) and the first Mystery (Enthusiasmos). The libretto (p. 10) tells us that they 'are made up from pre-recorded fragments of Orpheus' first song. They represent the voice of Apollo teaching Orpheus.' It is clear from the start, then, that the rising sun is not just a birth or creation symbol but is also associated with the sun-god Apollo, the god of music and poetry. We have seen in the previous chapter that certain tellings of the Orpheus myth represent Apollo as Orpheus' father, and in this work Apollo plays a central role; indeed, it is Apollo, not Orpheus, who is present at beginning and end and who stands both for an idea of time in eternity and, particularly, of music. '[Apollo's] highly polished golden throne had magical inscriptions carved all over it, a back shaped like a lyre, and a python skin to sit on. Above hung a golden sundisk with twenty-one rays shaped like arrows, because he pretended to manage the sun.'[4]

In fact, the ideas presented in the libretto were not entirely realized in the score. The sketches and the first fair copy show additional parts for psalteries, a medieval kind of harp, but these have vanished from the final edition, presumably on logistical grounds as they were to be used nowhere else. The sounds we hear in the Parados relate in general to Apollo, his lyre and the sun: the electronic background Summer Aura (present throughout much of Act I, and here sounding perhaps like a far-off

---

[2]   Ovid [Publius Ovidius Naso], *Metamorphoses*, tr. A.D. Melville (Oxford: Oxford University Press, 1986), Book I (p. 1).

[3]   Robert Graves, *The Greek Myths* (London: Penguin, 1992 [1960]), 30.

[4]   Robert Graves, *Greek Gods and Heroes* (New York: Dell Laurel-Leaf, 1960), 9.

swarm of bees or the indistinct pre-nascent humming from within the womb); the distant (electronic) voice of Apollo speaking – in his own invented language – the word 'OFOARIF' (meaning 'remember'); Apollo's gong-like punctuating signals, which are in fact generated entirely from sampled harp sounds; and the chimes of the (indeterminately) pitched Noh harps. I am unable to find any evidence of pre-recorded fragments of Orpheus's first song for use here, though Apollo's word makes links with the 'remembering' with which the first Poem of Reminiscence is concerned.

The function of the Parados is both to provide a frame and to set up – in a pre-literate realm – the central themes of birth, memory and music. It is from the formlessness of this world where

> the countenance
> Of nature was the same, all one, well named
> Chaos, a raw and undivided mass … [5]

that words, then music, then song emerge. The entrance of Orpheus Man is 'like a human sunrise' (score, p. 2).

Act I, scene 1

The true beginning of Act I is marked by Orpheus' first utterances, which are just isolated syllables, primitive grunts to himself, 'as if searching for words'. The words towards which he is groping are eventually revealed, and, retrospectively, we understand that his initial inchoate sounds in fact come from the first line of his Poem of Reminiscence: 'The King stands highest [over fifty men]', the king being Jason, and the men being his Argonauts, among whom numbered Orpheus himself. These, then, are the fragments of Orpheus' first song to which the libretto alluded; the work thus begins with a pre-echo (memory) of an act of remembering.

The libretto tells us that the 'evolution of speech via recitative to aria through mumbling and incoherence is gradual' (p. 11). This process takes place audibly before us. Into Orpheus' inward grunts are interjected shouted syllables, out of which emerge single words spoken in an elongated and exaggerated manner. Eventually, 'with natural speech inflection', he learns how to utter a complete and connected sentence, and this marks the beginning proper of the first Poem of Reminiscence (score, fig. 12, p. 8). We are already some eight minutes into the work.

But there are other sounds accompanying this representation of Orpheus' development. His grunts are punctuated by the voice and signals of Apollo, who urges Orpheus to 'remember' and commands him to 'speak' ('DREID'), which eventually he does. Orpheus Myth (Puppet) simultaneously begins to speak his

---

[5] Ovid, *Metamorphoses*, Book I (p. 1).

recitative, a further set of memories recounting the sounds, feelings and experiences of his expedition on the *Argo*. 'I remember …', the Myth repeats, persistently. This, then, is a third kind of remembering. In the libretto Orpheus Myth repeats the telling phrase, 'I remember remembering' (p. 11), though this is not set in the score. When eventually Orpheus Man begins to speak the five stanzas of his Poem ('an allegory on the same journey'), though clear enough at the start, it soon begins to break up.

As far as it is possible to tell, this moment may well have been the starting-point for Birtwistle's long compositional journey. His earliest sketches show him playing not with pitches but with the words. Illustration 2.1 relates to the fifth verse of the first Poem of Reminiscence, through which we would appear to have access to some of his first thoughts. These are elegant doodles, improvisations, the trying out of ideas with text alone to see where they might lead: 'that's how most of my pieces begin. I indulge my fantasies: I allow intuition to take over'.[6] Here, each line of the verse is numbered in order from 1 to 6, and each syllable of each line is similarly numbered in sequence. Then both the order of (selected) syllables within each line and the ordering of the complete lines are subjected to a reordering according to a scheme that is not given, but that would seem to be a kind of interversion routine similar to that of Messiaen (and possibly familiar to Birtwistle from Messiaen).[7]

The result is a line of text that throws a new perspective on the original poetic verse:

---

[6]   Birtwistle, quoted in Michael Hall, *Harrison Birtwistle* (London: Robson, 1984), 148.

[7]   The most straightforward kind of interversion is produced by reading from the centre to the extremes of a string of numbers, e.g., where 1–2–3–4–5 becomes 3–4–2–5–1 or 3–2–4–1–5, or from the extremes to the centre, e.g., where 1–2–3–4–5 becomes 5–1–4–2–3. These interversions can then themselves be subject to further processes of interversion. The processes Birtwistle adopts here are relatively informal, but – despite the complication of a changing number of syllables in successive lines – it should be clear how he gets from line 1 to line 6, e.g., line 3 is a direct 'centre outwards' interversion of line 2 where 5–3–1–2–4 becomes 1–3–2–5–4 with the additional '6' tagged on to the start. In general, the sketches for *Orpheus* are littered with number matrices that are the result of reordering through simple permutation procedures such as cyclic rotation. As will be seen later in this discussion, these matrices can be used to generate a wide range of pitch, durational, textural and other material. David Beard has made a detailed study of Birtwistle's use of number in the sketches for his works up to 1977, in particular of the evidence revealed by the so-called 'modual book' (dating from around 1970) in which are to be found, for instance, the working out of the permutation of three- and four-note contours. See Beard, 'An analysis and sketch study of the early instrumental music of Sir Harrison Birtwistle (*c*.1957–77)', DPhil dissertation, University of Oxford, 2000. Messiaen devotes a full discussion to interversion as part of a technique of 'symmetrical permutations' in Olivier Messiaen, *Traité de rythme, de couleur, et d'ornithologie (1949–1992)*, vol. 3, 5–76. Birtwistle's interest in Messiaen dates back to his student days in Manchester in the mid 1950s.

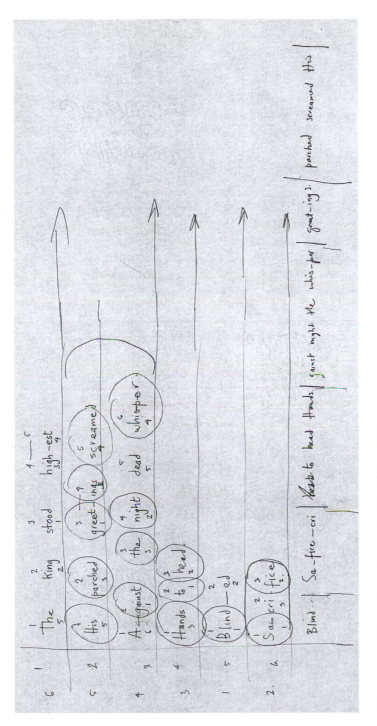

Illustration 2.1 Act I, early sketch (PSS 0530-0858)

Blind | Sa-fice-cri | to head Hands.| gainst night the whis-per | greet-ings.| parched screamed His |

Its semantics are (part-)destroyed, but there are still echoes of the original. To use an analogy of which the composer himself is fond,[8] it is a kind of Cubist take on the original text, a Cubist (re)telling of the tale. Birtwistle is not so much interested in the text *qua* text but as material with which he can work. As Paul Driver has written, 'in certain theatrical circumstances, Birtwistle can make a piece without using "actual" music at all, in a work such as ... *The Mask of Orpheus* ... he piles up material with a positively frightening appetite for resonance and context. In some ways *The Mask of Orpheus* is less an opera than a body of ... material.'[9] The reworking of the text is entirely in keeping with the way in which material elsewhere in the work is continually being re-presented, such as in the Time Shifts or in the presence of multiple Orpheuses. And given that this text is part of a Poem of Reminiscence, such a procedure would seem appropriate. The text is not, in a sense, being presented for the first time, but is being recalled, summoned from the past, fragmented and distorted in Orpheus' memory.

In actual fact, in the final version of the score the text appears closer to how Zinovieff wrote it and how it appears in the libretto. The sketches seem to suggest that, quite early on, Birtwistle abandoned such an extreme reordering of syllables. Perhaps a degree of narrative continuity was eventually found to be desirable. Certainly it appeared necessary to maintain a closer connection between the text of the poem and the 'commentary' on it in the recitative, because the presentation of the fifth verse of the poem is shared between Orpheus Man (Singer) and Myth (Puppet) (see score, after fig. 17, p. 11):

O_{singer} The King highest stood |		remember	the screaming |
O_{puppet}	| I	I remember	|
//			
O_S His parched greetings screamed,		| (against)(the whisper)	|
O_P	Against the night dead whisper. | The dark rocks splashing, |		
//			
O_S Hands to head. (Greetings) Blinded. (Screamed his) Sacrifice. | (Parched) ||			
O_P	The effortless	rowing.	| ||

The sketches here give glimpses into the compositional process and throw interesting light on the way in which Birtwistle deals with all his material: musical, textual

---

[8]   For example, he has spoken of the cyclic processes in his music as a 'sort of musical Cubism'. See Birtwistle, in Ross Lorraine, 'Territorial rites 2', *Musical Times*, 1857 (November 1997), 14.

[9]   Paul Driver, 'Sir Harrison Birtwistle – ein Porträt / Harrison Birtwistle – a portrait', in Basil Rogger (ed.), *Roche Commissions: Sir Harrison Birtwistle* (Lucerne: Roche, 2004), 15.

and dramatic. The division of text between voices explored in *Nenia: the Death of Orpheus* is here expanded on to a much larger canvas.

Birtwistle himself had a very clear visual sense of how this section of music should be structured, and this is revealed in a 'graphic representation' that is to be found among the sketches (see Illustration 2.2). The shape of the whole and the dramatic placement of key events (the entrance of Orpheus, his first coherent statement, the first interjection of Eurydice) were all thought through before he set to work on the music. It was already clear from earlier compositions – and his comments on them – that Birtwistle liked to conceive of the formal processes in his music in visual terms. *Tragoedia* is an instrumental work whose overall form is modelled on an abstract notion of ancient Greek tragedy, complete with an opening Prologue and Parodos, and a closing Exodos. These dramatic ideas took on explicitly theatrical life in *Verses for Ensembles* (1968–69), another entirely instrumental piece, in which the performers move about the concert platform according to a visual scheme given in the front of the score. *The Triumph of Time* takes its title from an etching of 1574 by Pieter Breughel the Elder and, although Birtwistle claims that he encountered the picture only after he had begun work on the piece, it stands as a striking visual metaphor for this musical 'procession made up of a (necessarily) linked chain of material objects which have no necessary connexion with each other'.[10]

Once again, the reality is rather different, the demands of actual composition overriding the initial abstract plans (though, no doubt, they continued to inform the process). Orpheus Puppet has already delivered half of his narrative before Orpheus Singer even begins his poem. They overlap through their simultaneous presentation rather than dovetailing neatly as in the sketch. This was perhaps to make possible a smoother transition from the timelessness of the Parados (an unarticulated sense of duration represented by its electronic 'Aura') into the first Poem of Reminiscence. Orpheus' emerging 'consciousness' is symbolized by the progressively more articulate (i.e., temporally specific) nature of the music. The pace of the drama is controlled by the increasing frequency of occurrence of key events, most notably Apollo's signals. Ten signals in a row ('DREID') prompt the beginning of Orpheus Man's poem (articulate speech) and, soon after, the first utterance of the name of Eurydice, shared between the two Orpheuses, in song. This is the birth of music. It is the first focused pitch to be heard in the work, the name being sung on the note g, anticipated just seconds before on a clarinet. (Is it possible to read this autobiographically? Orpheus gives voice to music, which appears first, as if 'from nothing', on Birtwistle's own instrument.) This then initiates a series of regularly pulsed clarinet mobiles that continue until the end of the section, as if Eurydice's name were echoing into the surrounding landscape. The unfolding of the recitative is interrupted on three further occasions by the singing of Eurydice's name, in just the same way as the lovers' names were interjected into the narration in *Nenia: the Death of Orpheus*. Each statement shows a progression as the Orpheuses become increasingly conscious of the presence of (the memory of)

---

[10] Birtwistle, quoted in Hall, *Harrison Birtwistle*, 175.

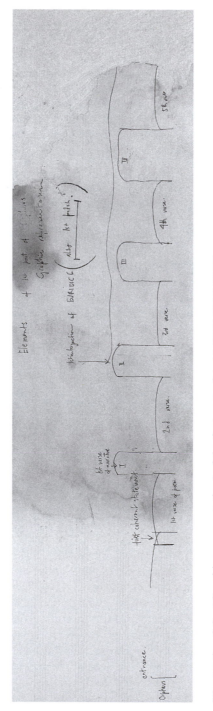

Illustration 2.2 'Graphic representation' of the first part of Act I (PSS 0530-0955) The stains visible on this sketch page are traces of mould, a consequence of the fact that the composer used to store his materials in a damp cellar.

Eurydice. The initial g♮ is later decorated in various ways by f♯, its neighbour, and b♭, a minor third above; the accompanying clarinet mobiles adapt accordingly. These fragments of song in the context of a narration anticipate what is to come, in that song blossoms in the aria that follows. The three pitches also present the incipit of that song's melody. One might say that a later memory (of love) is present in the present memory (of a journey).

In summary, this first part of *The Mask of Orpheus* – through text, music and dramaturgy – presents us, by means of the device of memory (multiply represented), with the allegory of a journey. It describes 'a slow transition from night to day (words to song, myth to man) using the metaphor of changes in the hands and eyes of Jason (the king) standing over the fifty Argonauts. This song gives rise to numerous echoes' (libretto, p. 11).

But before the song unfolds, we hear a very brief gesture (score, fig. 18, p. 12) that comes at the end of the Poem of Reminiscence as the Orpheuses finish their texts, as the clarinet mobiles slow down and fade into nothingness, and as the Summer Aura begins to reassert its presence. It is a 'pivot' that, musically, concludes what we have just heard but, dramatically, being designated the first Act of Love (Act of Tenderness), points to what is to follow: Eurydice reaches out her hand to Orpheus. Musically it is a clear point of punctuation; tellingly – both for Orpheus/ Apollo and for Birtwistle – it is coloured by harps. For Birtwistle, the harp has always played a role akin to that of a Baroque continuo instrument. At this moment in *Orpheus*, the harps and a Noh harp plus percussion play a three-beat cadence. A perfect fourth (c^1–f^1) on the marimbas, reinforced by the same rising fourth on two trumpets, clearly alludes to the archetypal cadential formula found at the end of so many Baroque recitatives. It has a strangely archaic effect here. It opens a kind of Stravinskian window on to an earlier era, but with which it is immediately clear it has no direct continuity. Like the Mozartian cadences in *The Rake's Progress*, the quotation marks are there for those who choose to hear them. This moment is ironic in that, as a formal, structural device, it distances the spectator from the narration.

First Duet of Love (Duet of Hope)

The first Love Duet follows on immediately from the poem. Its dominant form is marked as 'aria'. Whereas the preceding recitative was concerned principally with narrative (albeit of a compromised kind) in which text (in various guises) was given priority, this aria is primarily concerned with music. This discovery of music is a metaphor for the transition from night to day, and from myth to man. Birtwistle has often spoken of aria as the 'poetic flowering of the moment'. Here we have an act of reflection on a moment, a moment when the two lovers, Orpheus and Eurydice, stop to sing each other's names. Just for a moment, they are wrapped in each other and the world around them echoes to their love. As Ovid writes, Orpheus 'found Eurydice / And took her in his arms with leaping heart. / … hand in hand they stroll, the two together'.[11] The emotional depth of this moment is explored by means of extending it musically in time: it flowers not only here (over about five minutes) but across much of Act I in a series of extensions that interrupt events at key moments.

Aria is, by definition, about song. And at the heart of this duet is a simple melody (in fact, a pair of melodies). This is the thread on which the rest of the music hangs. This is confirmed by the sketches, where this melody appears to be the first element of this section to have been written.

The entire duet for Orpheus and Eurydice – devoid of the many interruptions and extensions as they appear in the final score – is written out in full, entirely in 5/4, for two voices across three pages of manuscript.[12] The two lines were obviously conceived together, for they continually interlace and overlap. Orpheus' melody is generated from sets of four, five and six notes; Eurydice's is slightly more complex, employing three- to seven-note sets. Each set corresponds with one sung statement of the names 'Orpheus' and 'Euridice'. The aurally apparent linearity – narrative consistency – of the melodies is confirmed by the sketches, which show an apparent logic to the way Birtwistle proceeds from one set to the next (see Illustration 2.3). The slur notation would seem to indicate the importance of the progression, that is, there is a generally high degree of invariance between the pitch classes of successive sets. Change takes place gradually. At first, the logic would appear to be that of a kind of stream of consciousness, suggesting that the melody could end up somewhere very different from where it started. But, in fact, the order in which each new pitch class is exposed (in Orpheus' melody) is according to a 'wedge' shape. This is a typical generative scheme used by Birtwistle, where a chromatic wedge opens out symmetrically from a central pitch class. It also suggests a progression from the simple (a single focal point) to the complex (the total chromatic), though in practice its realization can be much less clear than this would suggest. (Its pitch-class symmetry can often be just a generalized notion that lies behind the unfolding of actual pitches.) In the case of Orpheus' melody here, the symmetrical centre is initially absent (A♭), but the pair of semitones that are generated either side of it (F♯–G–[A♭]–A–B♭) have an important referential as well as expressive role in the aria. The entire wedge is given below; only the D♮ appears out of sequence:

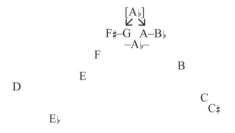

---

[11]   Ovid, *Metamorphoses*, Book XI (pp. 250–52).
[12]   Beginning at PSS 0531-0028.

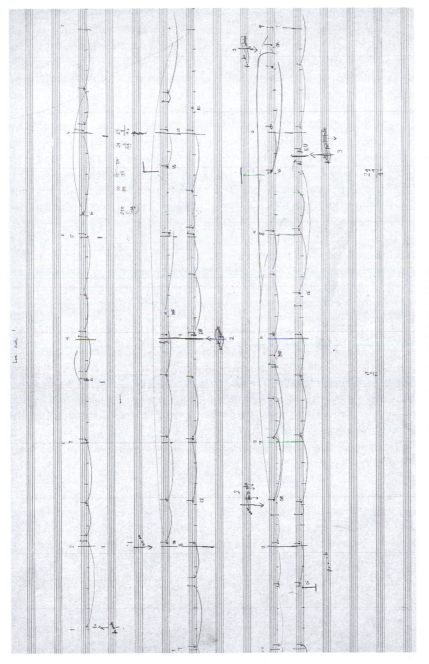

Illustration 2.3 Act I, scene 1, first Duet of Love, sketch (PSS 0530-0028)

The order of appearance of each new pitch class is, then, controlled by the chromatic wedge. But, in an apparent contradiction, the melody also finds it impossible to escape the influence of the initial four-note set: at least one pitch class from that original set is contained in all bar one of the 19 generated sets. So, far from presenting a line that moves into the future, it only gives the semblance of forward motion and in fact keeps turning back in on itself. This contradiction is extremely important, not just for this aria, but for the whole of *The Mask of Orpheus*, and for Birtwistle's music more generally. It is a notion that, around this time, the composer was to label 'stasis in progress', and it emerged explicitly in relation to his work for solo clarinet, harp and two string orchestras, *Melencolia I*, which was written just after he had suspended work on *Orpheus* in 1976. The phrase 'stasis in progress' was coined by and taken from a contemporary essay by Günther Grass which, like Birtwistle's piece, took the Dürer etching of the same name as its starting-point. Indeed, Grass's commentary on the picture could almost stand for this moment in the opera:

> Phases displaced individually and in relation to each other. Progress overtaken. Inactive amid instruments. As though geometry had outmeasured itself. As though the latest knowledge had bogged down in doubt after its first attempts to walk. As though science had canceled itself out. As though beauty were an empty fiction. As though only mythology would endure.[13]

'Stasis in progress' is an apt account of the concerns of the opera as a whole:

- Orpheus' quest to retrieve Eurydice from the underworld results only in his losing her again – he moves forward but ends up where he started;
- Orpheus is forever lamenting the loss of Eurydice, their love only being a memory, which he is constantly replaying;
- Orpheus appears to make journeys that, in fact, only take place in his imagination.

Here, as elsewhere in Birtwistle, the notion of progress does not necessarily carry with it any strong sense of development or teleology. It is more like the self-styled 'processionals' that he wrote in the 1970s (*Melencolia I* is a good illustration; *The Triumph of Time* is the exemplar). These are ceremonial events, linear but inherently repetitious. The titles of post-*Orpheus* works reveal that such a notion remains at the heart of Birtwistle's creative imagination: *Still Movement, Endless Parade, An Interrupted Endless Melody* – though, as Robert Adlington has pointed out, the

---

[13]   Günther Grass, 'On stasis in progress: variations on Albrecht Dürer's Melencolia I', in *From the Diary of a Snail*, tr. Ralph Manheim (London: Minerva, 1997 [first published in German in 1972; first English translation published 1974]), 298.

metaphor of the labyrinthine journey is perhaps more apt than that of the processional for more recent music,[14] as has emerged most explicitly in *The Minotaur*.

Much of this melody for Orpheus, and the counterpart for Eurydice, finds its way into the score, though there is some significant reworking of ideas between sketch and edition. Material originally written for Orpheus is sometimes transferred to Eurydice, and vice versa. But the important fact is that the melodies were conceived as one large span. In the final version two important metamorphoses take place. First, the melodies are cut into discrete chunks and then pasted across Act I, where, as we have seen, they are labelled extensions of the Love Duet (see Table 2.1).

Table 2.1   Summary of 'progress' of first Duet of Love across Act I

	Pages in score	**Rehearsal figs**	**Duration (crotchet beats)**	**Comment**
Duet opening (scene 1)	13–18	After fig. 18–before fig. 22	195	Interrupted by first Passing Cloud
Continuation	19–21	Figs 22–3	79	Continues after first Passing Cloud
First extension	29–30	From 2 bars before fig. 30	35	Interrupts first Ceremony
Second extension	36–7	Figs 35–6	30	Interrupts first Ceremony
Third extension	43–4	Figs 41–2	24	Interrupts first Ceremony
Fourth extension (scene 3)	98–9	Figs 93–4	24	Occurs after a long gap, immediately after the first Hysterical Aria
Fifth extension	104	Figs 99–100	30	Occurs after the first Hysterical Aria (interjection II) and interrupts the second Immortal Dance
Sixth extension	112–13	Fig. 109	22	Occurs after the first Hysterical Aria (interjection III)

In other words, in the course of the act, we keep re-encountering the singing lovers, but their context is always changing as the plot has moved on; new perspectives are offered. It is almost as if we keep glimpsing them as they process across the landscape. Such a 'cut and paste' approach would certainly seem to undermine any obvious narrative continuity, and it carries with it an anti-developmental pedigree that goes back at least as far as key early works by Stravinsky. In a seminal analytical article Edward T. Cone described these processes as 'stratification' and 'interlock', where a musical idea is stratified temporally through a work, but nonetheless makes

---

[14]   Robert Adlington, *The Music of Harrison Birtwistle* (Cambridge: Cambridge University Press, 2000), 116–17.

connections across the interruptions.[15] We will find many examples of this procedure in *The Mask of Orpheus*, reinforcing its sense of a fractured narrative.

The second change is that each of the two melodies bifurcates and is presented in the final version by *two* Orpheuses (Man and Myth) and *two* Eurydices (Woman and Myth). Thus two related but different perspectives on their love are also presented *simultaneously*. Once again, time and memory become central concerns. The end result is a poignant love song, where the music of the two lovers is intertwined. However, it is imbued throughout with a deep sense of melancholy. Theirs is a doomed love whose tragic outcome is known even before it begins. This sense of melancholy is, in part, achieved via the musical articulation of 'stasis in progress'. (It should be noted that Grass's essay on Dürer was, in fact, a reflection on melancholy.) It is further expressed through the insistent presence of the pair of semitones F♯–G and A–B♭, the *pianto* topic of grief or melancholy, discussed in Chapter 1.

Once again, the sketches reveal just how important this four-note set was for the composer. There are many pages of charts that permute the notes or intervals of this set to generate a wealth of material with which the composer can then work. Figure 2.1 gives just one such instance, where the four pitch classes are numbered from 1 to 4, which are then permuted in order to generate a 6 x 4 matrix of all 24 possible orderings – like some kind of bell-ringer's change patterns. The sketches do not appear to show directly how this ends up in the music, but it is not hard to see in general how, in this duet, the pitch classes are present in constantly changing guises, like some sort of kaleidoscope, continually being refigured.

Figure 2.1   Permutations of a four-note set[16]

F♯–G–A–B♭
1   2   3   4

2143	1243	1432	4213	1324	3241
2413	4231	4312	1234	3421	2314
2431	3412	1342	1423	2134	2341
3142	3124	3214	4123	4321	4132

But it is not just in the melodies that these semitones are prominent. They are in evidence in a number of other strands to this music, layers that (as the sketches reveal) were composed one after the other, and then added on top of the duet – a

---

[15]   Edward T. Cone, 'Stravinsky: the progress of a method', *Perspectives of New Music*, 1/1 (1962), 18–26.

[16]   Transcribed from PSS 0531-0005.

process that parallels the 'tiling' that Boulez identified in Stravinsky's *The Rite of Spring*.[17]

These pairs of semitones are echoed in the network of wind lines that proliferate outwards from the central melodies, resulting in a rich kind of heterophony. One might say that the landscape in which the lovers move is coloured by their love and its melancholic character. It also gives the impression that the voices can only articulate conscious memories through song, whereas the instrumental lines are able to summon up something deeper – it is in music, not words, that the fleeting realm of the ineffable is suggested.[18] There is something inherently Wagnerian about this, where the voices speak of (vaguely) conscious ideas but the depth of the unconscious is revealed by the orchestra.

Example 2.1 Act I, scene 1, first Duet of Love, piccolo figure

There are also a number of independent layers that present commentaries on the central musical material. Most striking is a dancing triplet piccolo line in counterpoint (Example 2.1), which – from time to time – moves in and out of a more sustained figure that presents a rising and falling semitone, D–E♭–D. This clearly makes connections with the central melodies. This is especially intriguing in the context of recent processional works, *The Shadow of Night* and *Night's Black Bird*, where – as mentioned in Chapter 1 – the composer points to the same chromatic motif (again, a piccolo solo) as a quotation of the first three notes of Dowland's *In Darkness Let Me Dwell*. It infuses the entire score. Thus, by 2001, the motif has become an explicit expression of melancholy related to, *inter alia*, Dürer's *Melencolia I*, the Elizabethan preoccupation with the 'humour of the night' and, more generally, the notion of stasis in progress:

---

[17] See Pierre Boulez, 'Stravinsky remains', in *Stocktakings from an Apprenticeship*, tr. Stephen Walsh (Oxford: Clarendon Press, 1991), 55–110.

[18] 'the ineffable … cannot be explained because there are infinite and interminable things to be said of it: such is … the inexhaustible mystery of love … . The ineffable unleashes a state of verve.' Vladimir Jankélévitch, *Music and the Ineffable*, tr. Carolyn Abbate (Princeton: Princeton University Press, 2003), 72. Jankélévitch also writes – in relation to Fauré, but the comment also seems apt here – of music 'charged with the ineffable nostalgia of a past that has, once more, flown away' (p. 75).

> This motif, which rises a semitone and down again, is woven into the fabric of
> the work and also alluded to figuratively: lines split and later reunite, the notes of
> a chord move away and back again, and longer melodic lines are interrupted and
> resumed like the moon shining through a series of slowly passing clouds.[19]

He could easily have been writing about *Orpheus*, composed more than a quarter of
a century earlier, and about the Duet of Love in particular.

Further layers reinforce the musical and affective ideas already discussed.
The tuned percussion (vibraphones and marimbas) play a series of mobiles,
each rhythmically distinct, each taking the pitches from the central melodies. By
definition, such music cannot progress. Here, as in *Nenia*, it could be understood to
be attempting to 'catch Eurydice in time' by usurping time. The immediate effect is
one of an echoing outwards of the lovers' song. And, while the mythic incarnations
of Orpheus and Eurydice (puppets) only sing, their human counterparts (singers)
utter spoken text in between sung statements of their lover's name. 'I remember my
singing', says Orpheus Myth, as we hear Orpheus Man doing just that. The melody
unfolds in time and yet its static character, in the context of a text that is concerned
with remembering, has a kind of mythologizing effect on the music, as if it were in
some kind of eternal present.

Each appearance of the first Duet of Love and its extensions is accompanied by
the electronic Summer Aura. It sets the mood of the season: 'I remember, Euridice,
this summer', says Orpheus Man. In that it is non-directional background sound,
it contributes to the heavy sense of stasis, like an oppressive, hot, summer wind.
But it also serves a kind of 'continuo' role, binding the various layers of the music
together and giving a sense of continuity. This is especially important for the duet's
extensions that interrupt the principal narrative. The Aura overlaps with the music
that stands either side of the extensions, suggesting a transition and mitigating the
harshness of the juxtaposition of very different kinds of music.

But even the linear continuity of the first part of the first Duet of Love is interrupted
and frozen by another electronic element: the first Passing Cloud of Abandon.

The Passing Clouds of Abandon and the Allegorical Flowers of Reason

There are three Passing Clouds of Abandon and three Allegorical Flowers of
Reason, discrete, self-contained musical sequences, each entirely electronic. Each
lasts approximately three minutes. They are distributed unevenly across the three
acts, and their appearance is intended to be unexpected: three in Act I, one in Act II
and two in Act III. Their function in the drama is to interrupt the principal narrative
and to provide the backdrop for the appearance of the Troupe of the Passing Clouds,

---

[19] Harrison Birtwistle, 'Composer's note', preface to the published score (London:
Boosey & Hawkes, 2003).

a mime group which silently enacts various mythical stories. The stories tell either of violent deaths involving Dionysus (the Passing Clouds, 'stories of subterfuge') or of lyrical love where the loved one dies and is transformed into a flower (the Allegorical Flowers, 'stories of purity').[20] The narrative disruption is exaggerated, according to the libretto (p. 2), by the way in which the violent Clouds occur at points of least tension and the lyrical Flowers at points of greatest tension. For example, the first Cloud interrupts and brutally contrasts with the gentle, lyrical Duet of Hope. The Clouds and Flowers are allegories within the larger allegory, plays within the play, having a symbiotic relationship to the main drama, in that they reflect the violence of the murder of Orpheus and the lyricism of his love (and sense of loss) for Eurydice.

According to Ovid, it was the grieving Orpheus himself who told lyrical stories in song to the trees after losing Eurydice for the second time:

> There was a hill, and on the hill a wide
> Level of open ground, all green with grass.
> The place lacked any shade. But when the bard,
> The heaven-born bard, sat there and touched his strings,
> Shade came in plenty. Every tree was there[21]

It is from the *Metamorphoses* that Zinovieff takes a number of these stories. But he was by no means the first to make the connection between the death of Orpheus and these other legends. For example, in his lost play about Orpheus, Aeschylus parallels the violent death of Orpheus at the hands of the Maenads with stories of the violent deaths of others who did not honour their god Dionysus, notably Lycurgus and Pentheus. While they are an essential part of the opera, in *The Mask of Orpheus* the stories remain independent. In that they (allegorically) anticipate and retell of the love and death of the protagonist, they represent another representation of memory, and enrich the work's complex network of temporal structures. Further, they play a key role in ritualizing the narrative.

Such procedures are encountered in more recent stage works by Birtwistle. Towards the end of *The Last Supper* (1998–99), for example, the main drama is interrupted by three Visions. While the stage action re-presents the events of the first Maundy Thursday in a generally chronological manner, the Visions are presented as tableaux that proceed in reverse order, beginning with a representation of the Crucifixion, which is followed by the Stations of the Cross, and finally the betrayal of Christ by Judas. They each take place in a different space on the stage[22] and, like

---

[20]   The stories they tell are given in Appendix A. Zinovieff's description of the Clouds and Flowers is to be found in the libretto, p. 47.

[21]   Ovid, *Metamorphoses*, Book X (p. 227).

[22]   In the original Berlin Staatsoper production (2000), directed by Martin Duncan and designed by Alison Chitty, the visual style of the Visions echoed the style of the representations

the Passing Clouds and Allegorical Flowers, offer a different time frame, another level of commentary on the principal story. The minimal action is mimed in slow motion, whereas the main action takes place in 'real' time. The music accompanying the Visions takes the form of three motets, sung by an *a cappella* chorus (on tape). The texts are the words of traditional Latin prayers and hymns from the thirteenth and fourteenth centuries: 'O bone Jesu', 'Pange lingua' and 'In supremae nocte cenae'. Only the last is directly concerned with the Last Supper, and yet all three are appropriate in that they form meditations on Christ's last hours. Just as their language is set apart from the language of the narrative, so their music – while working with the same materials as the rest of the opera – is in a quite different 'style': slow, quiet, sustained, with subtle counterpoint between the voices. It alludes to a much earlier style of motet writing (e.g., that of Palestrina), without ever imitating it. It is literally a 'holy' music in that it is 'special', 'set apart', but avoiding, as the composer has observed, the 'clichés of holy music'. While *The Last Supper* as a whole retells a familiar story, the interjected Visions serve to ritualize the narrative.

Such, too, is the function of the Passing Clouds and Allegorical Flowers. One might argue that the Troupe of the Passing Clouds has a function similar to that of the chorus in a Greek tragedy. There are times when the chorus has a structural function, punctuating the flow of the narrative and commenting on the action from outside it. The troupe here remains outside the main narrative and comments on it through its story-telling. Its appearances punctuate the flow of the narrative (as far as the narrative in this work ever flows), serving the purpose of distancing the audience from the emotions of the protagonists, making explicit the 'structural' nature of the work and – through the stylization of music and dance in a language at a remove from that found elsewhere – ritualizing the whole. Like a chorus, too, each Cloud and Flower presents a different version of the same thing; each is a musical variant of every other: they are always different yet always, in essence, the same. They are refrains. Verse-refrain structures abound in Birtwistle. He loves the idea of one repeating structure embedded in another, resulting in complex clock-like mechanisms. He also loves the idea of 'chorus', which he has explored in every one of his stage works. Dramatic or structural function always seems to come first in his conception of a work; subject matter comes at a later stage.

At the time of its production in the early 1980s, the music for the Passing Clouds and Allegorical Flowers, along with the Auras and the voice of Apollo, was at the limits of the capabilities of the world's most advanced computer programs; it remains among the most brilliant electronic music ever to have been made. The composer Nigel Osborne, who was present at the first informal presentation of *Orpheus*' electronic components in the summer of 1983, writes of the effect it had on its first auditors:

of Christ by the seventeenth-century Spanish painter Francisco de Zurbarán, an idea that (anecdotally) came from the composer. This further reinforced the separation of the tableaux from the main stage, whose set and costumes were in a contemporary style.

It was good to share in this small piece of music history. Everyone felt that something significant had happened. It involved no startling advances in computer technology but rather the stretching of possibilities already available to their very limits. Most important of all, it had musical authenticity. One felt that something already latent in Birtwistle's instrumental music (like the violent attacks, quasi-mechanical pulses and slowly evolving clusters) had assumed an inevitable further incarnation.[23]

The results, then, were astounding yet appropriate:

> and when he'd tried his strings
> And, as he tuned, was satisfied the notes,
> Though different, agreed in harmony,
> He sang this song … [24]

The worlds of the Clouds and Flowers resound to the sound of Orpheus' lyre. The music is formed from just four simple groups of sampled harp sounds: a high note, a low note, a simple chord and a complex chord. But from these building blocks an entirely new musical world is conjured, extending the sonic and expressive scope of the harp outwards through the audible spectrum and into the entire auditorium (into which all the electronic music is projected, mixed live with amplified voices and instruments). The spectra of the very first part of these sampled sounds (their 'attacks') were first analysed by Barry Anderson, using the IRCAM computer, broken up into their component parts and then re-synthesized and transformed in myriad ways. This involved adjusting frequency amplitude values using the phase vocoder program developed by Andy Moorer at Stanford University, along with various treatments such as looping and reverberation.[25] The result was the material with which Anderson was able to realize the complex scheme of rhythms and metres that Birtwistle had imagined.

I have been unable to trace any obvious sketch material for the Clouds and Flowers, or indeed for any of the work's electronic components. Among the materials in the Harrison Birtwistle Collection are documents that appear to show timings and details of the tape projection and which may well date from 1982, when Birtwistle and Anderson were working together intensively in Paris. Anderson confided to Nigel Osborne that he found working with Birtwistle 'tremendously inspiring'.[26] It was clearly a genuine collaboration in which ideas were being explored in the studio rather than on paper. Technical problems meant a number of return visits, Birtwistle's

---

[23]   Nigel Osborne, 'Orpheus in Paris', in programme book for premiere performances of *The Mask of Orpheus*, ed. Nicholas John (May 1986) [no page numbers].

[24]   Ovid, *Metamorphoses*, Book X (p. 229).

[25]   See Osborne, 'Orpheus in Paris'.

[26]   Ibid.

final trip to Paris to finish the tapes taking place in August 1983. Anderson returned many times more, often at his own expense, to oversee the final preparations of all the electronic elements.

Despite Zinovieff's statement concerning the contrasts between the violent and lyrical moments of the narrative with, respectively, the lyrical Flowers and violent Clouds, in practice the musical differences between these two types are not so marked. Indeed, a basic aural analysis reveals that each of these interludes is structured in a very similar way, involving extended verse sections (A) and shorter, punctuating refrains (B). All six share the same basic musical materials and, more specifically, they are grouped in pairs. In general, the sound of the Clouds is sharper, their volume louder and the density of events higher; the Flowers tend to be softer, their ideas more attenuated and the sound more distant, being subjected to a greater degree of reverberation. But these observations are really only generally true. The similarities between the pairs, and between the six sequences as a whole, are much more striking.

The first Cloud is the most violent. It has an overall ABABA shape. Its verses – varying in duration from $c.0'20''$ to $c.1'00''$ – consist of a series of extended trill-like figures accompanied by points of percussive sound panned across the stereophonic field.[27] The changes from one trill to the next are articulated by a *crescendo* flourish. The refrain punctuates these rather static verses with a sequence of nine loud, violent gestures of essentially percussive sound, high and low. The sequence is brought to an end by one of the signals of Apollo and a muffled echo of his disembodied voice.

Although Zinovieff directs that the 'sequences should follow the original [story] closely' (libretto, p. 47), in no sense does the music here attempt to represent or narrate the story being told, other than in a very general way of articulating the violent affect. The Clouds and Flowers are, in the broadest sense, metaphorical. This is typical of Birtwistle. He rarely indulges in obvious kinds of narrative or 'word painting'. As Adlington has commented, 'For Birtwistle a libretto presents not words but dramatic situations; and a libretto's cogency as a narrative, far from demanding a correspondingly coherent musical response, largely *relieves* music of precisely that responsibility.'[28] The composer has observed in relation to the *Three Brendel Settings* (2001–04) that, on setting poetry, he interprets the poems for himself, fixing a particular aspect in the music: 'you make it have an attitude'.[29] The same could be said of these electronic sequences, each of which is really concerned

---

[27]   The 'trills' and their treatment in this Cloud call to mind the trill-like figures that give Boulez's own work of this time its characteristically static character – see especially *Répons*, which was begun at IRCAM in 1981 at almost exactly the same time as Birtwistle and Anderson were working there.

[28]   Adlington, *The Music of Harrison Birtwistle*, 36.

[29]   Birtwistle in conversation with the author (21 June 2004), quoted in the programme note by the author to accompany the world premiere performance at the BBC Proms on 17 August 2004.

with only one idea, mood or emotion. In this sense, reinforced by the fact that they are danced by a 'collective', they might be understood to have a function similar to the chorales in a Baroque Passion, which similarly interrupt and punctuate the flow of the narrative.

Key is the fact that their verse-refrain structures echo in microcosm the formalized structures of the work as a whole. Even in these short sequences, the material is able to comment on itself, in that each verse is a variant of itself, as is each refrain; they present multiple perspectives on an idea that is never actually present in an 'original' form. Further, each verse in the entire set of six sequences appears to be a variant of every other, as is each refrain. (Comparison with *Verses for Ensembles* – especially its central section of wind grounds and brass ritornellos – is fruitful, this being one of Birtwistle's boldest structural(ist) designs.) The second Allegorical Flower is the softer counterpart of the first Cloud. It occurs at the end of Act II, after the densest and most violent music in the opera, and marks Orpheus's first Terrible Death by Suicide. The Flower shares the first Cloud's ABABA shape, its verses are constructed from a similar series of 'trills', and the refrain is made up of five clear string- or bell-like punctuations. It is as if the first Cloud is being viewed through a prism.

The sequences that are most alike are the third Cloud and third Flower, which occur in Act III. They are of identical length, as are their constituent verses and refrains. In both cases, the refrains take the form of the five string- or bell-like punctuations (plus low echoes) mentioned above. The verses are characterized by rhythmic repetition, firstly of pitches or chords (cf. the second Cloud and first Flower), later of rocking pairs of sounds. One is an obvious reflection of the other, only the third Flower is softer, more distanced, as a consequence of the reverberation. Similarly, the second Cloud and first Flower are parallels. The first Flower has the familiar string-like refrains, while the rhythmically repeated chords of the verse turn into a kind of reinvention of the Monteverdian trillo, with punctuating gong-like sounds and intervening silences. The second Cloud has the violent ninefold refrain chords of the first Cloud, and its verses also turn repeated chords into trillos, moving generally upwards and punctuated by a violent falling figure.

Orpheus turned. He keeps returning to the memory from which there is no escape. Even these stories that he tells, which seem to speak of something other, merely bring him back in touch with his loss. (Allegory, from the Greek *allos* + *agoria*, means literally 'speaking otherwise than one seems to speak'). Being made from the sound of his own instrument, and being built from music that through repetition and variation is continually turning back on itself, the Passing Clouds and Allegorical Flowers stand as a mirror to Orpheus in which he sees a version of himself, distorted through grief.

First Ceremony (The Wedding)

> Thence Hymen came, in saffron mantle clad,
> At Orpheus' summons through the boundless sky
> To Thessaly, but vain the summons proved.
> True he was present, but no hallowed words
> He brought nor happy smiles nor lucky sign;
> Even the torch he held spluttered throughout
> With smarting smoke, and caught no living flame
> For all his brandishing. The ill-starred rite
> Led to a grimmer end.[30]

Hymen, the god of marriage, 'was supposed to bring good luck at weddings' (libretto, p. 46). As Ovid tells it, although Orpheus had invited Hymen to his wedding to Eurydice, their marriage was doomed from the start, and, in Zinovieff's retelling, the lovers' fate is foretold in a number of bad omens. During the first Ceremony, the Troupe of Ceremony presents a mystical, ritualized representation of the wedding, which takes the form of a series of three exchanges (questions and answers) between Orpheus Singer and the Priests and Caller. All we hear from Eurydice is her vow, 'I will!', to a simple falling major third (g^1–$e\flat^1$).[31] The Ceremony culminates in Orpheus' first Song of Magic and the lovers' wedding dance (the first Immortal Dance), which brings scene 1 to a close.

To the piercing sound of three (indeterminately) pitched conch shells, the trio of Priests summon Hymen to begin the Ceremony. Immediately, three percussionists strike up on drums, temple blocks and cow bells, and continue to play incessantly throughout the Ceremony. These are all clear signs of the ritual character of this event. Where the Poem of Reminiscence had in essence been concerned with text, and the Love Duet with melody (with no obviously perceptible metre), this music is shocking in the absolute regularity of its pulse (at $\downarrow$ = c.138). This signals the importance of dance to this event. 'The Ceremonies are secret ritualistic dances, which by repetition and exposition of a gross and inner detailed structure, gradually become revealed as parts of a sacrificial murder' (libretto, p. 46). The regular pulse here also suggests a much more obviously time-bound moment in the drama, which stands in stark contrast to the seemingly timeless extensions of the Love Duet that periodically interrupt the course of the Ceremony.

This music is constructed from clearly defined layers. Each element in itself may be relatively simple, certainly involving a high degree of repetition; combined, the result is a complex structure that matches the structural nature of the exchanges taking place in the text. This can be heard in microcosm in the percussion parts. Each player

---

[30]   Ovid, *Metamorphoses*, Book X (p. 225).

[31]   This occurs at the end of both the first and second exchanges, but because in the performances the second exchange was cut, Eurydice is heard only once in the recording.

has simple repeating patterns in groups of threes and twos that together produce a compound rhythmic continuum (a kind of rhythmic drone) where the accents are always shifting. It also gives the music an energy that drives the drama forwards. This entirely rhythmic layer is, intermittently, reinforced by trios of pitched instruments – initially, bassoons, harps and tuned percussion – which, severally, pick up the quaver patterns of the 'drone' and extend them into the pitch domain with permutated groups of pitches having a generally rising character. Again, the sketches reveal that these fragments were separately composed and then 'pasted' into the score.

The layered structure here was evidently in Birtwistle's mind at the earliest planning stage. Among the sketches of the first Ceremony is to be found the following note:

levels = melodic —— how many groups
             percussion —   "
             priest ———   "

He was concerned to find ways of distinguishing the layers clearly to reflect their dramatic function. One way in which this was achieved was by ensuring that each layer worked within a distinct pitch field, that is, with specific scale fragments that are labelled in the sketches as 'modes' (circled in red). Much more recently he has commented that 'modality … still interests me. A mode is not about its notes – its essence is in its intervals. These intervals pervade the music, giving it a distinctive flavour.'[32]

A separate continuum layer is made up of long sustained chords, very low or very high (groaning trombones and squealing clarinets), cultivated extensions, perhaps, of the conch calls, thereby identifying themselves with the trio of Priests. Other wind instruments join in. And, in the midst of this, the ritual questioning of Orpheus takes place, a series of exchange patterns that 'are a sort of cryptic conversation between the Troupe of Ceremony and Orpheus. The Priests and the Caller require answers and make statements that, although making some alchemical sense, also set up a pattern for a dance' (libretto, p. 46). Questions are called out by the Priests; the Caller speaks and sings answers that involve symbolic numbers.

In rhythmic unison the chorus of Priests sings the first Complicated Question (The Cypher) (see Figure 2.2). Its meaning is opaque. The words have an almost shamanistic effect. The libretto (1997) gives the text and then indicates that, in its subsequent three repetitions, the words can appear in any order, chopped up (p. 21). In fact, Birtwistle begins this process from the start, using the text as a pool of words, irrespective of order, for their sensuous qualities. The words recur in different combinations on each of the four occasions. The same is true of the music, where each

---

[32] Birtwistle in conversation with the author, in 'The piano music of Harrison Birtwistle', liner notes for *The Axe Manual: Complete Piano Works* (London: Metronome Recordings, 2004, MET CD 1074), 7.

subsequent repetition is a variant of the first (or, more accurately, each is a variant of every other, there being no obvious 'original'). And this process is replicated across the three Ceremonies. Compare the second Complicated Question (The Riddle), as it occurs in the second Ceremony in Act I, scene 3 with the first question, and it is clear how the second has been rewritten as a kind of shattered echo of the first by means of reordering words, giving new rhymes and so on. The third question, whose verses extend across Act III, shows the process taken to a further extreme of fragmentation and attenuation.

Figure 2.2   The Complicated Questions

Wedding (Act I, scene 1): first Complicated Question	Funeral (Act I, scene 3): second Complicated Question	Sacrifice (Act III): third Complicated Question
Cull bright	Storm-white,	Scream luckwards.
Carefully	Coin-mouthed, spat.	Gold.
King-caged.	Direct:	Fierce fire-time.
Luckwards turning.	Shout luck-screams,	
Recognise	Sun's night rise;	Lose luck-screams.
Discovered, dead	Clean sky-spark.	Spark.
Dull Talisman.		Dark. Dead. Stung.
	Guide quite	
	Tongue-dumbed, lost.	
	Select:	
	Gold mind-bells,	
	Cracked doom-ice,	
	Fierce fire-time.	
	Child's light:	King. Caged.
	King-caged, caught.	Cold.
	Reflect:	Clear. Sky. Skull.
	Eyes, hard-held,	
	Cold water-cries,	
	Dark dead-stung.	
		Sun. Night. Rise.
		Eyes.
		Crack. Doom. Ice.

The same is true, in general, of the music. The first verse of the first question as presented by the three Priests is given in Example 2.2b (score, figs 26–8, pp. 25–7). A sketch for this passage (Example 2.2a) shows how the pitches in each voice are derived from intervallically distinctive scales (modes), from which Birtwistle chooses to work with overlapping four-note groups.[33] Thus a^1 gives the pitches for the first phrase of Priest 1, a^2 the pitches for Priest 2, and a^3 for priest 3 (though here

---

[33]   The brackets are Birtwistle's; the identifying labels are mine.

a 'rogue' B♮ is initially substituted for the D♮). They combine to form a sequence of chords, with the effect of a kind of chorale. The opening superimposed perfect 5ths signal the ceremonial, fanfare character of the Priests' calls, reinforced by the three clarinets, which double the voices an 18th or a 19th (i.e., two octaves and a fourth or fifth) higher, like some kind of organum, invoking a pre-modern music and its associated ritual practices. Birtwistle then moves one step to the left in his modal models to give him the pitches for the second phrase (b$^{1-3}$). Thus, just as the words of the second phrase are a variant on the first, containing some words that are the same and some new ('Cull bright bright [sic] talisman luckwards turning', 'Cull bright Dull Talisman carefully discovered'), so in the second musical phrase some pitches and rhythmic figures are repeated, some are new. When the text is reinterpreted in the second Ceremony, this is matched by a similar procedure of reconfiguration of the music from the first Ceremony (see below).

Example 2.2 Act I, scene 1, first Complicated Question
(PSS 0531-0103)

(a) Sketch

(b) Score

Table 2.2 attempts to represent the organization of the first Ceremony as a whole. It has a cyclic structure, though it should be noted that this is somewhat at odds with the structure as presented in the libretto (pp. 12–13). Evidently a certain degree of rethinking took place between the completion of the libretto and the composition of the music. Changes were also made to the text: lines are sung and spoken in the second and third exchanges that do not appear in the libretto. Table 2.2 highlights the structuralist nature of the Ceremony. It is, according to Zinovieff, 'secret', but its meaning may be glimpsed through number. The number 3 (the symbolic number of the Christian Trinity; the ritualistic number of Tamino's trials in *The Magic Flute*; and so on) is everywhere. The three-ness of the dramatic structure is echoed in the 'choirs' of three instruments in the music. The text of the exchanges is full of numbers.

Such cyclic structures are not unfamiliar. Birtwistle's first opera, *Punch and Judy*, was built almost entirely from such cycles. And the opera that followed *Orpheus, Yan Tan Tethera*, is in essence about number. The parallels between the recurrent Passion Chorales in *Punch* (to a libretto by Stephen Pruslin) and the text of the Complicated Questions in *Orpheus* are striking. Birtwistle's response to the structuralist text of the Passion Chorales was to underscore it with a music that behaved in an entirely contrary manner: to lines of text that reduce successively by one syllable is added a counter-balancing trumpet figure that gets progressively longer. What Table 2.2 conceals is the powerful forward momentum of the music (the percussive layer discussed above) that cuts across many of the dramatic divisions. It has an energy all of its own. It is as if the music is attempting to resist the pull of the drama that keeps turning back on itself, just as Orpheus attempts to rewrite his own, fatal, turning back.

Table 2.2　　　Structural summary of first Ceremony

Exchange	First Complicated Question	Silence	First Duet of Love
First exchange	Verse 1	Spontaneous Remark	Extension 1
Second exchange	Verse 2		Extension 2
	Verse 2 (continued)	Silence in Vow	
Third exchange (interrupted)			Extension 3
Third exchange (continued)	Verse 3		
Third exchange (continued)	Verse 4 (+ Summer Aura)	'Silence' (The Voice of Apollo)	

'Such questions. Such answers.' Orpheus sings a sustained response to the Caller and the Priests, though it is as if he is addressing someone else. He understands it is a trial he has to undergo, as he has done many times before: 'I remember these questions'. The first Ceremony is brought to an end by the voice of Apollo, to which Orpheus listens, motionless: 'OFEIUS', 'SUIIA', 'OFOARIF' ('Orpheus', 'Hear', 'Remember').

First Song of Magic

The first Song of Magic is a solo aria for Orpheus, a familiar moment in Birtwistle's major stage works. Such arias usually represent a moment of deep personal reflection, often of melancholic character, and generally allude to a Baroque mode of expression, that is, they are concerned with a single affect. Compare this with, for example, Judy's aria 'Be silent, strings of my heart' from *Punch and Judy*, Inanna's aria 'All my life and all my death' from *The Second Mrs Kong* or Judas's aria 'I looked upon his silver face and wept' from *The Last Supper*. The Baroque traits of the first Song of Magic are clear. Orpheus sings a sustained and expressive melody. There is an elaborate continuo group designated (in the sketches[34] but not in the score) the 'harp of Orpheus'. It is made up of (i) three harps, crotales and vibraphone, and (ii) a seven-string metal harp, a Noh harp, and maracas, claves and tambourines. Sub-group (ii) accompanies Orpheus directly (conductor I), providing a harmonic background for his melodic line. Sub-group (i) operates independently at a different tempo (conductor II) and presents a set of layered mobiles; in the sketches this sub-group is headed the 'dance group'. At the top of the texture is an obbligato piccolo line, slow and sustained, that offers counterpoint to (and commentary on) Orpheus' singing.

The song emerges from a snatch of spoken recitative which, once again, is a reminiscence of the Argonautic journey, when Jason's ship was saved many times through the magic of Orpheus' singing. Here, the beautiful song saved the day at the wedding, but it nonetheless has a melancholy air. 'Soar into darkness', he begins, echoing once more the sentiments of the Elizabethan poets.[35] The line takes on an arch shape, achieving its highest point about three-quarters of the way through ('... curved corners where mirrors reflect ...'). The pitches unfold according to an informal wedge shape, underlining the song's linearity. The melodic interval of the semitone is given particular emphasis, closing (with the word 'sympathy') on a neighbour-note figure – here d^1–$c\#^1$–d^1 – that is taken up in the second verse.

The piccolo as an obbligato instrument has already been encountered in the first statement of the Duet of Love. As pipes, the flute and its smaller sister have obvious pastoral connotations, appropriate to the skill of Orpheus in charming nature. Since Antiquity, the shepherd has been represented playing the pipe. And perhaps because of its association with sheep and lambs, the flute also has connections with spring, new life and dancing. William Blake recognized this: 'Sound the Flute! ... Birds

---

[34]   PSS 0531-0219.

[35]   The libretto (p. 13) gives this line as 'Soar into madness'.

delight / Day and Night; … Merrily to welcome in the Year.'[36] Birtwistle's flutes often dance, symbolizing love. It is the flute that begins *Secret Theatre*, in keeping with the excerpt from Robert Graves's poem from which the work takes its title and which prefaces the score:

> It is hours past midnight now; a flute signals
> Far off; we mount the stage as though at random,
> Boldly ring down the curtain, then dance out our love.

Inanna's aria, supported by a dancing accordion continuo part (her lyre, if you like) and low string ostinatos, is accompanied by a triplet flute obbligato line that has much in common with the opening of *Secret Theatre*. The aria as a whole parallels Orpheus' Song of Magic in fascinating ways. Punch's quests after Pretty Polly centre on his serenades for her, in which a flute leads dances for Polly (first a gavotte, then an allemande). At the end, when Punch finally triumphs, Polly sings in her aria of the arrival of spring, again to the accompaniment of a dancing flute. Yet in both these works, the joyful dance of love is compromised: Inanna is yearning for Kong, whom she knows she can never have; until the very end of the opera, Punch's advances are spurned by Polly. The flute signals a melancholic colouring to love. For Blake, sorrow is prefigured even in the seemingly happy song of the innocent child: innocence can be understood only in the context of its opposite. For Birtwistle, too, love is dialectical.

The flute can also be understood as a symbol of the feminine. In Mozart and Schikaneder's Orphic *The Magic Flute*, it is the Three Ladies who give Tamino the magic flute which ultimately enables him to be united with Pamina. As Wilfrid Mellers has observed,

> The regenerative flute is thus associated with the female principle … the flute, if rationally Apollonian in Tamino's eighteenth century hands, preserves too its ancestral magic by way of its female donors. The libretto possibly, Mozart's music certainly, tells us that enlightened reason is inoperative without intuitive magic, the two being associated with male and female principles respectively.[37]

There are clear parallels with the role of the flute in *Orpheus*.

Of course, the flute (like other wind instruments) has also frequently been used in Western music to represent birdsong. Virgil makes the comparison between a specific bird's mournful songs and Orpheus' lamenting:

---

[36]   'Spring', from *Songs of Innocence* [1789], in William Blake, *Selected Poems*, ed. P.H. Butler (London: Dent, 1991), 19.

[37]   Wilfrid Mellers, *The Masks of Orpheus: Seven Stages in the Story of European Music* (Manchester: Manchester University Press, 1987), 116.

… as the nightingale
Mourning beneath the shade of a poplar-tree
Laments lost young ones whom a heartless ploughman
Has spied unfledged in the nest and plundered. She
Weeps all night long and perched upon a bough
Repeats her piteous plaint, and far and wide
Fills all the air with grief.[38]

In the Song of Magic, the piccolo's mournful line inflects Orpheus' singing, pointing – even on his wedding day – towards the tragic future: he will forever be lamenting his lost young lover. The piccolo fills the air with grief.

The link between the flute and dancing manifests itself more explicitly in the second verse of the song, as Orpheus and Eurydice dance their wedding dance (the first Immortal Dance). According to the libretto, the 'dance towards which each Ceremony pushes consists of six figures. In each exchange more and more of these figures are revealed. The dance takes place around the imaginary limbs of a horizontal Tree of Life. The words refer to these symbolic and metaphorical positions' (p. 46). It is perhaps difficult to imagine precisely how these ideas are to be realized on the stage, but the strange, distant music provides a context for their mysteriousness. At one level, the harp and percussion ostinatos and mobiles and repeated harp chords (distinct acoustic echoes of the electronic Clouds and Flowers) that accompany the sustained but rhythmically lopsided flute line play a slow, stately waltz. Yet with its bell-like accompaniment and prominent grace-note decorations of the sparse melody, this waltz – far from the Viennese tradition! – takes on the stylized aspects of an oriental ritual such as might be found, say, in a Noh drama.[39] It is not a passionate love dance.

The vocal line (from score fig. 50, p. 53) has an upward trajectory – each peak note is one semitone higher than the last – and ends with intense melismas that form an impassioned plea to Apollo. Piercing flourishes at the top of the piccolo range echo Orpheus' call, after which the music fades away to nothing. The strangeness of this music adds to the air of uncertainty.

---

[38] Virgil [Publius Virgilius Maro], *The Georgics*, tr. L.P. Wilkinson (London: Penguin, 1982), Book IV, ll. 511–16 (pp. 141–2).

[39] *Bow Down*, written for the National Theatre during the hiatus in the composition of *Orpheus*, is explicitly indebted to Noh drama. In the classical Noh tradition, the highly stylized ceremony is accompanied by a rarefied music for bamboo flute and three drummers. The scoring of *Bow Down* for five actors and four musicians includes a bamboo flute and percussion. In its retelling of multiple versions of the traditional balled of the 'Two Sisters' it obviously shares common territory with *The Mask of Orpheus*. Birtwistle discusses the influence of Noh theatre on *The Mask of Orpheus* in Chapter 6.

Act I, scene 2

Scene 2 is the first extended section of the opera where the story as described in the libretto and represented in the stage action is not directly embodied in text and music. 'In this scene there is only one song with words: when Aristaeus explains Euridice's death to an invisible Orpheus' (libretto 1997, p. 23). The scene shows the death of Eurydice, presented as a 'simple synchrony': we hear two Eurydices (Singer on stage, Puppet off) and we see two Eurydices (Singer and Mime). The action as given in the libretto is as follows:

> Euridice Singer is first noticed standing by the vertical river. She yawns (1st Cry of Memory). She is followed by Euridice Mime who stands on the other side of the river. Orpheus Singer is then noticed on the left. He remains as a static observer until after Euridice's death.
>
> Aristaeus Mime then enters and first tries to seduce one Euridice and then the next. Euridice Singer rejects Aristaeus but Euridice Mime is seduced by him. Finally both Euridices run away from him. He follows but a snake rears out the water from the horizontal and the vertical rivers and strikes first one then the other Euridice. Aristaeus tries to revive them to no avail. He kills the snake. Aristaeus tells Orpheus of Euridice's death. (Libretto 1997, p. 23)

One clear source for these stories is Virgil, the fourth book of whose *Georgics* is, in essence, about bees. Aristaeus was the 'first' beekeeper and Virgil recounts Aristaeus' part in the death of Orpheus' wife: 'You were the cause'.[40] The place of the Orpheus story in this book is fascinating. It occurs in the context of a narrative about Aristaeus' loss of his bees; the story of Orpheus' loss of his Eurydice parallels the main narrative in much the same way that the tales of the Clouds and Flowers parallel the main narrative in *Orpheus*.

Aristaeus' bees are present throughout much of scene 2 as another electronic Aura. Eurydice only sings vowel sounds that, obscurely, are 'very onomatopoeic of summer'. Again, obscurely, the first five vowel sounds (AOUEI) are meant to represent the five strings of Orpheus' lyre, while the last two (E' and O') are the two extra strings he added. It could be that the seven ringing notes on tape that sound as a rising scale across the first part of the scene (score, pp. 56–60) also represent the (chromatic) lyre of Orpheus (d^2–$d\sharp^2$–e^2–f^2–$f\sharp^2$–g^2–$b\flat^2$), who otherwise takes no part in the action. Especially striking here is the sound of the chorus. At first, the tenors and basses punctuate Eurydice's vocalizations with 'grunts' that match the low trombone chords; later, the whole SATB choir echoes, *divisi*, Eurydice's line in dense chord clusters, culminating (score, fig. 62, p. 68) in an extraordinary indeterminate passage where nearly all instruments are playing but very softly (*pppp*). It is a comparatively rare moment in Birtwistle reminiscent of the controlled

---

[40]   Virgil, *The Georgics*, Book IV, l. 457 (p. 140).

aleatoricism of the European avant-garde of the 1950s and 1960s. It lends an air of suspense to the drama at this point.

The instrumental music that surrounds Eurydice's vocalizations is built mainly from increasingly dense layers of ostinatos, layers which in themselves are constructed from relatively simple repeating material (scale fragments, highly regular rhythms). When combined, the result is a complex texture, but one in which each layer is still clearly audible. These slowly shifting strata are highly characteristic of Birtwistle's orchestral writing of the 1970s and 1980s, already in evidence in *The Triumph of Time* and culminating in *Earth Dances* (1985–86), which received its premiere in the same year as the opera. Typical also are the darkly coloured falling lines that weave their way through this texture, beginning with the oboe d'amore and cor anglais and later moving to the oboe. The cor anglais is another of Birtwistle's favourite obbligato instruments, with a sultry, melancholic character, and the use of the archaic oboe d'amore here carries obvious associations with Baroque music in general, and arias from the passions of Bach in particular. Despite being wordless, Eurydice's Cry of Memory is nonetheless designated 'aria'.

The Cry of Memory is interrupted twice: during Eurydice's 'yawn' by the violent Second Passing Cloud, and during her death by the more lyrical first Allegorical Flower. In the second part of the scene, the first Look of Loneliness (from fig. 63, p. 69), we hear the voice of Aristaeus (Man) for the first time, mainly delivering his text in a kind of rhythmicized speech. He turns to song only in order to sing Orpheus' name to a neighbour-note figure c^1–b^1($-c^1$) (fig. 68, p. 74; fig. 72, p. 77) and to deliver his final statement in response to a distant vocalization from Eurydice Singer (vowel sounds that close also with the c^2–b^1–c^2 neighbour figure associated with Orpheus' name):

> What memories.
> What tears forcing blood from the yellow sand.

This focused musical line, built from a characteristically symmetrical five-note set (f–g–a♭–a♮–b) and marked '*tenuto, sotto voce*, sadly', has that wistful character to which Birtwistle was to return in his next major operatic role for baritone, the Green Knight in *Gawain*.

As at the end of scene 1, the music fades away into silence.

Act I, scene 3

The scene begins with the first Time Shift. This is the most complex instance so far of a separation between drama and music – in other words, where for the most part drama and music proceed relatively independently, according to their own concerns. The libretto specifies the 'narrative' and stage action; no attempt is made to represent this directly in the music.

> Scene 3 introduces complex simultaneity (contrasted events seen at the same time); time distortion (the repeat of Euridice's death); size distortion (Euridice as a singer, mime, puppet and doll); the Golden Carriage of Mirrors; the first Journey and Metamorphosis; the first puppet (Euridice); The Oracle of the Dead (as a skull); vertical separation word echoes and pre-echoes. ...
>
> The scene opens with Orpheus Mime chasing Euridice Mime. The sun is high and slowly sets as the exaggeratedly slow action goes through Euridice's death once again. Aristaeus Singer offstage sings the 1st Human Lie while the mime action takes place on the stage. As Orpheus chases Euridice a huge snake rears up and strikes her dead. Euridice repeats this action several times over. She dies again and again. Finally Euridice replaces herself with a lifeless doll. Orpheus Mime then kills the snake and tries to revive the limp doll. These actions are all caricatures of the similar actions by Aristaeus in the last scene. Orpheus then lets the doll drop and this is the signal for the purely musical 1st Whisper of Change – The Whisper of Death. (Libretto, p. 16)

The stage actions are left to speak for themselves[41] while the music concerns itself entirely with Aristaeus' first Human Lie. One might wonder why music is necessary at all here if it has apparently nothing to do with the drama. As we have seen earlier, Birtwistle has no interest in mimesis; simply to echo the action in music would, in his view, make the music redundant. The one element – itself a kind of 'time shift' – on which the composer focuses stands in general for the way in which past events are reinterpreted in the present, in which memory has an inevitable capacity to distort and, as a consequence, in which exact repetition is an impossibility. This echoes the composer's practice elsewhere during this period: he will virtually never repeat music exactly.

> If I arrive at a context where a procedure is required, I will always invent or re-invent a procedure. I will never look back [he has a stronger will than Orpheus!] to see how I did it before. That would be too academic. ... So, apart from very rare exceptions, I either create something new or call on memory in order to make every situation unique. ... I would never copy something out from another page.[42]

The most obvious element of 'time shift' here is in Zinovieff's text, in which the 'words are an echo of the 1st Look of Loneliness where Aristaeus first tells Orpheus of Euridice's death' (libretto, p. 16). They are now sung by Aristaeus Myth.

---

[41]   It should be noted that not all of the given stage instructions were necessarily realized in the first production.

[42]   Birtwistle, quoted in Hall, *Harrison Birtwistle*, 151–2.

First Look of Loneliness	**First Human Lie**
(Act I, scene 2)	**(Act I, scene 3)**
Kissed by the snake,	Kiss the snake,
Cracked shadow.	Cracked memory.
Speak to the water.	Speak to the dire land!
Kicked in the dust,	Cry in the dust,
Dead shadow.	Dead tears.
Listen to the dried grass.	Listen to the silent grass!
Killed by the river,	Kill by the river,
Dark shadow …	Dark blood.
What tears forcing blood	Remember the yellow sand!
	from the yellow sand.

But the music does not provide such immediate echoes of the first Look of Loneliness. There are clearly significant connections, but there are also many differences: this is more than just the simple variation that the text alone might suggest. The delivery of the text is more focused than before, generally in *Sprechstimme* but, for key words ('Speak', 'Dead tears', 'Kill', etc.), alighting on specific pitches. It is the singing of the name of Orpheus that elicits the most precise 'memory', beginning as before with the semitone b–c^1 but now extended to end on g♯. In general, this is a 'softer' presentation of the ideas: whereas in scene 2 the accompanying percussion was loud and for hard-edged metallic instruments, in scene 3 it is at a softer dynamic level and for wooden instruments. The sustained chords (bassoons, horns, trombones) are still present, reworked, almost as if echoing the singing of Orpheus' name, but a new swirling layer in flutes and clarinets is also added. The duration of this section is also much shorter than its predecessor. Thus, as the libretto suggests, what the music offers here is a distortion of the end of scene 2. To take up Zinovieff's metaphor of mirrors, the music is not subject to a simple reflection in a flat-surface mirror but, rather, the original is deformed as if seen in a mirror of multiple surfaces so that some features remain virtually the same while others are reshaped almost beyond recognition. So, although the precise echoing of text and events is not directly represented in the music, their respective transformation processes are nonetheless well matched. The music performs a 'time shift' in its own terms that offers a commentary on the textual and dramatic Time Shift with which it is associated. Music and text remain complementary rather than analogous.

The function of the brief first Whisper of Change is that of a dissolve – music that, on stage or in film, signals a return from the 'past' to the 'present' (though clearly the meaning of such terms in this work is complex). Very soft (*pppp*), gently undulating clusters of sound for wordless chorus and harps are bound together by virtually inaudible rolls on bass drums and a new, whispering electronic Aura. Time seems to stand still. It is a moment of eerie near-silence. Birtwistle the theatre composer judges such moments to perfection. And out of this dead stillness emerges, hardly audibly at first, what seems like the faint sound of life again, a heartbeat ($\downarrow$ = *c*.60) on a bass drum. But ironically this sign of the living is to accompany a ritual for the dead: the drum beat becomes the motif of a funeral march and marks the beginning of the second Ceremony.

Second Ceremony (The Funeral)

Table 2.3 shows a summary of the structure of the second Ceremony that brings Act I to its conclusion.

Table 2.3   Structural summary of second Ceremony

Exchange	Orpheus	Second Complicated Question	First Hysterical Aria	First Duet of Love
First exchange	First Song of Failure (A)			
First exchange (continued) (including second Immortal Dance, vv. 1–3)		Verse 1	Interjection I	Extension 4
Second exchange		Verse 2	Interjection II	
Funeral Dance				Extension 5
	First Spoken Argument (R)			
Third exchange (including Funeral Dance) (continued)		Verse 3	Interjection III	Extension 6
	Second Statement of Reason (A)		Verse 2	
	First Magic Formula (A)		Interjection [IV]	
	First Shout of Gratitude (R)		Interjection [V]	

Comparison with Table 2.2 reveals a similar organization in three cycles. Three further extensions of the first Duet of Love interrupt the course of the Ceremony. The brief, contemplative silences that punctuated the first Ceremony are here replaced with their opposite: loud, screeched statements of the Hysterical Aria from the Oracle of the Dead, accompanied by the Ensemble of Hell.[43] Her singing is unpitched and consists of 'incomprehensible interjections from syllables in the words STAND, WAIT, HIDE, HANDS, REACH, PRESS' (libretto, p. 17), a nightmarish reconfiguration of the by now familiar Argonautic journey. There are clear echoes here of Punch's War Cries in *Punch and Judy*, screamed seemingly from his bowels just before he commits each murder, and early pre-echoes of the screams of the Harpie-like Keres in *The Minotaur* who feast on the life-organs ripped from the bodies of the Minotaur's victims. But, in these wordless cries at the upper limits of this high soprano's range, there are older operatic echoes too of the Oracle's hysterical forebear, the Queen of the Night. Only towards the end of the Ceremony do the Oracle's words become intelligible when she offers Orpheus the three rules that should govern his (dreamed) journey in Act II:

Face the way of the sun.
Choose without choosing.
Speak indirectly.

Thus she presents the condition – look not back – of Orpheus' entry into the underworld. She guards the cave at Taenarus, believed to be an entrance to Hades, and, according to Zinovieff's self-styled 'children's' prose version of the plot, she is jealous of Orpheus' power over rocks, trees and animals through music (see libretto 1997, pp. 10–12). It is through his magical song, the first Magic Formula, that he reveals to the Oracle the secret of his music and so wins her over. The Oracle tries to imitate him, but all she can utter is a horrible screeching. Too late she realizes that Orpheus has tricked his way into the cave.

In general the pace of this Ceremony is slow, the dynamic soft, the mood subdued. We immediately recognize that it is a kind of repetition of the first Ceremony when we hear the Priests' call of 'Answer'. But the energy of that occasion has been dissipated. The rhythmically insistent, ritual drumming that accompanied the calls and wedding dance during the first Ceremony becomes here something much more hesitant. It is as if this Ceremony is taking place in the ruins of the wedding. It is only in the Oracle's violent interjections that we are reminded of the Dionysian aspect to Eurydice's funeral rite. 'The dancing gradually became wilder and wilder. The mourners put on grotesque Dionysian masks of women and effigies of Euridice were torn apart in her memory. This wild abandon was in the old tradition and celebrated the re-birth of Dionysus by the sacrifice of Euridice' (libretto 1997, p. 11). In the midst of this stands Orpheus, whose extended arias and recitatives mark the most significant difference between the two Ceremonies. He tries to ignore the funeral.

---

[43]   Birtwistle uses this designation (often abbreviated to 'EoH') in the sketches to refer to the continuum mobiles that are presented at the start of Act II, but it can also be understood to relate to the music associated with the Oracle at the end of Act I. The only time the designation is used in the score is in Act II, scene 2 (see fig. 49, p. 202).

Central to this Ceremony, and (as I shall argue in Chapter 5) to a wider understanding of the opera as an expression of ideas of late modernity, is Orpheus' first Song of Failure (score, fig. 81, p. 86).

> Window into hard rain.
> Touch me sooner.
> Overlaid with golden ribbons …
> Jewels. …

Orpheus is overcome by grief at Eurydice's death. He had tried in vain to revive her (though this is not depicted here). 'This was the first time of three that Orpheus' magic music failed' (libretto 1997, p. 10). His loss is desperate and his grief at his failure is palpable in this Baroque-like song, redolent with echoes of a Bach Passion aria ('Es ist vollbracht', 'It is finished').

Although the melody is a free and expressive chromatic line, moving towards climactic high notes on key words, the accompaniment remains static, almost mechanical. Indeed, the accompaniment merely takes over ideas from the start of the first exchange, out of which it emerges; they echo throughout the Ceremony. The funereal bass drum strokes have become a regular repeated-note, *crescendo* figure heard, variously, on trios of electric plucked string instruments, flutes (of various sizes) and metal tuned percussion, the last doubled by a scalar line on tape similar to that heard in scene 2. Here, though, there are only four notes chosen from the seven heard earlier, presented as a sequence of rising, expanding intervals: e^2–f^2–g^2–$b\flat^2$. Increasing emphasis is given to the first of these pitches as the aria proceeds, and it is to a repeated e that Orpheus' melody drops on his final phrase, 'dumbed by death'. However hard he may try, he cannot escape his predicament and his failure becomes all the more apparent. As before, the tape sound may refer to a lyre, and in this aria it could represent Apollo, to whom Orpheus appealed in vain. The clear, ringing sounds of tape and percussion may also be understood as a colouring of the aria prompted by the prominence of such words as 'rain' and 'jewel'.

A familiar trio of clarinet, bass clarinet and contrabass clarinet extend the repeating figure throughout most of the aria, providing continuity and setting a melancholic mood, while the harps counteract the rising tape figure with a falling punctuating device. Most conspicuous of all is a three-note motif on the piccolo that floats high above the melody line. It is Birtwistle's 'signature' chromatic motif,[44] a variant on

---

[44]   In his discussion of Stravinsky's serial music, Joseph Straus identifies an important motivic cell he names the 'twist motive', which is identical to Birtwistle's motif here, i.e., the combined tone and semitone pointing in different directions. See Straus, *Stravinsky's Late Music* (Cambridge: Cambridge University Press, 2001), 90 ff. The tone-semitone motif is, for example, an obsessive surface feature of *Agon* (in both its serial and non-serial sections). Birtwistle made an extensive study of *Agon* while he was a Harkness Fellow at Princeton University in the mid 1960s, and the work has had a profound impact on his subsequent

the 'Dowland' chromatic motif discussed above, which here occurs four times in the four possible permutations of rising or falling tone and semitone:

$$f^3-g^3-f\sharp^3 \mid c^3-d\flat^3-b^2 \mid e^3-d\sharp^3-f^3 \mid c\sharp^3-b^2-c^3$$

As we saw in scene 1, both the motif and the instrument are a signifier of the melancholic, as well as pointing to the love that has been lost. Links are made with the Love Duet, whose extensions we are shortly to hear again as a further reminder, and in which this piccolo motif is again prominent. In fact the piccolo is a virtually continuous presence throughout the Ceremony to the end of the act. It achieves its fullest melodic identity as the top and most audible voice in the chorale that supports the first Shout of Gratitude (see below), but elsewhere one can hear piccolo melodies built, for example, as in the third exchange (score, fig. 104 ff., pp. 108 ff.), of chained sequences of the signature motif.

Example 2.3 Act I, scene 3, second Complicated Question, Priests

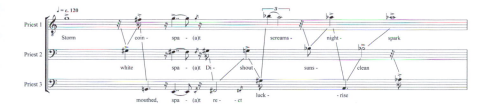

Space does not permit here a detailed discussion of each component part of the Ceremony – indeed, it should be noted that in all performances to date, a substantial section of this music has been cut (see Appendix B). Worthy of particular comment is the second Complicated Question, a 'variant' of the first Complicated Question. The confident rhythmic unison of the first question is clearly undone here as the text is passed between the three voices in a procedure reminiscent of medieval hocketing (see Example 2.3). This, too, echoes a very similar situation in *Punch and Judy* where, in Passion Aria I, high tenor (Lawyer) and low bass (Doctor) share a line, to parodistic effect. The pitch content represents a rethinking of the modal segments in the first question: each line here is built from a (now more explicitly chromatic) scale segment:

Priest 1:   F♯–G–A♭–A♮–B♭
Priest 2:   F♯–G–G♯–   –B♭
Priest 3: E–F♯–G–G♯–A♮

musical thinking (see Jonathan Cross, *Harrison Birtwistle: Man, Mind, Music* (London: Faber and Faber, 2000), 36–43).

The second Ceremony also contains the most complex instances so far of temporal simultaneity where two ensembles (under two conductors) present entirely distinct music. The motivation for this is simple: Orpheus addresses his songs to the Oracle of the Dead. 'In each case he leaves the area [of the stage] assigned to the Funeral Ceremony and moves over to the side of the Oracle. Both sets of words move towards the Act 2 arch songs' (libretto, p. 18). While such a procedure is not new in opera, its realization here is striking. (Precedents are to be found in, for instance, Zimmermann's *Die Soldaten* and Henze's *We Come to the River*, while Stockhausen's *Gruppen* for three orchestras and three conductors remains a work of great importance for Birtwistle.) It is another manifestation of the playing with time that is central to the opera – the challenging of the model of linear time, of 'time's arrow', as Karol Berger has described it, that has been the 'essential subject matter' of music since the later eighteenth century.[45] In *Orpheus*, (musical) time appears to turn back on itself, to repeat itself, to stand still; and in these instances time is represented as multiple rather than singular. The recitative text of the first Spoken Argument (score, fig. 100, p. 105) is delivered in a clipped, rhythmic manner (*molto secco*) with a similarly clipped hocketing accompaniment from four trumpets and five untuned percussion. The effect is of continuous, rapid semiquaver movement at a tempo of $\flat = c.160$. This is superimposed on to the music of the Funeral Dance, which provides a background continuity at $\flat = c.112$, and across whose regular dance rhythms a mournful soprano saxophone sings its melody. Orpheus' second Statement of Reason (score, fig. 110, p. 114) is a fretful aria anticipating his future fate ('My limbs are now wrenched from their sockets'). Accompanied by three harps playing strange musical fragments, the music is in an anxious state of flux, alternating or moving (by means of *rall.* or *accel.*) between tempos of $\downarrow = c.112$ (conductor I) and $\downarrow = c.63$ (conductor II). The vocal line switches between *Sprechstimme* and song, and leaps widely across the singer's range. At the end of each short verse the music is suspended, only (strangely) to resume by repeating the previous bar, as if some sort of tape had to be rewound a centimetre or two before the music could resume. It lends an uncanny air. Meanwhile, the large ensemble provides continuity (at $\downarrow = c.60$) with sustained, mainly falling lines associated principally with the exchanges and Funeral Dance and not unrelated to the accompanying lines in the Love Duet. There is also a third temporal layer here: in the pauses between Orpheus' verses a group of percussionists sounds a figure (always in temporal flux, variously marked *accel.* or *rall.*) that escapes the tempos of both conductors. It is a complex moment. The aria ends with the solemn announcement of the Caller that 'The soil is now ready for a new child'.

---

[45]   Karol Berger, 'Time's arrow and the advent of musical modernity', in Karol Berger and Anthony Newcomb (eds), *Music and the Aesthetics of Modernity: Essays* (Cambridge, MA: Harvard University Press, 2005), 14. These ideas are developed at length in Karol Berger, *Bach's Cycle, Mozart's Arrow: an Essay on the Origins of Musical Modernity* (Berkeley: University of California Press, 2007).

Orpheus' final song to the Oracle – in response to her crazed request to 'Tell me a secret!' – is the first Magic Formula that we have already encountered (score, fig. 117, p. 120). The text speaks of:

> Magic mirrors corner,
> Turn, flashing memories.
> Reflections, burning hottest …

and Birtwistle responds with a magic music of mirrors: glistening flourishes on metallic percussion and harps, with watery mobiles in flutes and clarinets continuously turning. It is little wonder that the Oracle is enchanted, not least because Orpheus engages in a subtle kind of flattery: the wind and brass layers that accompany the Oracle's screeches are themselves made up of similar oscillating mobiles. Although the immediate differences between their music are obvious in their juxtaposition, at a deeper level the knowledge possessed by the Apollonian Orpheus and the Dionysian Oracle would appear to be merely two sides of the same coin.

The act ends with Orpheus' first Shout of Gratitude, a moment of triumph in his being able to pass through the gate to the underworld. It marks a transition between the end of this act and the beginning of the next, and between the land of the living and the land of the dead. As the libretto states (p. 19), it is 'the start of the dream and nightmare sequence that makes up Act 2': indeed, the majority of Act II might be understood to be an elaboration, a 'composing out' of the ideas set out in the shout. The text, which is in two principal parts, describes the structure of the Arches, first in general, then with more detailed characteristics of each of the 17 arches. The Arches are never physically present but remain a structure of Orpheus' imagination, of his memory. 'I remember the arches', he tells us. He has been there before. What we are to see in Act II is only a dream.

This text is delivered in a manner quite unlike a shout. (It is the Oracle who shouts.) It is spoken clearly and deliberately. It is accompanied by a thick-textured wind chorale (quadruple woodwind, horns and trumpets) that marks, appropriately, the end of the passion, that is, the conclusion of Eurydice's funeral rite. Its melody is played throughout in seven simultaneous octaves (the first pitch class sounds in each octave all the way up from F$\sharp^1$ on the contrabassoon to f$\sharp^4$ on the piccolo, and so on). The result is a strange kind of organum, rather like one of Messiaen's chorales, evocative of a disembodied, full swell organ with all its couplers and mixtures in use but with swell box tightly shut. (Distant echoes, perhaps, of Debussy's *Cathédrale engloutie*?) The chorale melody, too, has a Messiaen-like character as if it were a chant twisted through a strange, chromatic mode. It moves mainly by seconds and thirds (semitones predominate) with occasional larger leaps, and all its pitches are contained within the narrow chromatic range of a minor sixth between B♭ and G♭. Starting on F♯ (the insistently repeated pitch class with which the second Ceremony has begun) and ending on B♮, there is an intriguing focus on the bare fifth that reinforces the ancient air to this music. And the chorale comes to an end on an unexpected sustained single pitch class, B, marked with a searing *crescendo* from *p* to *fff*. (Not-so-distant echoes, perhaps, of Berg's variations on the same note in *Wozzeck*?) Overall, its sense of quiet, timeless, stillness has an other-worldly quality that is in keeping both with its dream nature and with its role as an almost Shakespearean foil to the violent events that are to be represented in Act II. The melody is shown in Example 2.4.

Example 2.4 Act I, scene 3, melody of final chorale

The sketches for this chorale[46] reveal that Birtwistle worked out the durational scheme first. A sequence of 36 durations, each individually numbered, is written out in full, complete with bar numbers and time signatures, just as it occurs in the final score. The predominance of open note-heads not only indicates that the chorale proceeds at a relatively slow, meditative pace, but in its appearance also evokes, again, something ancient. It is juxtaposed in an extreme fashion with the short-value black notation of the Ensemble of Hell that precedes and succeeds it. Being associated directly with Orpheus and the Arches, it has an Apollonian (male) order that contrasts sharply with the extreme Dionysian nature of the Oracle's (female) hysteria.

And it is with this hysteria that the act ends, as the screeches of the Oracle of the Dead return. Layer is added upon repeating layer at a high dynamic level in a statement of pure, visceral energy: rhythm dominates pitch, noise dominates sense. At the end the almost literally unbearable music just stops as if it has been suddenly and violently ripped apart. In this, it anticipates the violent death of Orpheus. It is music to be felt with the body, not understood with the mind. It overwhelms us; we have no choice but to submit to its savageness.

---

[46]　　Around PSS 0531-0360.

Chapter 3
The Mask of Orpheus: Act II

Synopsis

The act opens with the second Time Shift, in which Orpheus witnesses another representation of Eurydice's death. The lovers, as Myths (Puppets), sing their second Love Duet. Then Orpheus' imaginary journey begins. Orpheus Man sings his vast second Song of Magic while watching Orpheus Hero's descent into the underworld (scene 1: Arches 1–9) and return (scene 2: Arches 10–15). As in a nightmare, characters from Act I reappear in distorted forms: Orpheus sees himself as Hades, Eurydice as Persephone and the Oracle of the Dead as Hecate. A searing, screaming musical climax accompanies Orpheus' awakening from his dream: he realizes that he never descended into the underworld and that, in turning, he has lost Eurydice for ever. Scene 3 (Arches 16 and 17) represents the awareness of his loneliness. Orpheus Hero suffers his first Terrible Death by Suicide.

The structure of Act II is very different from that of Act I. Whereas in Act I each larger section remained relatively discrete and each scene asserted its own identity, the shape of the whole appearing somewhat diffuse, Act II describes one large arch from beginning to end, overriding any nice distinction between scenes. The overall effect of the act is of a gradual and continuous increase in musical and dramatic intensity up to its climactic high point at the end of scene 2, and then of a reverse move to the stillness of its ending. It projects, therefore, a conventional and familiar expressive trajectory. Despite the obvious strophic structure offered by the libretto via the 17 verses of Orpheus' second Song of Magic (the Song of Arches), the music gives the contrary impression of being forward-moving. Thus the conflict between the essential circularity of the text and the essential linearity of the music results in a productive tension that colours the whole act and is entirely in keeping with the representation of Orpheus' heroic journey that ends in failure. Once again, it raises fascinating interpretative questions.

As Robert Adlington observes, 'rarely can a composer have been presented with such a prescriptive statement as Zinovieff's … text, down to split-second timings for the entire course of Act II'.[1] In this regard, the description in the introduction to the 1974 'Explanatory Document' of the text as 'more like a film scenario than a conventional libretto' rings true. Like a film shooting script, this document lays

---

[1] Robert Adlington, *The Music of Harrison Birtwistle* (Cambridge: Cambridge University Press, 2000), 19.

out the events of each act in a detailed graphic scenario, a plan in which the relative temporal position of each event is explicitly given. The charts in the published libretto offer a simplified version of these scenarios. What is interesting is how Birtwistle interprets the timings that Zinovieff offers him. Largely the composer follows them to the second, like a film composer; sometimes, however, he uses the specific durations in the libretto as a more general stimulus for the development and opposition of specifically musical ideas. The framework is useful to the composer only up to a point: unlike a film composer, he has the freedom to ignore it if it suits his musical purposes. This exemplifies a conflict central to the opera as a whole, namely that between the fundamentally structuralist and formalist concerns of the libretto and the overtly expressive concerns of the music. Act II is therefore a prime illustration of Birtwistle's statement that he has 'made a distinction between a series of closed forms which define the stage action, and a much more organic, through-composed substructure belonging exclusively to the orchestra'.[2]

The detail of this relationship between text and music, between structure and expression, will be explored in the body of this chapter. The main consequence of such oppositions in performance is a sense of distance between what is heard taking place in the music and what is seen taking place on the stage. The music, as has already been noted, generally represents a progression towards and away from a climactic point, an imaginary journey that culminates in Orpheus' first suicide by hanging. But this linearity is complexly expressed – indeed, the spatial metaphor of the spiral might be more appropriate than that of the line. Though the overall trajectory is forward-moving, each verse appears to begin again, despite the fact that the music never returns to the same place. Hall briefly explores the possibility of the spiral metaphor in relation to Birtwistle's strophic structures and notes that 'the route through Hades which Orpheus follows is traditionally an inward-winding spiral or labyrinth, as is the route for all who wish to transcend time, the spiral being a symbol for the progress of the soul towards eternity'.[3] Orpheus' quest in Act II is an imaginary one, coloured by memories of the past: he re-encounters people and music from Act I, but transformed or distorted as in a dream or nightmare. The spiral metaphor is therefore further relevant in that Act II is concerned with memory – a return is made to earlier music and events but viewed from new perspectives.

The principal events are familiar elements from the story of Orpheus' descent into the underworld, and are depicted on the stage but only alluded to intermittently in the music. Various texts are heard, sung by the characters whom Orpheus Hero encounters and interspersed with or superimposed on to the verses of his Song of Magic, which is the primary focus of attention. In scene 1, Orpheus' singing enables him first to pass Charon, the ferryman who rows souls across the river Styx (the

---

[2]   Birtwistle, in discussion with Michael Hall, 'Composer and producer speak', in the programme book for the premiere performances of *The Mask of Orpheus*, ed. Nicholas John (May 1986) [no page numbers].

[3]   Michael Hall, *Harrison Birtwistle* (London, Robson 1984), 109–10.

River of Fire); next the Furies; then the Judges of the Dead. Visions of Eurydice (as a puppet) keep appearing. Once in the underworld he encounters the terrible trio of Hades (the god of Death), Persephone (wife of Hades, daughter of Demeter) and Hecate (the old witch-goddess). Now that Orpheus has reached Eurydice, scene 2 marks the return, in which 'one form of Euridice gradually changes into another ... Orpheus follows Euridice as she becomes more lifelike' (libretto, p. 28). They reach the River of Fire, which is extinguished. Orpheus awakes. He turns to see Eurydice already slipping away from his grasp. 'He realises that he never descended to the underworld' (p. 29). In scene 3, Orpheus is alone. He understands that he has been dreaming and that, real or otherwise, he has lost Eurydice for a second time. The events of the first 13 Arches are replayed again, 'even more archetypally' (p. 30), as a shadow play. After singing the 17th verse of his song, 'Orpheus Mime enters from right, crosses the stage and deliberately hangs himself. Orpheus Singer faces away towards the underworld' (p. 30).

While the events that one would expect to see represented in any telling of the story of Orpheus' journey to the underworld are obviously present, they ultimately remain tangential. They are the background plot against which the principal concerns of the act are explored, namely singing, dreaming and memory. This might initially seem an inversion of the facts. After all, Orpheus' singing is, in the first place, motivated by the plot through his need to charm his way, artfully, past the characters who impede his progress towards Eurydice. But unlike Monteverdi's Orfeo, Orpheus ultimately makes no progress here because the journey is only a dream. He sings because he can, as a mode of self-expression. It might certainly be argued of Monteverdi's 'Possente spirito' that it, too, is as much about the art of the singer as it is about the singer's ability to charm. But in that case Orpheus does at least address his song to Charon in a passionate entreaty to allow him to pass across the river, and implores the gods of Tartarus to return his love to him: 'Rendetemi il mio ben'. Birtwistle's Orpheus sings only, obscurely, of the characteristics of the Arches, of strange feelings and of half-grasped memories. For each arch he intones, 'I remember'. His dreamed journey to the underworld parallels an earlier journey made with the Argonauts, and echoes of it are heard throughout. In the ninth Arch, recalling the beginning of Act I, Orpheus sings: 'I remember the fifty men: / Their parched greetings screamed / Against the night-dead whisper'. Orpheus' Song of Magic appears, then, to be about himself. As I shall argue in more detail in Chapter 5, Orpheus' song represents a late-modern quest after self. The music yearns for a continuity and completeness (a unified sense of self, the constitutive subject) that is continually frustrated in its verse structure and the fragmentation of the text. Orpheus sings of the very crisis of modernism. His own failure stands also for the failure of modernism.

That this journey is imagined is reinforced by the fact that Orpheus continues to encounter music and people he has met before. Characters who appeared in Act I reappear in new guises, as in a dream or nightmare. Charon is sung by Aristaeus Myth, echoing the first Look of Loneliness (first Human Lie) of Act I. (Both characters stand, as it were, between Orpheus and Eurydice.) Hecate's screeching is that of the Oracle of the Dead; Persephone sings with Eurydice's voice and words from the first Love Duet; and in Hades Orpheus sees himself. The Judges of the Dead are inverses of the Troupe of Ceremony, and although the three Furies are new, they will later reappear in Act III. It is not unknown for opera to play with such doublings.[4] The paralleling of characters in Acts I and III of Berg's *Lulu* is perhaps the most famous example. And just as Berg there intended to make connections between the characters thus paired, so here the couplings signify an aspect of Orpheus' imagination in the way in which characters he has already met are reconfigured. The resulting confusion of past and present is a vivid representation of memory. That this is achieved through the medium of music which, since the late eighteenth century at least, has attempted to articulate the passage of time in strictly linear terms – from past through present to future[5] – says important things not only about Birtwistle's art but also about post-Freudian understanding of the mind.

These many ideas are all, as the libretto (p. 22) puts it, 'contained in the tight structure of the Arches'. The progression of the story from dream to nightmare is built by the librettist into the temporal structure of each arch, that is, each verse of the Song of Magic. The increase in intensity across the 17 verses is also built into the structure, in that the duration of each successive arch is three seconds shorter than its predecessor. Thus the first Arch is specified as lasting 2'36", and the final Arch as lasting 1'48". The entire song should thus last 37'24".[6]

Each verse is like a self-contained aria. Each arch is made of a different substance; each represents different aspects of the world as Orpheus knows it, as he has already declared at the end of Act I; each is also associated with a particular affect or emotion – though this association becomes increasingly opaquely articulated as we progress across the Arches. Thus the first Arch is the arch of countryside, associated with hesitancy; the second is the arch of crowds, associated with confidence; and so on. The 17th and final Arch is of fear and relates to misery. In addition, the text as sung by Orpheus suggests further related characteristics. For example, each arch has a

---

[4]   The doubling of parts by a single actor, a task facilitated by the wearing of masks, was not unknown even in ancient time.

[5]   See Karol Berger on 'time's arrow', discussed above in Chapter 2. Interestingly, Berger gives the trial scene in *The Magic Flute* as an exemplar of this linearity, with its 'transition from the dark archaic minor to the bright modern major' (Berger, 'Time's arrow and the advent of musical modernity', in Karol Berger and Anthony Newcomb (eds), *Music and the Aesthetics of Modernity: Essays* (Cambridge, MA: Harvard University Press, 2005), 19). Birtwistle and Zinovieff may well be alluding to and subverting Mozart's Orphic work here, not least in their play of threes. *The Mask of Orpheus* is a kind of negative *Magic Flute* moving from light to darkness, a late-modern critique of Mozart's Enlightenment opera.

[6]   In practice, the music follows the spirit of this structure in its increasing intensity, but not necessarily the specific timings. That said, using the timings on the CD as a rough guide, the total duration of the song in performance is 38'22", which, allowing for the additional time taken by signals and pauses that are not part of Zinovieff's calculations, is remarkably close to the libretto's total specified duration.

'purpose': the first Arch 'is the arch for love', the second 'the arch for anger', and so on. A detailed chart in the libretto (pp. 50–51) spells out precisely the senses, objects and symbols for each arch, making explicit just how structurally conceived they are. As will be seen below, Birtwistle strives to differentiate between these ideas musically.

Each arch is itself made up of four component parts. The libretto explains:

> The fabric of each arch is divided into 4 sections: fact, fantasy, distortion and awakening. These form in turn two overlapping types of expression: dream (made up of fact and fantasy) and nightmare (made up of fantasy and distortion). The awakening is instantaneous. … The style of words and music changes according to each part of the wave: the fact is aria, the fantasy is recitative and the distortion is speech. Interjections or appearances of the underworld characters are accompanied by a musical indication – the Ensemble of Hell (abbreviated to EOH). Other signals and pauses force the tension of the structure and occur in fixed positions. Each arch has an overall mood. (p. 49)

This specification of an 'overall mood' confirms the Baroque-like nature of each verse of the song, reinforced by the subdivision into dream and nightmare sections – opposite sides of the same coin reminiscent of the A and B sections of a *da capo* aria.

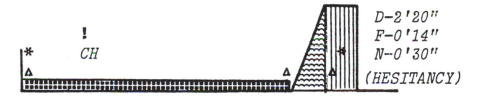

Figure 3.1   Act II, scene 1, durational proportions of first Arch (libretto, p. 23)

In the published libretti, each verse of the Song of Magic is accompanied by a small diagram that gives precise timings for each section of each verse, drawn to scale (the example of the first Arch is given in Figure 3.1). What these indicate is how the relative proportions of each section change gradually over the course of the song. Thus in the first Arch, in which dream predominates, the dream portion (D) is given as 2′20″, fantasy (F) 0′14″ and nightmare (N) 0′30″. By the time we have reached the climax of the song and the moment of Orpheus' awakening at the 15th Arch, in which nightmare predominates, D has been reduced to only 0′07″, F is just 0′06″ and N has increased to 1′53″. The durations for each arch are given in Table 3.1. It will be noted immediately that simply adding up the three durations for each verse does not produce the totals specified by Zinovieff, that is, for the first Arch, 2′20″ + 0′14″ + 0′30″ does not equal 2′36″. The answer to this lies in the explanation quoted above where 'two overlapping types of expression: dream

Table 3.1 Durations of the sections of the 17 Arches as given in the libretto, and the differences in duration between successive sections (a positive number represents increasing duration, a negative number decreasing duration)

Arch	1	2	3	4	5	6	7	8	9	10	11	12	13	14	15	16	17
Dream	2'20"	2'15"	2'08"	2'00"	1'54"	1'46"	1'39"	1'30"	1'22"	1'12"	1'03"	0'53"	0'41"	0'25"	0'07"	1'29"	1'38"
difference		-5"	-7"	-8"	-6"	-8"	-7"	-9"	-8"	-10"	-9"	-10"	-12"	-16"	-18"		
Fantasy	0'14"	0'21"	0'26"	0'30"	0'34"	0'36"	0'39"	0'40"	0'41"	0'48"	0'45"	0'40"	0'33"	0'21"	0'06"	1'08"	1'19"
difference		7"	5"	4"	4"	2"	3"	1"	1"	7"	-3"	-5"	-7"	-12"	-15"		
Nightmare	0'30"	0'39"	0'48"	0'57"	1'04"	1'11"	1'18"	1'25"	1'31"	1'45"	1'48"	1'50"	1'52"	1'53"	1'53"	1'30"	1'29"
difference		9"	9"	9"	7"	7"	7"	7"	6"	14"	3"	2"	2"	1"	0		
Arch total	2'36"	2'33"	2'30"	2'27"	2'24"	2'21"	2'18"	2'15"	2'12"	2'09"	2'06"	2'03"	2'00"	1'57"	1'54"	1'51"	1'48"

←——— scene 1 ———→ ←—— scene 2 ——→ ←— scene 3 —→

(made up of fact and fantasy) and nightmare (made up of fantasy and distortion)' are specified. In other words, the Fantasy section F is common to both D and N: deduct the 14 seconds of overlapping F from D, and the sums work! (Even so, Birtwistle's interpretation of these durations results in a longer section than specified – see below for an explanation.)

The diagrams also indicate the positions of other events. The most prominent of these are certain electronic signals that generally mark the start of each verse. They take the form of an electronic flourish (transformed harp sounds), the voice of Apollo speaking in his invented Orphic language and a burst of the Winter Aura. Additional electronic sounds interject periodically. In scene 1, Apollo utters the words 'FIS' ('high'), 'RIS' ('tide') and 'IES' (no meaning given, though it sounds like the word 'yes'). In scene 2, Apollo on each occasion speaks only the words 'OFEIUS OFOARIF' ('Orpheus remember'), as he did at the end of the first Ceremony. This has a double meaning. Orpheus must remember the instructions of the Oracle and not turn or else he will lose Eurydice. But, as we know, his entire journey is also in itself an act of remembering. In scene 3, Orpheus has lost Eurydice; Apollo remains silent.

This is only a brief introduction to some of the concerns of the Arches. The published libretto gives further information, while in the original 'Explanatory Document' ideas are elaborated in far greater detail. Much is included with regard to the specifics of production, such as the positions of actors on the stage, the movement of the Golden Carriage of Mirrors in which Orpheus descends to and returns from the underworld, the use of puppets and masks, and so on. Space does not permit fuller discussion here; suffice it to say that, in the spirit of *Gesamtkunstwerk*, in conceiving the work, matters of staging were as carefully (and structurally) thought through as were text and music. Many of these details remained unrealized in the original stage production, partly as a consequence of financial constraints. As always in opera, while text and music remain (relatively) fixed, any future producer would be free to rethink the way the ideas could be presented on the stage. (Clearly, more recent developments in theatre technology now offer the potential for new stagings very different from that of the premiere.)

The question also inevitably arises, with a libretto and scenario as complex and multi-layered as these, of how many of the ideas it is possible to perceive in performance. The finer points of sectional proportions, for example, are entirely a (private) matter of poetics but will impinge on the audience if they are made relevant. To the extent that, as I have argued, the music articulates the general trajectory of the organization of the text in its increasing urgency, then both the structural concerns of librettist and the expressive concerns of composer have a direct impact. That the presentation of the story seems to work 'in counterpoint' to the musical unfolding is, it could be argued, a rethinking of the principles of Greek tragedy, where the plot was already known to an audience more interested in the telling than in the tale. Here, music and text serve the function of throwing new light on the well-known story. Not everything can be grasped immediately, nor should we expect it to be. But the many repetitions built into the work mean that we gradually become familiar with the repertoire of ideas and devices that the creators are exploring as the opera unfolds.

Act II, scene 1

Act II begins with the second Time Shift and the sound of the continuum. This particular word has a special resonance for Birtwistle and is usually paired with the word 'cantus'.[7] The first explicit use of the two terms together appeared in *Secret Theatre*, where the continuous melody line, played by soloists who stand on a raised dais at the back of the performing space, is labelled 'cantus', while the main ensemble, seated, forms the 'continuum'. In notes made prior to composing *Secret Theatre*, the composer mused:

> MELODY/ACCOMPANIMENT … bad analogy, suggesting one more important than the other … CANTUS/CONTINUUM – better way to think – a bit academic maybe – *important* – think, explore notion – FOREGROUND/BACKGROUND (juxtaposition of opposites again … CONTINUUM equals vertical music (rhythmic development) CANTUS equals horizontal music (melodic development) CONTINUUM to be made up from invented ostinato forms, plus solos.[8]

The important distinction, then, between cantus and continuum, however complexly each may be constituted, is one of function. Cantus is a kind of melody, horizontal, linear, forward-moving; continuum is more rhythmically conceived, circular. The simultaneity of linear and circular process in Birtwistle's music is evident in his earliest works.[9] In Chapter 2 this was explored in relation to Günther Grass's notion of 'stasis in progress'. In relation to Act II, especially the second Song of Magic, it is an apposite musical metaphor both for what is being represented on stage and for the strophic nature of the song: Orpheus appears to be moving forward but is continually turning back on himself. And the sketches of *The Mask of Orpheus* reveal Birtwistle working with the two terms. For example, on the verso of a leaf that begins to sketch out the long woodwind melody that extends across much of scene 2 (starting at 5 bars before fig. 43, p. 193) is written in large capitals 'CANTUS'. At the same time we see in the score the presence of the 'EOH', an entirely rhythmic layer, which later is labelled explicitly the 'Continuum of the Ensemble of Hell' (score, fig. 49, p. 202)

---

[7]   This term is first used by Birtwistle to designate the melodic line in *Entr'actes and Sappho Fragments* (1964).

[8]   Reproduced in the London Sinfonietta programme book 'Response' (1987), 19. It ends with a caveat: 'The ideas set down in these random jottings do not necessarily appear in the finished composition. H.B.'

[9]   For a discussion of this issue, see Jonathan Cross, 'Lines and circles: on Birtwistle's *Punch and Judy* and *Secret Theatre*', *Music Analysis*, 13/2–3 (1994), 203–25.

and whose insistent repetitions dominate the remainder of the scene. The separation of the functions of cantus and continuum in *Orpheus* is further achieved, from time to time, by presenting the ideas at different simultaneous speeds, each group under the direction of a separate conductor.

The continuum at the start of Act II is scored for a 'rhythm group' of plucked instruments consisting of electric mandolin, electric guitar, electric bass, harp and Noh harp. The sounds are all filtered, the amplitude and length of delay being specified in the score and diffused into the auditorium. The players are presented with a 'labyrinth' of lines (each of which is a variant on every other) through which they choose various routes according to a number of specified schemes. The continuum thus presents a series of 'mobiles', repeating ostinatos whose repetitions are never quite the same twice. It is joined by the electronic Winter Aura. Under the control of conductor II at a strict tempo of $\downarrow$ = 92, the continuum is present (though not necessarily always audibly) throughout the first statement of the second Time Shift. As this Time Shift presents another version of Eurydice's death, but now seen through Orpheus' eyes, the sound of the continuum may well be heard as a distorted representation of Orpheus' lyre: its insistent presence is a reminder of Orpheus' lament even while he and Eurydice are singing the second Love Duet. The fact that the mobiles and the Aura sound entirely static (undirected) gives the feeling, entirely appropriate to the Time Shift, that 'normal' time has been suspended.

The second Love Duet, sung by Orpheus Puppet (off-stage) and Eurydice Puppet, sets the frame for the act and, as with the first Love Duet, its echoes can be heard across the act. Its first presentation here is as a strophic song, its three almost identical verses being sung principally by Eurydice. These strophes are framed by a kind of brief 'parodos' and 'exodos', entry and exit music for SATB chorus. The duet thus presents the structure of the act in microcosm.

At first, the sounds of the chorus appear to grow out of the continuum and Aura. At a very low dynamic level (*pppp*) a dense chord cluster is built up, which is then sustained, interrupted only by occasional louder (*p*) grace-note flourishes. These echo outwards into the semiquaver and trilled flourishes of upper woodwind and percussion. The chorus provides a backdrop for Eurydice's melisma on the word 'come' in that the hum and vowel sound sung are an echo of that word. The flourishes establish a generic representation of key words in what Eurydice is to sing: 'fountain', 'mirrors', tinkles', brazen bells'. Water is the predominant image of the text (referring to the river by which Eurydice died); the 'watery' sounds of parodos and exodos capture this in music. The filtering of the music adds a further watery edge to the sounds, and this serves the double function of distancing what we hear. This is, after all, a memory, and the duet is subtitled 'Duet of Distance'.

Eurydice's melismatic line begins on the note E. The significance of this note for the composer was explored in Chapter 1, and its Phrygian association is further in evidence in Eurydice's melisma, in that it is bounded by the notes e^2 and f^1. It also suggests an expressively directed line, a cantus, in contradistinction to the repetitions of the continuum. In terms of its pitch organization, this is explicitly the case: it is essentially a chromatic line that rises from the initial E, though clouded by octave displacements (and with the exception of the D♯ a semitone below the starting-point, and the 'rogue' C♮):

↗ f² f♯¹ f♯²   g¹ g♯² g♯¹ a¹ (c²) b♭¹ (f¹)

e²

↘   d♯²

(The actual melody occurs at fig. 1, pp. 133–4.) Its rising nature and the wide leaps give the melody both an urgent and an anxiously ecstatic flavour. It is answered by Orpheus' question (fig. 2, p. 135), 'Are we alone?', which has a complementary falling shape, from g¹ to f♯ and again, quasi-sequentially, from f♯¹ to f, the same pitch class on which Eurydice ended.

Each of Eurydice's three verses has the same melody.[10] It is constructed according to a very clear example of a chromatic pitch wedge, a favoured technique of Birtwistle that we encountered in the first Love Duet. In contrast with the melisma melody, there is no octave displacement here, so the way in which the melody unfolds from the starting a¹ is clearly audible. In fact, the sketches reveal that this particular wedge is centred on b♭¹ and moves out to the octave E♮s either side of it. Example 3.1 shows a transcription of the sketch.

Example 3.1 Act II, scene 1, second Love Duet, Eurydice

(a) Sketch (PSS 0531-0851)

(b) Score

It shows the composer writing out the wedge once, then starting again, but 'fizzling out' before the end. He then adds stems and beams to make groups of

---

[10]   The very slight differences – amounting to two pitches a tone lower in strophe 2 and a naturalized pitch in strophe 3 – are insignificant; indeed, they could easily just be copying errors.

five notes, which he annotates according to a matrix of numbers already prepared. These then, in principle, determine the order in which the pitches occur. Thus the order of notes taken from the first group of five should be: a^1–$b\flat^1$–$a\flat^1$–$b\natural^1$–c^2. The qualification 'in principle' is necessary because, as always with Birtwistle, he is never a slave to his self-determined system. Compare the beginning of the melody with the first five notes of the sketch, for example, and you will see that the third note is $a\natural^1$, not $a\flat^1$. This is probably just a mistake, and it is a relatively trivial one. The system matters only in so far as it generates material with which the composer can work. The overall shape and effect of Eurydice's melody are unaffected by this or other 'misreadings' of the model. Yet, as the reams of grids of numbers in his sketches attest, Birtwistle remains fascinated with the 'technology' of generating notes and rhythms (a symptom of his modernity), even if what it generates has an unpredictable bearing on the finished artistic result. And why is the wedge technique appropriate here? In part, as in the 'parodos', because it produces something obviously linear in keeping with the idea of cantus; in part, I imagine, the mirrors of the text ('I can see mirrors in the water') prompted a melodic line that is itself mirrored about its central axis, $b\flat$.

The melody is marked 'nervously'. This effect is produced by the clipped style of writing, where many notes (and therefore syllables) are separated by rests. The isolated *staccatissimo* semiquavers in the accompanying orchestral hocketing figures take on an even more exaggerated idea of nervousness. The rhythmic organization of the vocal melody also gives the effect of being unnaturally stiff. Again employing a favourite procedure, Birtwistle selects just three durations – (i) dotted quaver preceded by a semiquaver rest, (ii) dotted crotchet and (iii) dotted quaver – and applies them in blocks to the pitches: three of (i), two of (ii), two of (i) again, two of (iii), and so on.

The end of each of Eurydice's first and second strophes overlaps with two more quasi-sequential, repeated phrases from Orpheus. Each is a variant on the other; each is identifiably the same thing. The end of Eurydice's third strophe continues directly into the 'exodos', a more elaborate, more melismatic version of the 'parodos'. The transition from the remembered past of the Time Shift to the present narrative reality is, as in Act I, effected by means of the Whisper of Change. This is – exceptionally – identical to its first appearance. The only changes are those made to the percussion, from (funereal) bass drums to (watery) tam-tams, and the addition of Eurydice intoning Orpheus' name on a repeated f^1. This lends a rhythmic layer to continuum music that is otherwise entirely ametric and static. The appropriate lack of identifiable pulse is achieved in the chorus by a dense superimposition of rhythmic layers, all seeming to move at different speeds.

Second Song of Magic (The Song of Arches)

And so Orpheus dreams. His journey to the underworld begins.

As already discussed, the second Song of Magic presents an irresolvable dialectic between the desire of the strophic text continually to turn back on itself and the desire of the music for forward-moving continuity. We shall see as we proceed through the song that the text is doubly backward-looking in that it presents, in essence, a reconfiguration – a remembering – of words, sounds and images familiar from Act I. The music is, for the most part, entirely new.

The most astonishing feature of the music for the dream sequences of the nine verses that constitute scene 1 is that it was first written as a continuous whole. The same is true for the nightmare sequences. Only later were these cut into sections and redistributed according to Zinovieff's scheme. Birtwistle's compositional method, as revealed in the sketches, confirms our sense of the music as experienced: that is, a yearning for continuity, for wholeness and connectedness, which is ultimately thwarted. Continuity is strived for, but fails. Orpheus strives to be reconnected with Eurydice, but fails.

The composer clearly began by conceiving the structure of the whole in visual terms. An early chart maps out an idea of the Arches across 17 large sections, subdivided into 75 smaller units.[11] Another graph is to be found among the sketches marked 'continuum of dream'.[12] Here the composer maps out the whole of the dream sequence. The timing of each of the 17 dream sections is carefully marked, as in the libretto – 2'20", 2'15", 2'08" and so on, though with a few small inconsistencies – totalling, as he notes, 24'15". Overlaid is a different scheme, comprising eleven units as follows:

2'20" – 2'30" – 2'22" – 2'28" – 2'27" – 2'12" – 2'06" – 2'16" – 1'30" – 2'28" – 1'36"

This also totals 24'15". This is a more erratic ordering of durations than the consistently diminishing pattern of the first scheme. The bearing this has on the final score is unclear, but it again suggests a desire for a larger continuity that cuts across the smaller divisions of the Arches.

Next Birtwistle begins to sketch out the detailed structure of Orpheus' song. Illustration 3.1 shows the first page. What we see is a kind of durational grid. The Fact portion of the first dream needs to last 2'06" (i.e., 2'20" for the dream minus the 0'14" specified for the Fantasy section). This works out as 28 bars of 3/4 at ♩ =40, or 84 crotchet beats, which are measured out and numbered. This can be seen in the fourth stave up from the bottom as a line of dotted minims (metre) subdivided

---

[11]   PSS 0530-0749–51. This sketch is drawn on landscape pages attached together with adhesive tape. By means of continuous straight lines it also shows some sort of movement across octaves, though how this relates to the final structure of the Song of Magic is unclear. (It appears more like the conception of the movement of the Tides in Act III.)

[12]   Beginning at PSS 0531-0694–5.

into crotchet beats (pulse). On to this are superimposed various other schemes. At a later stage, a sketch of the shape of Orpheus' melody is added (fifth stave up), mainly in rhythms but with a sense of contour and a few key pitches in response to the text. Only at a further stage (not in evidence in this sketch) are all the pitches added, determined by reference to one of the many sheets of pitch matrices he has generated. Thus the sequence of composition would appear to be from the general to the particular, from overall shape, via rhythmic continuity graph and contour of song, to pitch.

A heavy barline marks the end of the 84th beat, but the grid continues in like manner for a further 9 crotchet beats (i.e., at ♩ = 40 this is the nearest he can get to the additional 0′14″ of the Fantasy), ending with a double bar. Then the sketch moves directly on to map out the second dream section, and so on, until the end of the ninth verse. The nightmare sequence is separately mapped out in similar fashion.

The sketches thus disclose the primacy given to metric continuity across the second Song of Magic. It is this that paces the drama, as observed above, not the narrative developments of plot. In other words, Act II is structured *musically*. It is opera, not film. The sketches make transparent Birtwistle's layered approach to composition during this period, where ideas are conceived apparently independently and then are later brought together in the context of a controlling (temporal) scheme. The narrative, it might be argued, is just one of these layers.

Arch 1

> The 1st Arch is the arch of countryside, meaning to see. The 1st Arch touches the living …

As appropriate to the start of a journey into the unknown, Orpheus Singer speaks 'hesitantly, clipped, as if peering into the dark'. Gaps between words give a stuttering effect. The accompanying woodwind chords behave in the same way: they are very short and quiet, clipped, seemingly irregular. This is another kind of continuum. Each part is made up of three- or four-note (mainly) chromatic motifs, that is, varied ostinatos that keep turning; these motifs are indicated in the score by dotted slurs. Their pitches can be seen to be derived from the three-note cells sketched on the seventh stave up from the bottom of Illustration 3.1. This provides the backdrop for the cantus, Orpheus' song. The verse's presiding emotion of hesitancy is thus caught in the general affect of the music. A different kind of continuity is provided by a continuous layer for stopped horns. They symbolize the countryside, and the pairs of intervals they create – major and minor seconds and perfect fourths – are a distant echo of the pastoral horn call. The durations of this layer – a scheme of

Illustration 3.1   Act II, scene 1, draft of first Arch, first page (PSS 0531-0580)

triplet quavers – are sketched out in Illustration 3.1 (see the lowest three staves; the attached pitches bear little relation to the final score).[13]

When Orpheus moves from speech to song, his melody becomes free-flowing. Like Eurydice's call in the second Love Duet, it starts on an E and opens outwards. This E is swiftly taken up by three soprano saxophones, who bend it and distort it in between Orpheus' phrases. Perhaps, then, the saxophones represent a disturbed memory of Eurydice. The Ensemble of Hell punctuates progress; the musical energy increases as we move into the Fiction segment. Charon appears and violently croaks out fragmented words from Aristaeus' first Look of Loneliness: 'Kissed, Cracked, Killed, Clipped'. The saxophones *crescendo* to a point of savagery; they provide a degree of continuity with the nightmare section, which follows immediately, and continue to wail throughout it. The nightmare's hellish music of repetition stands as the opposite of the dream. The wind ostinatos are crude and direct, consisting of repeating pairs of notes in clear rhythmic layers. This is the kind of music Birtwistle reserves for his most violent moments. Except for the world 'love', Orpheus is unable to sing and returns to speech (*Sprechstimme*): the musician's true nightmare. The voice of Apollo marks the end of this verse and the beginning of the next. The opposition of dream and nightmare is at its clearest at the start of this vast Song of Magic, where dream is associated with melody (cantus) and the nightmare is mechanical (continuum). The differences between them are progressively eroded as the song unfolds – revealing a structural organization that Birtwistle was later to explore again in *Secret Theatre*.

The proportions of the verse, for the most part, follow Zinovieff's scheme. The first section (Fact) lasts 2′06″ (see above). The final Distortion (nightmare) consists of six bars of 4/4 at ♩ = 90, that is, 16″, which is the 30″ given for the nightmare minus the 14″ of the Fantasy section. It is only this Fantasy that does not conform to the plan (or, indeed, to the sketch as discussed above). In fact, it lasts three times longer than planned (*c.*42″), as if Birtwistle had been calculating at a rate of ♩ = 120, the tempo at which Charon sings, not the ♩ = 40 of the main ensemble. One can only speculate as to why, in certain instances, Birtwistle overrides the scheme and so distorts the proportions; in this instance, 14″ simply did not give him enough time.

Arch 2

The 2nd arch shows people. It is the arch of crowds, meaning to hear ...

The proportions of the second verse coincide precisely with those specified in the libretto. The first Fact section (from fig. 13, p. 145) consists of 25 bars of 3/4 at ♩ = 40,

---

[13]   In his very brief account of these sketches, Michael Taylor shows how the precise durations for the horns are 'produced by the superimposition of the continuous dotted minims, and an unpredictable element formed by counting alternate single and tied triplet quavers'. ('Narrative and musical structures in Harrison Birtwistle's *The Mask of Orpheus* and *Yan Tan Tethera*', in Hermann Danuser and Matthias Kassel (eds), *Musiktheater heute* (Mainz: Schott, 2003), 177–8).

that is, a total of 1'54". A single 'transition' pause bar (indicated by an asterisk in Zinovieff's graph) leads to the second Fantasy section (from a bar after fig. 15, p. 148) and consists of seven bars of 4/4 at ♩ = 80, that is, 0'21". Unlike the first verse, this has no tripling of durational values. Thus the total duration of the dream section of Fact and Fantasy is 2'15", exactly as in the libretto. The third section (Distortion) (from fig. 16, p. 149) consists of nine bars of 3/4 at ♩ = 90, that is, 0'18". If this duration is added to that of the overlapping Fantasy section, then it gives a total duration of 0'39", again exactly as in the libretto. The sum of Fact, Fantasy and Distortion is 2'33", precisely as specified.

As in the first verse, the different elements here are clearly layered. We see the three Furies, represented by masks 'in a pale watery light', but in Orpheus' dream they all look like Eurydice: their sad song contains echoes of Eurydice's words in the second Love Duet. Like Charon, they are charmed by Orpheus' song, and it is this – for the first time ever, it is said – that moves them to tears. They sing in rhythmic unison in a kind of organum that lends a gravity to their singing, reinforced by a complementary, similarly homorhythmic layer in the wind. Bassoons present a clipped continuum layer. The song of Orpheus, who also sings of water, weaves its way through the singing of the trio. Thus an unexpectedly close relationship between Orpheus and the Furies emerges. It is, perhaps, a very distant echo of the relationship between the Three Ladies (servants of the Queen of the Night) and Tamino in *The Magic Flute*. The sadness of both Orpheus and the women is captured in a brief weeping figure with a familiar contour, $e\flat^2$–$e\natural^2$–$d\flat^2$, which is heard on the saxophone at the end of the Fact section and again (doubled) at the end of the Fantasy. The second Distortion is even more rhythmic and mechanical, more nightmarish, than the first.

Very occasionally, the Ensemble of Hell bursts in. These interruptions are just like strokes of a very strong colour that slash across the canvas, seemingly at random. They do not belong with the rest of the music. (Here we hear first a violent gesture on metal tubes, then a rasped trombone chord; see score, p. 147). Such gestures are typical of Birtwistle. He has remarked about similar 'chance' gestures in the painting of Francis Bacon, whose contained violence he admires.[14]

Arch 3

The 3rd arch narrows, it is the arch of evening ...

As the arch narrows, the music becomes much denser. There are now more – and more active – layers than at the start, louder and more insistent. A sense of progress across the Arches is already palpable. The dominant emotion of this arch is one of anger.

Orpheus's memory here is of the Ceremonies. The Priests of the Troupe of Ceremony with their Caller reappear in the guise of the Judges of the Dead. Their

---

[14]   See Birtwistle, in Ross Lorraine, 'Territorial rites 2', *Musical Times*, 1857 (November 1997), 16.

words are an exact repeat of the text (as given in the libretto) of the first Complicated Question from the Wedding Ceremony. (It should be recalled, however, that the words appeared in a different order in their actual setting in Act I.) The musical setting here, while reminiscent of Act I in its rhythmic unison and rocking melismas, is not identical but reworked. As in memory, too, it no longer forms the main focus but becomes clouded by other simultaneous events. Orpheus' singing style is very different: his line, marked 'weighted and intense', proceeds primarily in straight crotchets, giddily leaping across the singer's range. It is almost as if he is distracted, the music seemingly having no relevance to the text being sung. The Ensemble of Hell punctuates the lowering of masks of, successively, Hymen, Hermes and Dionysus. Further layers are made up of resounding repeated or trilled wind and brass chords (echoes of the ritual of the Ceremonies, but also of similarly ceremonial brass writing in *Verses for Ensembles*); the wailing saxophone trio from the first Arch; a soaring line for piccolos, flutes and oboes in rhythmic unison. As with the equivalent moment in Act I, the layering of ideas here (and Birtwistle's desire to distinguish clearly between the different layers) expresses the multiplicity of present emotions and memories of the past being explored in text and drama.

The Furies reappear with an extension of their trio (another indicator of the desire for continuity across the individual arches), singing as before in rhythmic unison. But their music now seems more like that of the Judges of the Dead, with whom they alternate. Orpheus' phrase 'I remember' is notably sung to a high sustained f♯^{1}, a musical memory of that pitch, which played a central role in the second Ceremony. The Furies also sing in the Distortion section, first with clipped, rhythmic ostinatos to match the surrounding nightmare music, before returning to their more sustained style.

Arch 4

The 4th Arch is the arch of Contrast, meaning to hope …

The fourth Arch has a gentler character throughout both dream and nightmare sections. Its texture is thinner, there are fewer layers, and the music is generally more static. It suggests, therefore, that the emotional progress to the climax of the Song of Magic in verse 15 proceeds more in waves than in a straight line.

Both Orpheus and Eurydice are present in their manifestations as Singers and Puppets. In terms of staging, this is a complex representation of aspects of Orpheus' memory of Eurydice and of her death. The libretto tells us that 'Orpheus mime drinks from the Pool of Memory and does not drink from the Pool of Forgetfulness' (p. 25). We see Eurydice Mime, and we hear her wordless utterances: on-stage consonants (sibilants) and off-stage vowels. This is obviously an echo of the first Cry of Memory in Act I, scene 2, which presented Eurydice's death and in which she sang only five vowel sounds (representing the strings of Orpheus' lyre), while Orpheus again remained a static observer. Eurydice does not sing identical music in

Act II, but the slow, soft, falling, *portamento* character of her line is clearly the same. She is supported and given continuity by additional soft, sustained lines in horns and low trombones. The wailing soprano saxophone is again present, and it too presents a line that slowly descends. Eurydice remains in the distance.

In the foreground we hear Orpheus singing the fourth verse of his song. Each short phrase ends with a sustained note. He is accompanied by four woodwind instruments, which imitate him at a semiquaver's distance. The sketches for this passage throw interesting light on a significant change made between the preparation of the first fair copy of the score and the production of the final edition, namely the composer's decision to rethink the role of Orpheus as a tenor rather than as a baritone. In the sketches, each of the woodwind instruments is given a string of pitches (without rhythms at this stage), divided into groups of six. Each group of six corresponds to one of Orpheus' phrases. The pitches of Orpheus' line are identical to those of the piccolo, two octaves lower, written in the bass clef (see Example 3.2a); compare this with his pitches as they occur in the final edition, written in the treble clef (Example 3.2b). The piccolo line, however, remains unchanged. It is almost as if, in copying out the singer's line, Birtwistle or his copyist has misread the clef, but otherwise continued oblivious! (Re-read Example 3.2b in the bass clef, and you will see this.) But it is obviously not a mere copying error, as, for example, changes to accidentals are made to the final version. What is fascinating is that, in deciding to alter Orpheus' voice, Birtwistle simply transposed the relevant line up (in this case by the interval of a sixth). This did not generally entail making any further changes to the prevailing musical context. So, whereas in the original version of verse 4 the singer is doubled at the double octave, in the final version we end up with a kind of organum instead. What does this tell us about Birtwistle's attitude to pitch? It is important not to generalize from this one example, as context is crucial. However, in this particular case, it would be possible to argue that the precise pitches sung by Orpheus are unimportant to the extent that they need fit only with the heterophony of all the voices here. Of course, we have already encountered other occasions where an actual pitch is extremely significant, and in these instances a different kind of recomposition takes place to accommodate the change in the singer's register.

Example 3.2 Act II, scene 1, fourth Arch, Orpheus' melody

(a) First fair copy of score

The   arch   is   split   wa - ter   tou - ches   the   fire

(b) Final version of score

A violent stroke from the Ensemble of Hell and an electronic signal mark the change to the Fantasy section. Three saxophones take over the woodwind figures, while Eurydice Puppet's sibilants come to the fore. In the Distortion of the nightmare section, Eurydice Singer's mournful vowels are heard more prominently, surrounded by the expected wind and brass mechanical ostinatos, but softer, less aggressive, than in Arch 3.

Arch 5

> The 5th Arch is the arch of dying. It is narrower still. There is no water …

The fifth verse continues the affect of the previous arch – it is again concerned with memories of Eurydice – and there are a number of obvious musical continuities. Eurydice sings vowels that eventually form into the name of Orpheus, supported as before by falling wind lines. The woodwind figures at the start of the previous verse, still associated with Orpheus, are now transferred to tuned percussion. These watery sounds (in the context of Orpheus' description of the arch as being devoid of water) immediately recall the accompaniment to the second Love Duet at the start of the act. They preface Orpheus Puppet's singing of an extension of that Love Duet, taking over Eurydice's line directly (an exact transposition) with its nervous, clipped style. Orpheus Singer continues his song. The general mood reflects the predominant emotion of loneliness. Ominous, low repeated notes on tuba, electric bass and percussion are a distant reminder of hell.

Hell moves further to the foreground in the Fantasy section as the tuba and bass line turns into a more insistent ostinato; the woodwind lines turn ugly. This process of distortion continues into the nightmare, where the tuba, joined by other low instruments, now becomes a continuous line. A disturbing wordless chorus enters with undulating pitches. Orpheus' singing is increasingly agitated, while in the second part of the nightmare he cries out with renewed force, 'I remember', punctuated by horrific noises – the 'gigantic periodic sound of hell'. The continuous mechanical ostinatos of previous nightmares are disrupted here. The chorus sings across the signal and into the next verse as the emotional intensity continues to build.

The proportions of this arch diverge noticeably from those in the plan as a consequence of a blurring of boundaries between sections. Fact blends into Fantasy, so reducing the duration of the Fact section by the duration of the Fantasy (i.e., it is 34″

short). The Distortion is subdivided into two distinct segments of 10″ and 20″, both having the nightmarish characteristic of repetitious ostinatos. Thus the total duration of the arch (1′54″) is that given for just the dream segment in the libretto. Continuity across the entire arch becomes distinctly more important, as does continuity with the ensuing arch as the dream begins to take on a more nightmarish quality.

Arch 6

The 6th Arch is of Wings. It smoulders …

'The heads of Hades, Persephone and Hecate terrifyingly appear' (libretto, p. 26). The entry of each is marked by the violent interjection of the Ensemble of Hell, echoing out into the ensemble and giving the dream as a whole a more hellish hue. The layering is marked. The chorus strand is prominent, supported by low wind and brass lines. A continuum layer in plucked instruments (again anticipating the opening of *Secret Theatre*) offers the backdrop to Orpheus' cantus. A regular six-beat figure in trombones adds another strand while long, sustained notes in the upper woodwind add to the sense of greater intensity.

The Fantasy is entirely without text (instruments and wordless chorus). The layers from the Fact section continue, and the intensity increases as a further ostinato layer is added for tuned percussion. This prepares the way for the Distortion, which is again in two distinct parts. The first part (figs 31–2, pp. 171–2) is entirely instrumental and is the most densely and exclusively mechanical music heard in the work. Series of regular ostinatos are layered one on top of the other like different-sized cogs in a clock mechanism to produce a complex result. It is a clear moment of Stravinskian machine music. In the short second part of the Distortion section, to the accompaniment of a slower 'clock' (a distortion of the Distortion, you might say), Orpheus sings of the sixth Arch as 'the arch for birds'. The equation of nature with the mechanical here is fascinating. It carries Stravinskian echoes of a 'hard' pastoral (the exemplar being *The Rite of Spring*), which was to be explored in an extreme way by Birtwistle in his most explicitly Stravinskian work, *Carmen Arcadiae mechanicae perpetuum* (1977–78). Composed shortly after the suspension of composition on *The Mask of Orpheus*, it is based on the imaginary song of a mechanical bird, after Paul Klee's 1922 painting *The Twittering Machine*. It is a fine example of what, in the context of his later opera *Yan, Tan, Tethera* he was to name 'mechanical pastoral'. Here, this symbolizes the core of Orpheus' modern dilemma in his song, namely that the emotional (subject) can be articulated only via the mechanical (object), that the only way of understanding melancholy is via geometry. It is the negative dialectic of 'stasis in progress'.

Arch 7

The 7th Arch is the arch of Colour. It is the arch of the River …

As Orpheus tells us, he has now reached the highest point of the structure and is almost at the centre. The river flows through the seventh Arch from the past to the present. The mood of fury is caught as the characters of the underworld, whose heads were seen in the last arch, now begin to sing. Their words and music are familiar. Orpheus hears Hecate uttering parts of the Oracle of the Dead's first Hysterical Aria. Her words are, first, half-remembered fragments ('DUST STARS DEAD') of Aristaeus' first Look of Loneliness in Act I, scene 2 (a recitative that 'gives rise to numerous word echoes later'; libretto, p. 15), then a recollection of the Oracle's own fragments from scene 3 (themselves remembered fragments of Orpheus' Argonautic journey). Her line begins with a strangely murmured breathing, and then moves to a sequence of expanding intervals, ending with her characteristic four-note scream, before returning to a murmuring that continues to the end of the verse. The Fantasy is coloured by the strange low murmurings of Hades, sung by Orpheus Puppet, again (inscrutable) words as fragments of memories of the Argonautic journey. All the while, the main body of the ensemble plays an independent music of points and lines that continues for the entire duration of the dream section (Fact and Fantasy). Rather than representing the affect of fury, it appears to suggest Orpheus' forward progress despite the vivid remembrance of the past in this verse. The Distortion is unlike any heard so far. It is built from eccentrically repeated ostinatos for plucked and struck instruments, which fade away almost to nothing, allowing Hecate's moans to be heard clearly. Ominous, sustained notes – low semitonal pairs – remain in the background. Orpheus' singing, by contrast, is loud and agitated: 'Hands reach out calling'.

Arch 8

The 8th Arch is the arch of Secrecy. This is the arch for heads …

Orpheus' encounter with the characters of the underworld continues as he now witnesses Persephone singing words that Eurydice spoke in the first Love Duet. The slow, falling, *legato* line, in its own tempo, is characteristic in general of Eurydice's melancholic music and recalls the spirit of the melodies in the first Love Duet. It is built simply from three-note cells, which will have been generated via number matrices and which are strung together. Each cell is made up of a falling second (i.e., interval class 1 or 2) and a falling perfect interval or tritone (i.e., interval class 5 or 6):

$$g^2 – f\sharp^2 – c^2 \mid f\sharp^2 – f\natural^2 – b\flat^1 \mid e^2 – d^2 – a^1 \mid d\sharp^2 – a^1 – g\sharp^1 \mid \text{etc.}$$

The first note of each successive cell is also (with one exception) either a semitone or a tone lower than the previous one. For the first half of the melody, the connecting interval between cells is a tritone. In this way, harmonic and expressive consistency is maintained while allowing the line to cover a two-octave trajectory (from g^2 to g). Persephone's line continues across both Fact and Fantasy sections of the dream. The main ensemble also plays long lines across the entire dream, their falling character expressively echoing Persephone's melody. There is a clear continuity here with the previous dream section, as well as with the music that accompanied the first Love Duet in the first scene of Act I.

Percussion ostinatos – remnants of the nightmare of verse 7 – are a constant reminder of hell and continue, *ppp*, throughout the Fact section. The Fantasy, while not sharply differentiated from the Fact, is marked by the addition of a new independent layer in the harps that simply replaces the percussion. This supports a change in the mood of Orpheus' song text. He sings for the first time directly of himself – 'I can see my own eyes staring at my own eyes. My thoughts are hidden in the cold dream-water' – and the sound of his own instrument symbolizes this. The sketches for this layer[15] give another glimpse into the ways in which Birtwistle uses numbers as part of his compositional method. He first produces three sets of eight pitches, one for each harp, from which pitches are chosen and arranged into a matrix. He next generates a number grid. This is then mapped on to the pitch matrix, so determining the ordering of the pitch content of each harp part. But across the top of the sketch page is a further line of numbers:

$$11\ 13\ 15\ 12\ 11\ 10\ 10\ 12\ 6\ 10\ 14\ 6\ 12\ 14\ 10\ 14$$

How these numbers are generated is not clear, but they produce an interesting wave pattern. Each numeral determines the number of events in each block of harp activity which is allocated a single rhythmic value. Thus the first block consists of 11 successive demisemiquavers, the second block 13 semiquavers, the third block 15 sextuplet semiquavers, and so on, each successive block separated by rests of varying durations. This layer is then superimposed on to the other continuing musical layers. The pages and pages of number charts in the sketches for this and virtually every work by Birtwistle are evidence that numbers do much significant work for the composer: among other things, they can generate intervals, pitches and rhythms; they can determine the number and order of events; they can even determine how many events should be happening at any particular moment. Number, too, represents a hidden logic, a 'geometry of tragedy', to borrow Stravinsky's phrase,[16] which suggests a centripetal force working to frame the centrifugal force that is attempting to rip narrative, music and Orpheus apart.

---

[15]   PSS 0532-0090.

[16]   Igor Stravinsky and Robert Craft, *Dialogues* (London: Faber and Faber, 1982), 24.

Just as Persephone's singing linked Fact and Fiction (dream), so these harp blocks provide continuity between Fiction and Distortion (nightmare). Now, though, it is much more in the foreground as the layer is reinforced by other superimposed instrumental blocks (different pitches, same rhythms), alternating plucked instruments, woodwind and brass. The effect is of a continually shifting mosaic of coloured shapes. The absolute opposition of dream and nightmare that we saw at the start of the Song of Magic is being continually undermined as continuity across divisions becomes increasingly important.

Arch 9

The 9th Arch is the arch of Glass. It cannot be seen from the present. It shrinks …

This verse marks the end of scene 1 and the beginning of Orpheus and Eurydice's journey of darkness. It is temporally complex. Off-stage, Orpheus Puppet sings the second extension of the second Love Duet – virtually identical to the first extension – in his own tempo. Eurydice Puppet sings across both dream and nightmare sections with her own floating extension of the Love Duet ('Orpheus I am alone'). In the nightmare this becomes just a distant, repeated melisma calling Orpheus' name. Her music, however, is much closer to the first Love Duet than to the second: as in Act I, she begins to sing her lover's name on a sustained g^1 and her line slowly unfolds. As in Act I also, her line echoes out into the orchestra, where it is doubled and darkly coloured by alto flutes, clarinets and horns. This lyrical strain is a melancholic reminder both of what Orpheus has lost and what he yearns to recapture, expressed in the forceful intensity of his own (present) song here. The importance of Eurydice's line to the composer's conception of this verse is confirmed by the fact that it is present in the original continuous sketch for scene 1 as part of Orpheus's song.[17] The remaining layers here are strangely mechanical, distant.

The sound of hell re-enters in the Fantasy with a repeated figure for three percussionists playing (i) seven suspended cymbals, (ii) seven small drums and (iii) seven temple blocks. Even here, both the sequence in which each player strikes the seven instruments and the order in which each player plays are determined by matrices of number rotations.[18] In the Distortion, the mechanical sound of hell continues, eventually fading away. Orpheus shouts out yet another memory of his time on the *Argo*. But, all the while, Eurydice continues to sing: the lyrical (dreams of past and future) and mechanical (present nightmare) cannot be reconciled. This sense is compounded by the appearance at the end of a solo piccolo with a short line built from a seven-note chromatic segment. Its symbolism (as discussed in Chapter 2, a complex of associations with Eurydice, love, dance and melancholy) draws the scene to a close. We hear the voice of Apollo three times, as if urging Orpheus on.

---

[17] PSS 0531-0613.
[18] PSS 0532-0075.

Act II, scene 2

The new scene signals the return journey of Orpheus from the underworld. The durational structure of the Arches has a built-in progression away from dream and in favour of nightmare, reaching its climax at Arch 15. Scene 1 betrayed a subtle and gradual breaking down of boundaries between these two elements within each arch and a move towards continuity, both across internal divisions and from one arch to the next. These features rapidly become exaggerated in scene 2 as activity accelerates. The text of each verse begins to break up, so that by verse 17 we are left with only isolated words. Explicit meaning becomes more and more elusive. Having flowed in expressive waves in scene 1, the music now begins a gradual and relentless build-up in intensity towards its shattering climax at the end of this scene.

Arch 10

The 10th arch is of Buildings …

On stage are still to be seen the masks of the characters of the underworld. All the forms of Eurydice are revealed. But we hear only Orpheus singing throughout, and the musical features are relatively familiar ones. In many respects this Arch is similar to the first verse, and so symbolizes a beginning again as Orpheus commences his return journey. It is therefore fitting that one strand of the music begins on an E, first in tubas and trombone (composed as a separate layer in its entirety, including dynamics, in the sketches). The only reminder of hell is at the very start, in the insistent semiquavers of brass and percussion, and in the wailing saxophones. The ending is characteristically mechanical. Otherwise, it is a lyrical verse, where Orpheus' line is complemented by long, arching melodies in the upper wind.

Arch 11

The eleventh arch is of Weather …

The most notable feature of the 11th Arch is the entry of the Continuum of the Ensemble of Hell during the nightmare. This is an entirely unpitched percussive layer that provides a fast quaver pulse under the direction of conductor II. It starts at ♩ = 120 and at a very soft dynamic level (*pppp*). While it is in a continual state of flux (*accel.* or *rall.*, *cresc.* or *dim.*), it nonetheless charts a general growth in intensity from its quiet start here to the climax at the end of the scene. It is a constant and increasingly dominant presence. Its hellishness thus becomes increasingly apparent. As a purely rhythmic strand, the total absence of pitch or of anything resembling melody suggests the annihilation of the subject. Like the 'Danse sacrale' at the end of Stravinsky's *Rite of Spring*, in which rhythm also predominates, the consequences are terrible. In the case of the young girl of the *Rite*, it is a dance to death: through the relentless foregrounding of rhythm, of the forces of the collective, she becomes 'dehumanised', 'depersonalised', as Adorno argued. 'Through [the immutable rigidity of convulsive blows and shocks in the 'Danse sacrale'] the individual becomes conscious of his nothingness in the face of the gigantic machine of the entire system.'[19] Orpheus, too, is subjected to these terrible forces and is unable to overcome them. He is swallowed up by the sounds of hell. His individual desires are overwhelmed by the collective machine. His quest to find Eurydice, to find himself, fails; when he awakes from his nightmare, he comes to understand his failure, and in the moment of that realization he hangs himself. This is hell indeed.

In verse 11 Orpheus' song is mournful. It is slow and sustained, built essentially from a seven-note chromatic segment. It is supported by long pairs of wind lines in contrary motion, which provide musical continuity across the entire arch and into the next. Their essence is caught in the repeating pairs of notes (voice exchange) that are 'frozen' at the end of the verse. At the same time, at the same speed but in a different metre (3/4), Eurydice dances, according to the libretto 'as in the wedding'. In fact, her dance music here is much closer to that of the funeral dance in Act I, scene 3. It is in almost the same slow tempo ($\downarrow = c.45$), it has similar patterns in its continuum, and it is joined by a simple, mournful, bluesy saxophone line built from just three notes, $c^2–e\flat^2–f^2$. Representative of Eurydice, the saxophone weaves itself around Orpheus' song, lending it a mournful colour. This is the second Look of Loneliness: Orpheus and Eurydice turn away from each other. The meaning of this moment is underscored, once again, by a prominent appearance at the start of the Fantasy of the signature motif ($e\flat^3–d^3–f^3$), hauntingly declared by three *ffff* unison piccolos.

Arch 12

> The twelfth is of eyes. Cliff-child. Excreta. In dawn-peep shadows flatten. Lust-
> arch. Drawn flash-claws.

All hell now breaks loose. Orpheus is unable to sing and can only stutter out words that seem to be drawn from deep in his memory, reformed into inscrutable phrases. As he follows Eurydice, he re-encounters the characters of the underworld. In his dream he hears Hecate again, a distorted version of himself grunting, as in the seventh Arch, low, unintelligible, isolated words. It builds to an ugly scream. While wind lines from the previous verse continue through the section, other layers made up of more mechanical repeating figures tend to dominate, turning even the dream into a nightmare. The hysterical screeches of Hecate colour the Fantasy; they proliferate outwards into a dense texture of (mainly) repeating musical layers, while the rhythms of the Continuum of the Ensemble of Hell (*ffff*) urge the music forwards to a terrible, noisy climax: five huge strokes (strident chords) and tape signals. Only

---

[19]   Theodor W. Adorno, *Philosophy of Modern Music* [1948], tr. A.G. Mitchell and W.G. Blomster (London: Sheed & Ward, 1973), 156.

in the Distortion section does the dynamic level drop as we hear Persephone intoning Orpheus' name to an oscillating semitone (e^2–f^2). For the moment, the continuum subsides back to *pppp* and ♩ = 90.

Arch 13

> Thirteen is knives. Falling tongues. Wood pattern. Machinery. Turn open the yellow sand. Earth-tooth.

The 13th verse is similar to the 12th. The music is predominantly Dionysian. While there is, of course, an underlying (Apollonian) order provided by the structure, it is increasingly difficult to perceive because each segment is so darkly coloured by the characteristics of nightmare and by the inescapable presence of the continuum. The desire for musical continuity now overrides any obvious concern to differentiate between the moods of successive verses.

Orpheus re-encounters the trio of Furies, the Judges of the Dead and, finally, Charon as his dream seems to take him back to his starting-point. The music of the Furies has harmonic links with its appearance in the second Arch, but their singing is now less lyrical, as if they have been influenced by Hecate/the Oracle. 'I prophesy', we hear them shout; 'I prophesy dumb darkness'. They seem to have forgotten that Orpheus earlier charmed them to sorrow, and are now reverting to their traditional role as custodians of the punishment ground. In turn, the Judges (oscillating semitones) and Charon (an oscillating minor third) call for an answer, as their counterparts did in the Ceremonies. The surrounding music remains highly active and difficult to grasp – ideas pass at great speed, but just as Orpheus is hardly able to sing any longer, so this music is incapable of sustaining or developing itself. A mysterious ostinato turns in the electric bass; aggressive wind figures surge rapidly from soft to very loud; an ominous trumpet calls out, rising in semitonal waves; saxophones wail; dense layers of fragmented music contribute to the growing sense of anxiety and dislocation. Only at the end of the verse does Orpheus find his singing voice. 'Turn open the yellow sand', he cries to a sustained $f\sharp^1$, his words recalling Aristaeus' first narration of Eurydice's death and his pitch offering a musical memory (as in the third verse) of the Funeral Ceremony. However, the fragmentation of musical and textual material here is so great that we, like Orpheus, do not consciously register these references. Memory calls up feelings of the past; we respond in an instinctual way.

Arch 14

> Fourteen is animals. Slime-summer. Scream learn. Lost seeds-pain. Book-terror. Torn-tiger.

The terror continues to grow. Fears and memories follow one another in rapid succession or are piled on top of each another in a dense musical layering. The sun is very bright. We hear the voice of Apollo urging Orpheus on – it is only through the power of song that he will overcome the forces of darkness – and the voice of Orpheus Singer on tape struggles to keep going. Eurydice Puppet spits out consonants (Cry of Memory). As Orpheus sees himself turning round to look at Eurydice, she gives out blood-curdling screams that span from the bottom to the top of her range, and already she starts to slip from his grasp. Wind instruments squeal high across the top of the orchestra, and only certain features can be clearly picked out from the hellish chaos, such as threatening low brass grunts or strident trumpet calls. The majority of layers are made up of rising ideas – such as the upward swirling semiquaver figures in the woodwind – that further contribute to the sense of urgency and unstoppable forward momentum. As before, isolated ideas seem unable to connect to make coherent utterances. It is a violent, expressionistic vision, a terrifying representation of the unconscious in which Orpheus' dream of hope has turned into a brutal nightmare.

The continuum persists at its own tempo, which fluctuates during the course of the verse in such a way that not even a regular pulse can be sensed. The only other continuous strand is made up of undulating lines for wordless female chorus, doubled in horns and saxophones. This becomes the Chorus of Awakening. Orpheus wakes from his dream with the screams of Eurydice still in his head. It is the moment both of *peripeteia* (turning) and of *anagnorisis* (realization/recognition):

> ... he halted
> And on the very brink of light, alas,
> Forgetful, yielding in his will, looked back
> At his own Eurydice. At the same instant
> All his endeavour foundered ... [20]

Orpheus turns to look at Eurydice, and in this moment the plot turns; it is the moment of tragic reversal. As he awakes, Orpheus realizes instantly he has only been dreaming. The term *anagnorisis* can be rendered in a variety of ways: recognition, revelation, self-recognition, wakening, illumination, recovery of knowledge.[21] Here, Orpheus awakes to the realization that Eurydice is lost for ever. 'His terrible series of dreams had been so realistic to him that he was still not sure that he had been dreaming. Real or not this was the second time that Orpheus had lost his wife Euridice' (libretto 1997, p. 11). Although he had dreamed of a descent to and return from the underworld, in fact the allegory of the Arches makes it clear that the journey could only take place in a single direction. The aqueduct crosses from the mountainside of the living to the side of the dead. There is no possibility of return to the living. This is what Orpheus learns in this moment of *anagnorisis*. Its tragic consequences are inevitable.

---

[20]   Virgil [Virgilius Publius Maro], *The Georgics*, tr. L.P. Wilkinson (London: Penguin, 1982), Book IV, ll. 488–92 (p. 141).

[21]   My understanding of the resonances of this term is indebted to Terence Cave, *Recognitions: a Study in Poetics* (Oxford: Clarendon Press, 1988).

Arch 15

Fift.een. Ro..p.es. Cl.ou.d ho.les. Tw.i.st.st.a.r.s. Li.ps li.ght.ca.tch.es. Sp.in.sn.akes,
THE KING STANDS HIGHEST.

Even individual words now break up. Orpheus' song has lost its magic. He stumbles over the text in hysterical pitched speech (just 13″, precisely according to Zinovieff's scheme). The music momentarily subsides as Orpheus takes in the immediate horror of his situation. There is a pause, a moment of stillness, when even the Continuum of the Ensemble of Hell suspends its activity. But reality floods back in: the Chorus of Awakening is a constant presence, singing – for the only time in the work – a text in Greek about the stars and about the god Ouranos, the personification of the sky.[22] Orpheus calls out Eurydice's name, over and over again. He begins, repeatedly, imploringly, on a sustained e^1. Then he starts to cry out like a terrified wild animal, his line opening in wedge-like fashion to expose 11 notes of the chromatic. He returns to the sustained e^1, conjoined with a g^1 (completing the chromatic), that interval of a minor third being the same as that to which he first sang Eurydice's name at the start of the first Love Duet. His cries become more and more terrified, more desperate, as his line continues to open outwards to the extremes of his range. The music surrounding his cries builds again to its climax, by means of layers of hurried ostinatos and urgent upward rushing scales. Towards the end the continuum accelerates to a final frantic speed as the voice of Apollo is heard above the din; in true expressionistic fashion, the whole of Orpheus' environment echoes to his wild scream.

The music comes to a sudden halt as the brass blare out the minor third, E–G, one final time. The cry goes unanswered. Eurydice is not there. All we hear is the empty Winter Aura as at the beginning of the act, and the presence still of the Chorus reminding Orpheus of the reality of his awakening. All he is left with is his memory. 'The King stands highest', he murmurs, ending on a falling third, g^1–e^1. 'OFEIUS OFOARIF', 'Orpheus, remember'. The sustained e^1 with which the scene ends points to Act III, in which Orpheus becomes Myth, meaning memory.

---

[22]   Zinovieff notes the entire text in his diary with commentary: 'Ouranos ano, ouranos kato. Astra ano, astra kato. Pan o ano touto kato. This and like a kid I have fallen into milk are probably the only Orphic fragments left. Willie Charlton [then Lecturer in Philosophy at Newcastle University] says that they can't be as they don't scan.' Peter Zinovieff, 'Electronic music diary summer 1976', *Bulletin of the Computer Arts Society* (May 1977), reproduced at http://members.tripod.com/werdav/vocpzino.htm (accessed 30 September 2008).

Act II, scene 3

In the short final scene Orpheus attempts to come to terms with what has happened, with what he has learned, with his own failure. He can still hear distant echoes of his imagined journey and, on stage, a 'shadow play illustrates even more archetypally the events of the ... arches' (libretto, p. 30). The scene is infused with a general atmosphere of lamenting, and the music takes on a quite different character. (It should be recalled that much of the music of this scene was written only after Birtwistle had resumed work on *The Mask of Orpheus* in the early 1980s. It betrays new ideas about compositional method and aesthetics which, as Hall has discussed, tend to respect the 'sanctity of the context'.[23]) The shape of these final two verses of the Song of Magic does not follow the progression that led to the climax at the end of the previous scene. While the libretto ostensibly divides each verse into dream and nightmare as before, in practice each has two parts and the arch song is heard only in the second part.

Arch 16

> Sixteen. Order. Stabs. Trembles. Sails. Creeps. I know the river. The detritus. I remember the sun. The nail. Sword-gut.

With after-shocks of the climax of the previous scene still reverberating in the percussion, Orpheus sings of his recognition of his new situation in the second Song of Failure. In a reversal of his murmur at the end of the previous verse, Orpheus calls out, 'No longer stands the King the highest over fifty men'. The phrase concludes appropriately with a reversal of the final interval of the last verse, e^1–g^1. A sinuous, heterophonic line for three piccolos provides a melancholic commentary on the situation. The Song of Failure (Orpheus Singer) intersects with extensions of both the Furies' mournful trio of tears and the second Love Duet (Orpheus and Eurydice Puppets). These memories are suddenly clear. The sequence of chords sung by the Furies is an exact repeat of the beginning of the trio in verse 2 and, although the context has changed, their tearful sentiments remain the same. The watery images of the trio complement the recurrence of an easily recognizable variant of the Love Duet ('I can see eyes in the jewelled water'). And, in a poignant moment, the calls by Eurydice of her lover's name are finally able to reach the ears of Orpheus Singer, who is briefly united musically with Eurydice Puppet in the final cries of his Song of Failure: 'I can see you'. The central perfect fifth of its diatonic setting (a^1–c^1–g^1–b) echoes outwards and is sustained by oboes

---

23   'I would never formalize, never predict what the piece is going to be, because the one sacred thing is the context'. Birtwistle speaking of *Still Movement* (1984), quoted in Michael Hall, 'The sanctity of the context: Birtwistle's recent music', *Musical Times*, 129/1 (January 1988), 14.

and saxophones. This becomes an increasing focus as the scene proceeds; such clear centricity has not been heard in the work to this point and is symptomatic of the composer's new (post-1980) way of thinking.

In the second section, the 16th verse of the Song of Magic is hurriedly sung to the accompaniment of Orpheus' own lyre – a continuum of harp and plucked instruments. But it is now, for the first time, Orpheus Puppet who presents this material. The Furies continue to weep, while a repetition of Orpheus Singer's 'I can see you' results, once again, in the saxophones picking up the C–G perfect fifth and carrying it over into the next verse.

Arch 17

> Seventeen. Fear. Caught. Time. Lost. The crystal. The water. The tremble. The death. The doll. Tide moan.

The music becomes softer, purged of its sense of fear, the further it moves from the climactic moment of realization. Orpheus continues to come to terms with his situation. In the first part of this final arch, he recites two Poems of Reminiscence: one, a poem of horror in response to the dead Eurydice; the other, a melancholic poem of love at the memory of Eurydice. But they are not distinguishable because the verses of each poem are interleaved. The texts are spoken rhythmically with the last word or words of each verse being sustained to a clear pitch or pitches (most notably the word 'memory', which is set to the significant interval of e^1–g^1). Again Orpheus appears to accompany his songs of loss on his lyre using rhythmicized aspects of just a single chord, punctuated by distant, muted trumpet calls.

But the principal feature here is purely instrumental. At a separate slow tempo of ♩ = 40, an elegiac melody for oboes and clarinets lends a desolate air to Orpheus' recitations. This line is in essence a piece of organum in free-flowing triplet rhythms. The constituent parallel elements are built from 11 notes of the chromatic divided into mutually exclusive sets of pitch classes:

>   oboes: G–A–B♭–B♮–C♮–C♯
>   clarinets: D♮–D♯–E–F♮–F♯

When combined, they produce mainly successive intervals of kinds of fourths and fifths, that is, interval classes 5 and 6. This echoes outwards in flutes and horns. It is, as it were, a composing-out of the possibilities of the central interval of a perfect fifth. It is out of this very interval on the saxophones at the end of the previous arch that this melody emerges, and, towards the end of Orpheus' recitations, it itself converges on to a sustained perfect fifth (now d^1–a^1). This interval colours the entire texture. It draws in the brass, which also sustain the fifth, while Orpheus delivers, in clipped style, his 17th Arch song.

* * *

This is the end of the Arches, the end of the Song of Magic. The nightmare has receded. Its mechanical music has now subsided into a static music of very different character. Orpheus' lamenting takes over, symbolized in the piercing emptiness of the bare fifth. It proliferates outwards into the whole orchestra as Eurydice's last distant calls of Orpheus' name are heard. The density, the blackness, the unrelenting rhythmic activity of the climax of Orpheus' journey has turned into its complete opposite: a simple, eternal whiteness of fifth-based music speaking of Orpheus' sorrow, of his failure, of his abandonment of hope. The forward momentum of Orpheus' yearning to be reunited with Eurydice is now replaced with a desolate, empty timelessness.

The second Allegorical Flower of Reason interjects unexpectedly. This is the most gentle of all the mimed electronic pieces. It acts as a kind of purge after the musical violence of much of Act II. Like the music of fifths that surrounds it, it has a mournful stasis which seems to represent the emptiness that follows the anger and sorrow of bereavement. It precedes Orpheus' suicide.

The concluding Whisper of Change, as on its previous appearances, represents transition. On this occasion, it marks the passage of Orpheus from life to death. The harp continuum and wordless chorus are identical with earlier manifestations of the Whisper of Change, but now a mournful unison woodwind melody sings over the top. A diatonic yet dissonant chord (C–D–E–G–A–B) for lower brass joins midway, out of which the upper brass softly pick the d^1–a^1 fifth in horns that has coloured the closing stages of the act. It is, as Adlington puts it, a 'beautiful and moving concluding device [that] is characteristic of an act that manages to amalgamate the pivotal moments of earlier Orphic operas – the graphic representation of hell, the lyrical urgency of Orpheus's song to win back Euridice, and his mournful lament at losing her – into a single [expressive] statement'.[24] Another fifth (E) is added above the horns. The *crescendo* is sudden and unexpected. It is as if a penetrating beam of light suddenly illuminates the reality of his situation. He can bear the sorrow no longer. He hangs himself. With five violent strokes, the act ends.

---

[24]   Adlington, *The Music of Harrison Birtwistle*, 21.

Chapter 4

The Mask of Orpheus: Act III

Synopsis

The structure of the final act is determined by the movements of the tide on a beach, though neither this nor the delineation of plot through the words of the stage characters is readily apparent. Much of the musical material is a reworking of ideas already revealed in the first two acts: it involves progressively greater degrees of repetition as the act proceeds. This is the most highly stylised act of the work and achieves an entirely new formal world.

Scene 1 consists of the final Time Shift, a wordless representation of the rebirth of Orpheus as a mythological figure. Act III is thus dominated by puppets.

As it is the tides which establish the order of events in scenes 2 and 3, no simple sequential account is possible. Nonetheless, from many perspectives, we are shown Eurydice's death, Orpheus' suicide, Orpheus' second Terrible Death by Thunderbolt, Orpheus' third Terrible Death at the hands of the Dionysian women and his dismemberment, and Orpheus' skull becoming an oracle and being silenced by Apollo. Orpheus' third Song of Magic, in the invented Orphic language, is woven into the structure of the tides. The Exodos parallels the work's opening Parados. Events become more and more attenuated as the myth of Orpheus decays into nothingness.

Act III, scene 1: Third Time Shift

The first two Time Shifts – at the beginning of Act I, scene 3 and at the opening of Act II – both reviewed the death of Eurydice. The third Time Shift, which opens the final act, reconsiders the death of Orpheus that occurred at the end of the preceding act and represents his emergence as a puppet, that is, in mythical form. The act as a whole is, according to librettist and composer, concerned with the mythological afterlife of Orpheus and the Orphic religion.

As before, none of this is directly represented in the music, which consists of an extended introduction for the whole orchestra. No words are spoken or sung. It concludes with the third Whisper of Change, which is virtually identical to the two previous occurrences, and serves the same function, that is, as a transition back to the main part of the act: still, soft undulations for wordless chorus and harps over a whispering aura and a (new) barely audible bass line.

What is most striking about this music is just how different it is from what has gone before. It announces in an uncompromising manner a new musical world. Just as Act III of Wagner's *Siegfried* opens with a much more mature music than that which closed Act II (there was a 12-year gap between the composition of the two acts), so here it is clear that Birtwistle's musical language has undergone a radical transformation in the six years since he had last worked on the opera. While this music shares some of the rhythmic energy of Orpheus' music from Act II, its balancing of voices, its constantly varied yet dynamic forward motion speaks with a fresh confidence and points to the new, through-composed structures of landmark works of the 1980s and early 1990s such as *Secret Theatre, Earth Dances* and, ultimately, *Gawain*. Cantus and continuum structures are still in evidence, but they are now used in a more subtle way: no longer are the two elements held in bold opposition, but rather the relationship between the vertical and the horizontal is constantly shifting, as cantabile lines emerge from and fade back into the body of the music. The frequent changes in tempo are deftly handled – often alternating ♩ = 126 and ♩= 168, that is, a ratio of 3:4 – so that the speed of the music appears to be in a continual state of flux. The music gives the impression of being much more organic.

Such a radically different music might appear out of place, but in fact it is entirely appropriate to the drama at this point. The concerns of the 'old world' have been left behind, exhausted, at the end of Act II. As Orpheus discovered, there was no going back. Now, a new musical language points to a new mythological existence for Orpheus. The musical concerns of Acts I and II are still present but are fundamentally transformed, in keeping with the way in which the previous Time Shifts re-evaluated earlier events. There is little music in the remainder of Act III that we have not already encountered in the previous acts, but it is never the same as before: it is music remembered, not repeated. Act III is about myth and memory. All this is signalled by the new music of the third Time Shift.

Act III, scenes 2 and 3

The main part of Act III is constructed from six 'sequences of death', which present Eurydice's death, various versions of the death of Orpheus and Orpheus' silencing by Apollo. By means of repetition these six sequences are organized into 15 'occurrences' shaped into a wave pattern, that is, a twofold rising and falling of the structure of the tides, which can be represented as follows:

```
                    6 6
                 5       5
       4 4          4         4
      3    3        3
           2    2
         1 1
```

This can also be seen in more detail in Table 4.1, which shows the detailed organization of the entire act. All bar one of the 15 occurrences are preceded by a statement of one of six short 'responses', which, as discussed below, represent six found objects. Woven into this structure are two other elements: the remaining mimed, electronic 'interruptions' (the third Allegorical Flower and the third Passing Cloud), and the six verses of the third Song of Magic sung by Orpheus in the language of Orphic devised by Zinovieff.

It is a complex structure that militates against any simple representation of narrative or presentation of drama. What one experiences in the theatre, through the many repetitions and allusions back to music and events from earlier acts, is a sense of a multi-dimensional, formalized ritual. It is almost as if the myth is being invented before us. For these reasons it is not possible here to present chronologically the various elements of the act. In the discussion that follows, I have chosen to isolate each of these various components for discussion, and I invite the reader to refer to Table 4.1 in order to gain a sense of where each element fits into the overall (tidal) structure.

Responses

The course of scenes 2 and 3 is punctuated by these six recurring refrains. In terms of the structure of the libretto, these responses correspond directly to six objects that lie on the shoreline and are covered and uncovered by the ebb and flow of the imaginary tides. Two of these objects relate to Orpheus' past, three to the present, and one to the future. Further, each object 'represents a "sequence" of death and decay' (libretto, p. 52). The objects take the shape of a fossil shell, an oar, a fishing net, a bird skull, a footprint and a rockfall. According to Zinovieff, they 'give clues to the words' of the sequences to which they relate (p. 52), and a chart provides word derivations and symbols (p. 62). The most direct connection between these symbolic objects and the sung text is revealed in the six verses of Orpheus' third Song of Magic, though even this connection is grasped with difficulty because the song is sung in Orphic. For example, the first verse responds to the object of the fossil shell, and its text translates as:

> Earth-pressed into time mould
> This tree-dance.
> Fruit-flower from day found.
> Death-grey into nightfall.
> Thought-lost-quartz-hid.
> Far-looked.
> Ring-feast-love-held.
>
> Taste.
> Remember.

Table 4.1 Overall structure of Act III

	Occurrence	Response	Sequence 1 (death of Euridice)	Sequence 2 (death by suicide)	Sequence 3 (death by thunderbolt)	Sequence 4 (death by sacrifice)	Sequence 5 (journey of skull)	Sequence 6 (Apollo silences skull)	3rd Song of Magic
Time Shift and Whisper of Change	1	Fishing Net			Recit of teaching, aria of prophecy, sentence of religion				
	2	Bird Skull				First exchange / Third Allegorical Flower			
	3	Bird Skull				Second exchange			
	4	Fishing Net			Repeat				
	5	Oar		'I remember the arches …'					
	6	Fossil Shell	Cry of Memory						Verse 1
	7	Fossil Shell	Repeat						Verse 2
	8	Oar		'The first arch is the widest …'					Verse 3
	9	Fishing Net			Repeat				Verse 4
	10	Bird Skull				Third exchange			Verse 5
	11	Footprint					Third Love Duet		Verse 6

No.	Item					
12	Rockfall					Oracle
13	Rockfall					Oracle Third Passing Cloud
14	Rockfall				Repeat of closing fragment	
15	Fossil Shell Rockfall Footprint Fossil Shell Oar Bird Skull Fishing Net			Fourth exchange		

A commentary in the libretto (p. 63) indicates that this is a representation of Orpheus' memory of the first Ceremony and his wedding dance. Certain words, such as the closing 'OFOARIF' ('Remember'), are at least familiar as a result of their repetition by Apollo in the previous act, and the final two words of each verse are also periodically whispered in English as part of the third Song of Failure. But, for the most part, the words and their meanings, and their relationship to the objects, remain obscure. The objects are both symbolic and structural devices; they have no physical presence in the theatre.

By contrast, the musical responses have a very clear role in articulating the structure of the act. They are the musical equivalents of found objects on which the composer has stumbled. They are the same on every occurrence. The visual analogy is one on which Birtwistle has often relied. He has frequently spoken of his musical materials as 'objects', and his listeners are invited to 'view' them from different angles. Of the central brass ritornellos in *Verses for Ensembles* he commented, 'It's like looking at an object: every view is unique, but the object exists irrespective of the way it's viewed. So it's the notion that this piece of music exists, just like an object.'[1] In *The Triumph of Time* two repeating musical objects (a saxophone motif and a cor anglais melody) are continually viewed from new perspectives as the piece unfolds. *Carmen Arcadiae mechanicae perpetuum* is constructed, object-like, from 'six musical mechanisms which are juxtaposed many times without any form of transition'.[2] More generally, these comments speak of the role played by repetition in Birtwistle's music. Repeating verse-refrain structures are to be found everywhere in his output, from *Refrains and Choruses*, via the strophic songs of so many of his stage works, to the subtle interleaving of 'friezes' and 'fantasias' and 'songs' in *Pulse Shadows* (1989–96). 'My attitude to time … is concerned with repetition – about how repetition changes our perception of how things happen.'[3]

Repetition as a means of representing time in new ways is a, if not *the*, central concern of *The Mask of Orpheus*. We have already seen many and various instances of this in, for example, the extensions of the first Love Duet in Act I, in the Arches of Act II or in the refrain-like Clouds and Flowers that occur across the whole work. But in Act III repetition becomes the primary *modus operandi*. Vast tracts of music are – unusually for Birtwistle – repeated exactly. The repeating object-responses function as refrains across the entire act. By the end, there is nothing left but the repetition of these refrains over the electronic aura in an increasingly attenuated musical environment. The punctuating refrains have now become the *only* musical material. Their inability to do anything other than repeat reinforces the musical and

---

[1]   Birtwistle, in Paul Griffiths, *New Sounds, New Personalities: British Composers of the 1980s* (London: Faber and Faber, 1985), 191.

[2]   Composer's note on the work – see Michael Hall, *Harrison Birtwistle* (London: Robson, 1984), 177.

[3]   Birtwistle, in Ross Lorraine, 'Territorial rites 2', *Musical Times*, 1857 (November 1997), 13.

dramatic stasis: they are like snatches of memory in an otherwise timeless world. Only memory persists.

Table 4.1 shows how the course of the act is punctuated by the recurrence of these refrains (reductions of which are given in Example 4.1): with one exception, they each mark clearly the beginning of one of the 15 'occurrences'. In general terms, because each refrain has the same function, all are alike. Each is short; each consists essentially of a single gesture that has a strong forward momentum; each occurs with an electronic signal and the voice of Apollo calling 'RUFI' ('Love'). Each also makes (different) use of the entire chromatic set: chromatic clusters occur in each, though this is not specific enough a feature in itself to suggest closer harmonic relationships. Beyond these similarities, however, each of the six responses is clearly differentiated in order that it is immediately identifiable to the listener. Each is an arbitrary signifier, in the sense that there is no necessary connection between its musical sound and structure and the signified object. Further, one stumbles upon the responses unexpectedly as *objets trouvés*, independent of their surroundings, apparently unrelated to the rest of the music of the act. The 'memorable' feature in each is quite different, for example, the rising line for trombone and tubas for 'fossil shell'; the dancing, woodwind melody for 'oar'; and so on. Each is at a different tempo, with no obvious relationship between one and the next.[4] The responses retain their object-like nature from the beginning of the act to the end. Although they remain fixed and are unable to develop, our perspective on them is always changing because they continually recur in new contexts.

Example 4.1 Act III: the six responses

(a) Rockfall

---

⁴   While Rockfall and Oar ostensibly share the same metronome mark of ♪ = *c*.112, their gestures and rhythms are entirely different, the one made of separate five-note demi-semiquaver figures, the other a continuous line of triplet quavers and semiquavers.

(b) Fossil Shell

(c) Oar

(d) Bird Skull

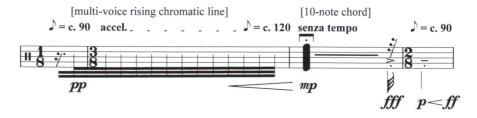

(e) Fishing Net

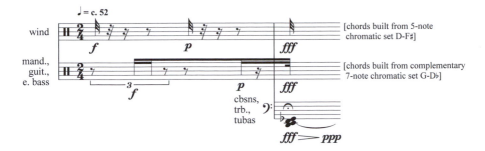

(f) Footprint

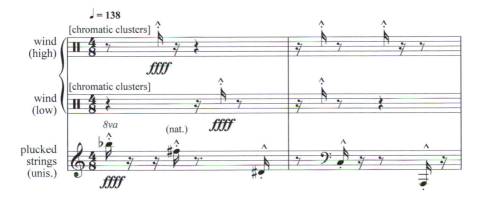

Example 4.1 sets out the nature of each musical object. A few further comments are in order here.

- Each of the four (five demi-semiquaver) gestures of Rockfall is an obvious variant on every other. There is a rich heterophony here of ten chromatically parallel woodwind lines. The high register (nothing sounds below middle c^1) and scoring for upper wind and tuned percussion make for the 'jewelled' sound associated with mirror and water imagery in Act II.
- Fossil Shell is scored for brass only. Its most striking feature is the rising trombone and tuba line: a five-note octatonic scale segment. (Its octatonicism is trivial, but it can easily be understood to be formed from overlapping statements of the 'signature' tone and semitone motif, ending with its most familiar Phrygian D–E–F incarnation.) It is accompanied by harsh, dense, chromatic clusters (again built by piling up tones and semitones) that, with the rising line, form 10-, 11- or 12-note chords.

- The Oar is most closely related to the Rockfall, being at the same tempo and scored for bright, 'jewelled' upper woodwind and tuned percussion. (If there is any dramatic connection between these two objects and their associated sequences, then it remains obscure.) The dance-like character of the leaping melodic line is striking, and it ends with a prominent sustained e^3.
- Bird Skull is a distinctive Birtwistle gesture that can be found in many different contexts in his music (in this sense, it is an object across which one has stumbled many times even outside *Orpheus*): a chromatic figure that rushes upwards through the instruments, a sustained ten-note chord and a closing punctuating gesture that allows a chromatic cluster to ring on, centred on E (D♮–D♯–E–F♯).
- The Fishing Net is made from (i) three repetitions of a five-note chromatic chord centred on E (D–E♭–E♮–F♮–F♯); (ii) corresponding gestures on amplified plucked instruments, using the complementary seven-note chromatic set (from G♮ to D♭); and (iii) a final, low, sustained cluster, again centred on E (D–E–F♮–F♯).
- The Footprint is a brief, chromatic gesture in 'contrary motion', in which the wind and brass move upwards from low to high, interlocking with the plucked instruments (including harps) which move downwards in unison from high to low.

Each refrain is thus discrete and distinctive. And yet the refrains' (generally) shared characteristics are also revealing. The fact that the majority of them appear to engage with the central pitch class E in one way or another suggests that they might be understood as a kind of 'composing out' of the latent possibilities of the background aura of the tides (focused on E). This becomes more explicit at the end of the act, when each refrain is heard to emerge in turn from the aura. But the pitch class E is also symbolic of both memory and loss, and so each of these isolated moments appears to relate to aspects of Orpheus' memory in which events – past, present and future – are endlessly repeated. Orpheus Man and Hero of Acts I and II has become Orpheus Myth. Myth is something that can exist only out of time, in memory. The close of Act III is an attempt to represent the Orphic myth in a seemingly timeless musical landscape where the only fixed points are those of memory.

Third Song of Magic and third Song of Failure

In Act I, Orpheus sang the first Song of Magic at his wedding, lending a moment of beauty to a situation otherwise heavy with bad omens. Act II was dominated by the 17 verses of the second Song of Magic, by means of which Orpheus charmed his way into the underworld (at least, so he dreamed). The third Song of Magic in the second half of Act III is rather different in that its singing appears to have no effect on those around Orpheus: both the Song of Magic and Song of Failure are sung by

Orpheus Singer, who is an observer only and takes no part in the action. Indeed, as can be seen in Table 4.1, it stands outside the main course of events, though it relates to them in that each of its six verses corresponds to one of the six sequences, and the end of each verse is punctuated, in turn, by each of the six objects and responses. The libretto describes the Song of Magic, and its corresponding Song of Failure, as '[j]igsawing into the plan of the Tides but having no real part of the structure' (p. 62).

The text of the Song of Magic is in Orphic. In practice, not one of its verses is heard in its entirety as a consequence of the additive structure of the song. The text of the Song of Failure is a rendition into 'a primitive type of English' of the verses of the Song of Magic. But aside from the occasional key word that is whispered inaudibly, none of this is set in the opera. In that the texts consist of the reworking of words already heard in Acts I and II, the songs are a commentary on past events. As an aspect of Orpheus' memory they underpin the scene, but in an abstract way only. As far as the auditor in the audience is concerned, the meaning of both songs is utterly inscrutable.

The question might then legitimately be put: why is this here at all? If the texts are neither audible nor intelligible, then what function can they possibly serve? One might argue – and not entirely flippantly – that inscrutable texts in a 'foreign' language are not necessarily an obstacle to an audience's comprehension of an opera's dramaturgy, even throughout the long history of the genre before the recent arrival in theatres of projected surtitles. One need only recall the immense popularity of Handel's Italian operas with early eighteenth-century London audiences in order to support such an argument. In the twentieth century there are instances of composers choosing to set texts in a language that it was hoped the audience would *not* comprehend. The most widely discussed example is Stravinsky's opera-oratorio *Oedipus rex*, to a French text by Cocteau translated into the 'dead' language of Latin. Stravinsky later recalled, in conversation with Robert Craft, that the 'idea was that a text for music might be endowed with a certain monumental character by translation backwards, so to speak, from a secular to a sacred language. … I thought that an older, even an imperfectly remembered, language must contain an incantatory element that could be exploited in music.'[5] While *Oedipus rex* may not have served as a direct model for *The Mask of Orpheus*, it was clearly known well to both Birtwistle and Zinovieff, and is a key precursor.

It is not that the words do not matter. But it is, for an audience, the musical context that gives the text dramatic relevance. Or, to put it in Stravinsky's terms, the music exploits the character of the language. In the case of Orpheus' Song of Magic, we hear an extraordinarily still and intense incantation. Even though we do not understand the words, we recognize the many repetitions that they contain and understand that, for the stage character, these words are meaningful. Like Stravinsky's Latin, the Orphic words here are endowed with a certain monumental character. They offer

---

[5]   Igor Stravinsky and Robert Craft, *Dialogues* (London: Faber and Faber, 1982), 21.

the composer the opportunity for a musical context that is, in a sense, 'sacred', that is, one that is ritualistic and that is quite different from the music elsewhere in the act. It not only stands outside the main structure, but also appears to be at a remove from the act's principal musical concerns. Such 'holy' music is appropriate to the mythical status of Orpheus in Act III. He became the focus of a religion. He sings in the language of the god Apollo.

The third Song of Magic has six verses, each of which consists of seven lines of Orphic text. But each line is preceded by a line from a fixed formula (also in Orphic) that presents a sequence of nouns (N) and questions (Q) that are then elaborated by the lines of the verse text (V). For example, verse 1 proceeds as follows:

[i]	[N] ID SAÀS	The object
	[Q] (FOD FO ID FEIS Ò)	(What lies on the beach?)
	[V] I SEI DEI FUI	*A fossil shell*
[ii]	[N] ID UEI SAÀS	The strange object
	[Q] (RI ID FOFUIIF EI Ò)	(What does the observer see?)
	[V] I DEI FSU SIA UD ROI DO EIDIFU	*A cast-up tree, laden with fruit and flowers*
[iii]	*Etc.*	

In its actual setting, the situation is less clear. The song as a whole has an additive structure; each verse gets longer as the song unfolds. Verse 1 sets only the first noun and question of the formula and the first line of text; verse 2 sets the first two nouns and questions, into which are interleaved the first two lines of text; and so on, all the way through to the six nouns, questions and text lines of verse 6. Given that there are seven nouns and questions in the formula and seven lines of text in each verse, the final lines are never sung. Each successive verse of the song, therefore, involves the repetition of all of the preceding verse with the addition of a final new section. But even within this 'curtailed' organization, not all the verses are heard.

Verse 1: line 1 of text of verse 4
Verse 2: lines 1–2 of text of verse 3
Verse 3: lines 1–3 of text of verse 2
Verse 4: lines 1–4 of text of verse 1
Verse 5: lines 1–5 of text of verse 4
Verse 6: lines 1–2 of text of verse 1[6]; lines 3–6 of text of verse 3

---

6   Given the high level of repetition from one verse to the next, and the obvious time-saving 'cut and paste' approach employed by the copyists in preparing the full score, it is likely that the presence of the text of verse 1 here instead of the expected verse 3 is a mistake.

Thus only elements of the text of the first four verses are used. Verses 5 and 6 are sung in their entirety without the interleaved nouns and questions of the formula as Orpheus' text for, respectively, the fifth and sixth sequences. In an even more extreme fashion, the text of the corresponding third Song of Failure remains a matter for the libretto alone: the fragments that are whispered cannot be heard, and the rest of the text is not set. At best, one might argue that its influence is felt in the affect of the Song of Magic.

Each verse of the song is accompanied by the Summer Aura, which provides continuity. The end of each verse is marked by an 'angry harp' signal (i.e., a loud, violent form of the familiar electronic signal) and the re-entry of the Aura of the Tides. This is immediately followed by the voice of Apollo calling 'RUFI', which heralds one of the responses. Each response has a double function, articulating the end of a verse as well as marking a return to the music of the sequences.

The music is unlike anything else in the opera. It seems to me that this music very much reflects the practical experience Birtwistle acquired while working at the National Theatre in that it responds directly to the dramatic moment and allows the melancholic singer to be heard. A background chord (*ppp*) provides the context for each 'phrase' (by which I mean each succession of N, Q and V) sung by Orpheus, to which, in turn, a group of supporting percussion instruments responds. A falling three-semiquaver harp cadence punctuates the end of the phrase and a change in background chord, and then Orpheus proceeds to his next phrase. It is a clear and simple idea. What Orpheus sings could hardly be described as a melody – its clipped style militates against any sense of a lyrical line – but the pitches of each phrase form a five-note wedge centred, alternately, on D (c^1–$d\flat^1$–$d\natural^1$–$e\flat^1$–$e\natural^1$) and G (f–$g\flat$–$g\natural$–$a\flat$–$a\natural$). The series of background chords for woodwind and horns is like a very slow chorale. The complete sequence, as it occurs in verse 6, is given in Example 4.2. Verse 1 is accompanied by just chord 1, verse 2 by chords 1 and 2, and so on, building up the complete chorale. My added slurs in the example propose that voice leading is significant, and it certainly does look like a cadential formula, with the upper voices forming a sequence of descending fifths and the lower voices suggesting a bass progression. Such (relatively) explicit tonal echoes are unusual in Birtwistle but are appropriate here in setting a musical mood that seems to belong to a different time and place: like Orpheus Singer, it stands outside the drama. The open harmonies, where every chord contains an instance of interval class 5 (as a perfect fourth or fifth), reinforce the sense of timeless ritual and point back to the open fifths at the end of Act II as well as forward to the 'emptiness' of the end of the work. An additional harmonic colour is provided by *tremolando* glockenspiels that, over the course of the six verses, expose all the notes of the chromatic.

Example 4.2 Act III, third Song of Magic, background chords

Sequence 4: Third Ceremony (The Sacrifice)

Sequence 4 occurs four times in the form of the exchanges of the Ceremony (occurrences 2, 3, 10 and 15).[7] It is principally a reworking of the text and music of the two previous ceremonies in Act I, though other elements, such as a further extension of the first Love Duet from Act I and the Trio of Women from Act II, are also woven into the structure. Zinovieff states that the action represents 'the culmination of the wedding and funeral ceremonies in that of the sacrifice. ... The ceremony itself is much brisker and less complicated than the other two' (libretto, p. 57).

As with the structure of the Arches in Act II, Zinovieff provided Birtwistle with a detailed scheme, including precise timings (to which, for the most part, Birtwistle adheres). Each exchange consists of 13 distinct parts of varying durations, ranging from the opening shout of 0′05″ to the main ceremonial dance lasting 0′25″. The total duration is given as 2′00″ for the 'uptide' exchanges (first and third) and 2′30″ for the 'downtides' (second and fourth). The 13 parts are as follows:

(i)   Shout (3 Priests: 'Answer!')
(ii)   Question (3 Priests: 'Where are the roots?')
(iii)   First Love Duet extension (Orpheus Singer, Eurydice Singer and Puppet)
(iv)   Demand (3 Priests: 'Answer!')
(v)   Invocation (Caller, third Complicated Question: 'Scream luckwards. Gold. Fierce fire-time')
(vi)   Statement (3 Priests: 'Here are the roots')
(vii)   Second Dangerous Murmur (SATB chorus: 'Stand, clutch, press, wait')
(viii) Reply (Caller: 'This is the answer!')
(ix)   Chorus of Crowds (SATB chorus: 'Stand, clutch, press, wait')
(x)   Third Immortal Dance
(xi)   Silence/pause
(xii)   Scream (3 Priests: 'Answer!')
(xiii) Third Hidden Trio (3 women: 'White sorrow we slowly breathe')

---

[7]   The libretto (p. 57) states that the '4th occurrence is very fragmentary' but this is not in fact the case in the final score, where a fourth complete sequence (exchange) is presented.

Birtwistle's first response was to produce his own more detailed visual scheme,[8] on to which he mapped to scale all of Zinovieff's events and timings (in the horizontal plane) and characters and groups (in the vertical plane), and from which he began to compose. It is a clear, simple structure, even if the resulting music is complex – a consequence of the dense layering of ideas. In this respect it is very much in keeping with the organization of the ceremonies in Act I.

All of the text is familiar to us from Acts I and II, though it is often refigured. None of the music is repeated directly but it clearly alludes to the musical ideas of the previous acts as if – once again – events from the past are being distorted in a present mosaic of memories. The shouts and responses of Caller and Priests (i, ii, iv, vi, viii, xii) are immediately recognizable, and they receive a rhythmic setting very similar to that in Act I. The third Complicated Question (v) reconfigures and compresses the text of the previous Complicated Questions but is now turned into a single-voice melodic invocation for the Caller, the organum in the original Priests parts in the first Ceremony now being transferred to sinuous lines in piccolos and saxophones, doubled at the fourth or fifth. The reappearances of the First Love Duet pick up the E♭s on which the sixth (and final) extension in Act I concluded, as if somehow the love song has been echoing across the work ever since. Orpheus and two Eurydices call each other's name, as before, in three complementary lines that open outwards from that E. The wind lines that accompany them betray the composer's new way of working in the 1980s. Instead of these wind lines working according to their own procedures, as was the case with the voices accompanying the singing lovers in Act I, they are now spawned directly from Eurydice's two lines, as shown in Example 4.3. Notes are selected (by means of numbers) from the original melodies and sustained to generate six new lines. Yet they are not really new at all: each wind line, if you like, interprets the two Eurydices' lines in a slightly different way. The result is a rich heterophony that offers multiple perspectives on an original idea.

A note on Birtwistle's sketched chart indicates that events (vii) and (ix) do not occur in the position specified by the libretto. The second Dangerous Murmur and the Chorus of Crowds appear out of sequence, being layered on to the calls of the Priests: thus the murmur (vii) coincides with the shout (i), and the Chorus (ix) with the statement (vi) and reply (viii). Both murmur and chorus share the same choral material and texts, which points back to the more nightmarish aspects of earlier acts. The most direct musical repetition here is of elements of the first Hysterical Aria at the end of Act I, where the chorus and wind supported the screeches of the Oracle of the Dead with clipped shouts of 'stand, clutch, press, wait', identical to the words sung here. However, rather than singing unpitched, as in Act I, each voice now has a single, repeated pitch, lending an anxiety to the (memory of the) moment. Upper woodwind provide, as before, matching points of sound.

The other choral element here is the third Hidden Trio, where the three women sing an obvious variant on the music of the Furies from Act II. Their mournful affect

8 PSS 0531-0957.

is also parallel ('White sorrow we slowly breathe'). They sing, as before, in rhythmic unison, with the upper two voices moving in an organum of fourths (perfect or augmented) and fifths. E♮ is again an important pitch centre, and thus makes links not only with the extension of the Love Duet, which is at a similarly slow tempo, but also with the E of the electronic tides. Three weeping wind lines (alto flute, cor anglais and saxophone) accompany the women, generated in the same way as the lines in Example 4.3.

The final, separate part of this Ceremony is the extended Immortal Dance (x), subtitled 'sacrificial dance'. Parallels with Stravinsky's famous 'Danse sacrale' are clear enough in the highly charged, rhythmic writing for squealing upper wind and xylophones. The memory invoked here is not so much the dances in the Act I

Example 4.3 Act III, scene 2, generation of new lines from Eurydice's melodies (fig. 23)

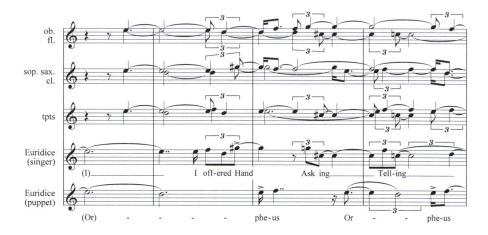

ceremonies, but the Dionysian climax to Act II. Neither wedding dance nor funeral dance, this seems to be more a brief, manic *Totentanz*, a dance to the death.

The overall impression of the Ceremony is of a mosaic of memories, some close to the words and music of previous acts, some transformed and therefore more distant. One part follows or overlaps with the next in rapid succession. Each is clearly characterized and differentiated musically, in terms of musical material, intensity and tempo. In each successive exchange everything is repeated exactly (with the exception of the continuum, discussed below). 'The exchanges are highly structured and are cyclical … Each exchange starts at a different point in the cycle' (libretto, p. 57). Thus the first exchange follows the given sequence from (i) to (xiii), though the end is extended, both to allow the third Allegorical Flower of Reason to be heard and to provide a transition to the second exchange, which follows immediately.[9] The second exchange begins with (iv) and cycles all the way round to a second statement of (iv); the third exchange begins at (xi), cycling round to (xi) and continuing with a second statement of (xii); and the fourth exchange begins at and cycles back to (x), which is repeated. Given that the third Ceremony as a whole is notionally concerned with sacrifice, it is dramatically highly effective to end the 15th and final occurrence of the sequences with this sacrificial dance.

This account so far might suggest something extremely fragmented where, no sooner has it started, than the music lurches on to a completely different idea, only in turn to be broken off for a third idea, and so on. This is certainly what is suggested by the libretto. Birtwistle provides an additional layer, however, which provides continuity and which has the familiar hallmarks of a continuum (even though, as a result of the many rests, it is not continuous). The sketches show how the third Ceremony was drafted on to a semiquaver rhythmic grid: a continuous sequence of semiquavers, grouped according to a changing time signature, and with various rhythmic patterns overlaid.[10] Then the vocal lines are sketched out and indications are given as to where instrumental groups will occur. And only then does he begin to compose the instrumental parts around this. In the final score, it is the plucked instruments (harps, and electric mandolin, guitar and bass), as a multi-faceted representation of Orpheus' lyre, that form the continuum group. It is a continuum not only in that it is made up of continually turning (albeit sparse) ostinatos, but also in that it has a continuity across the exchanges. In other words, the continuum operates according to its own scheme of repetition, independent of the cycles of repetition of the exchanges.

Sequence 1: Death of Eurydice

Sequence 1 consists of just two identical presentations of the first Cry of Memory from the beginning of Act I, scene 2 (occurrences 6 and 7), separated by the first verse of the third Song of Magic and the 'fossil shell' response. According to the libretto (p. 55) it forms 'a further re-interpretation of Euridice's death'. Zinovieff spells out the ways in which events are dramaturgically reconfigured in Act III (Orpheus is now the seducer), as well as the differences between the two occurrences. 'The action is a much condensed and simplified version of the action' in the earlier act.

---

[9]   In the performances to date, as well as in the recording, the first exchange is cut and so the Allegorical Flower is moved to a position later in the act – see Appendix B. The 'transition' here and also between the two consecutive occurrences of sequence 6 (see below) is specified in the libretto: 'Between each sequence on the falling tides there is a half-minute "transition" period. They take place in the dark and are without time' (p. 52). In fact, these transitions occur in these two instances only when a sequence is repeated immediately on the 'falling tide'.

[10]   Beginning at PSS 0531-0941.

But none of these differences – either between acts or occurrences – has any bearing on the music, which is a note-for-note repetition of the music as it was heard in Act I (compare sequence 1 with Act I, from fig. 52 until after fig. 56, pp. 57–61). Although only a curtailed segment of the Cry of Memory is twice repeated here, it is neither condensed nor simplified: nothing is added and nothing is taken away. It is the only extended direct repetition in Act III of material from Act I, and as such is striking. Even though, as the libretto states, the memory is 'the farthest back in chronological time', the music suggests that it is the most vivid of all Orpheus' recollections. The moment of his lover's death can be remembered precisely.

Sequence 2: Death by Suicide

This sequence refers to the Arches. The first occurrence of sequence 2 (occurrence 5), titled third Dream, uses the text of the first verse of the first Shout of Gratitude from the end of Act I ('I remember the arches'); its second appearance (occurrence 8), titled third Spoken Argument, uses the text of the second verse of the first Shout ('The first arch is the widest') (see Table 4.1). As in Act I, the text is spoken by Orpheus Puppet, only now it is given specific rhythms that correspond to the patterns of speech. Just as the appearance of this text in Act I prefigured the dreamed events of Act II, so here the 'action is very symbolic of the whole of act 2' (libretto, p. 55). In Act I the text was accompanied by a thick-textured wind chorale. Soft, slow-moving wind and brass lines also support the presentation of the text in Act III, representing a compositional reworking of Act I. But the most direct musical and expressive allusions are to the 17th Arch of Act II. Tempos, scoring, gestures and affect are virtually identical. In Act III, two time streams operate simultaneously, with wind, brass, two harps and one group of percussion under the direction of conductor II, and Orpheus, trumpet, harp, guitar and another group of percussion under the direction of conductor I.

In the first occurrence (third Dream) the text is supported, in the main, by a regular pulse on alternate beats in duple time. Periodic disruption of this pattern – to mark the end of a spoken phrase – is punctuated by a dry harp and guitar chord (as if Orpheus were accompanying himself) and a short flourish on the trumpet. Such gestures have become familiar to us in Birtwistle's post-*Orpheus* works, most notably in his 'trumpet concerto', *Endless Parade* (1986–87), whose recurrent opening motif punctuates the course of that musical procession. The ceremonial air thus lent to the presentation of the text has the effect of distancing Orpheus from his memory and the emotions associated with it. Appropriately, the text is 'spoken formally'. In the third Spoken Argument, the text is presented in the same way, with the same supporting instruments, but their movement is now less regular, more fragmentary, as if the certainty of the Dream had already started to decay.

Contrariwise, the identity of the complementary wind and brass group in the second occurrence (third Spoken Argument) is much clearer than in the Dream. On both occasions, the lines emerge from sustained E♮s, which in themselves seem to emerge from the E at the end of the 'oar' response. But in the case of the Spoken Argument, an unbroken unison melody sings across the occurrence, clearly the cousin of both the chorale melody from the equivalent moment in Act I and the mournful wind melody from the 17th Arch. Once again, this poignant music has a quiet timelessness as if one were hearing, for the first time in a long time, a familiar but distant melody. It is akin to the mournful shepherd's song at the start of Act III of *Tristan and Isolde*, 'die alte Weise', which evokes a desolate sense of emptiness, of a wasteland.[11] Orpheus, too, recognizes this. This second occurrence ends with a scream, his impassioned calling of Eurydice's name, just as at the end of Act II, scene 2. It is a cry of desperation. In the Dream, the wind and brass music is much less clearly formed, with no strong melodic identity. Its soft but thickly doubled lines continually rise from and merge back into the electronic aura. Its very ungraspability creates an underlying sense of uncertainty.

Sequence 5: Third Love Duet (Duet of Despair)

This sequence occurs twice towards the end of Act III (occurrences 11 and 14), and even then the second appearance is just an exact repeat of a final fragment (four bars lasting about 15 seconds, which have been cut in the performed versions). It is perhaps the 'purest' expression of melancholy in the entire work, consisting as it does almost exclusively of falling, lamenting lines. There are essentially three slow-moving, overlapping lines. Each moves at its own rate. Each represents an aspect of the same idea: although the pitches of each line are different, each is built from the same 'template', that is, falling intervals of semitones, tones and minor thirds. The texture is saturated with these intervals. Overall the music recalls the melancholy of the first and second Love Duets, and more generally the falling lines associated throughout with Eurydice/Persephone. Specifically, we hear:

- Overlapping lines for the three singers – mainly the two Eurydices calling Orpheus' name, occasionally joined by Orpheus Puppet; each word or phrase starts high in the singer's range and moves to the bottom. The music expresses the affect of the text ('white sorrow', 'into longing I fall'), which is

---

[11]   This sense of desolation was taken up by T.S. Eliot in 'The Burial of the Dead' from *The Waste Land* (1922), his exploration – in the aftermath of the First World War – of the spiritual barrenness of late-modern civilization: '— Yet when we came back, late, from the hyacinth garden, / Your arms full, and your hair wet, I could not / Speak, and my eyes failed. I was neither / Living nor dead, and I knew nothing, / Looking into the heart of light, the silence. / *Oed' und leer das Meer*.' ('The Burial of the Dead', ll. 37–42, from *The Waste Land* [1922], in T.S. Eliot, *Collected Poems 1909–1962* (London: Faber & Faber, pbk ed., 1974), 64.)

essentially a remembrance of words from previous Love Duets.
- A single line, expressed at slightly different rates in pairs of instruments simultaneously, falls progressively through the woodwind, starting high in the piccolo and working its way downwards through oboe, cor anglais and bass clarinet to contrabassoon. This takes place twice.
- A single line for two harps, taking alternate notes starting at the very top of their range and falling to the very bottom (on the first occasion from $e\flat^4$ to $E\flat^1$). This also takes place twice.

The remaining wind and brass instruments sustain a sequence of accompanying soft chords. But there is one additional layer. This is an entirely independent line for Orpheus Singer in which he presents the fifth verse of the third Song of Magic in Orphic (relating to the 'footprint' object). It is, as the libretto specifies, a gentle and continuous aria that cycles round the same set of pitches.

As far as the drama is concerned, Zinovieff (libretto, p. 60) tells us that the 'main action is the journey and metamorphosis of Orpheus' head down the river Hebrus into an Oracle on the island of Lesbos where it eventually came to rest'. Once again, there is no direct representation of these events in the music.

Sequence 6: Orpheus is Silenced by Apollo

The presentation of this sequence diverges from the pattern established by the other sequences. There are two consecutive occurrences (12 and 13), where the second is an extension rather than a repetition of the first; they are not separated by a statement of the expected 'rockfall' response. The libretto (p. 60) states that the 'two occurrences are separated by the Highest Tide and the one minute sustain (interrupted by the third Passing Cloud of Abandon) and the sixth transition during which the sixth verse of the third Song of Magic is sung by Orpheus Singer'. Between the two occurrences there is certainly contrasting material that involves a 'sustain' of sorts, but the Passing Cloud does not appear until the end of the second occurrence, while the verse of the Song of Magic, rather than being separate, in fact forms the substance of the first occurrence (sung by Orpheus Puppet in duet with the Oracle).

The sequence as a whole is predominantly rhythmic. This memory of the Dionysian music of the Ensemble of Hell is accompanied by the readily recognizable hysterical screeches of the Oracle of the Dead. It clearly points back to the climactic moments of both Acts I and II. Just as at the end of Act II, scene 2, Orpheus is left with only his memory of the Argonautic journey, so here the second occurrence subsides as we hear Orpheus stutter out the words 'The King stands highest'. This is appropriate to the drama in that the sequence is concerned with the silencing of Orpheus by Apollo.

In both occurrences, the large part of the ensemble forms the continuum group: a texture of semiquaver pulses in which the individual lines are formed from irregular two-, three- and four-note ostinatos. The cantus has two components, melody and counter-melody. The principal focus is the sixth verse of the Song of Magic, the most lyrical of all the verses, which is sung by Orpheus and doubled by the Oracle to form a line of organum. (The libretto suggests that the Oracle of the Dead here represents Orpheus as an oracle.[12]) Between phrases, and more extensively between the two halves of the verse, we hear the Oracle's high-pitched screeches, along with the voice of Apollo, who calls out 'ID FIS-IAD RIS' ('the highest tide'). The counter-melody is heard in the first occurrence on three unison saxophones that sing out a sustained, uninterrupted line starting on e^2 and opening out in an informal wedge shape. (Both the instrument and the pitch centre call Eurydice to mind.) The second occurrence is entirely instrumental. This time the cantus is a heterophonic melody for upper woodwind, upper brass and women's voices. The sketches show clearly how all the lines were generated from the 'top' line (the 'model') for unison flutes, oboes and clarinets: this is first split to create a second line (saxophones), and then from these two lines nine more are produced by distributing the pitches according to a number scheme across the other instruments and voices.

In the 'sustain' between the two occurrences we hear the voice of Apollo again, now calling out 'RUFI AS-RI DI' ('Love did it'), echoed by Orpheus. Orpheus has committed the ultimate act of hubris in using the very language of Apollo. The skull of Orpheus, which has turned into an oracle, must be silenced, and Apollo tells Orpheus to cease his singing. 'The skull cracks into three and this becomes the 3 pieced sun of the Exodos' (libretto, p. 60). This is followed by an overwhelming *crescendo*, starting on a sustained b^1 (thus recalling the equivalent *crescendo* at the end of Act I), out of which emerges a rising *accelerando* figure that is a common gesture of transition in Birtwistle's music, connecting the two occurrences.

Sequence 3: Death by Thunderbolt

Orpheus became a great teacher. He was revered as 'a maker of magic and, in some ways, a god' (libretto 1997, p. 12), revealing the gods' secrets to ordinary mortals. This provoked the anger of the gods and so, according to one legend, Orpheus was killed by a thunderbolt sent down by Zeus. In this sequence we see Orpheus as teacher; his disciple is represented by Aristaeus. Each occurrence consists of a Recitative of Teaching, an Aria of Prophesy and a Sentence of Religion. The words, taken principally from texts found in Acts I and II, are concerned mainly with religion (Orphism). Into these, appropriately, are woven the few extant Orphic sayings. Although the libretto shows textual and dramaturgical differences between the three occurrences (2, 3 and 10), each is musically identical.

---

[12]   'For at times it seemed as if Orpheus' magic had still not deserted him and this Oracle on Lesbos became a rival to Apollo's own Oracle at Delphi' (libretto 1997, p. 12).

The music is clearly layered, and the sketches show the writing separately of the vocal line (same rhythms as the final score but different pitches), the rhythms of the continuum group of percussion and plucked instruments, and then the meandering, narrow-ranged lines distributed through the wind and brass instruments. The final layer of sustained notes (wind, brass, chorus) was evidently added at a later stage. The overall effect here is of some kind of ancient ritual being staged. (One is tempted to call it a 'secret' ritual or theatre, especially since the writing here is similar to that of the virtually contemporaneous *Secret Theatre*.) The pitches of the vocal lines for Aristaeus and Orpheus echo those of the meandering wind lines. For example, Orpheus' short Aria of Prophecy moves around a five-note chromatic set, which lends it the air of an invocation or prayer, almost like a piece of plainchant. The repeating trumpet calls following the Sentence of Religion further reinforce the sense of ritual.

The sequence ends with the representation of the third Terrible Death by Thunderbolt. It is, quite simply, wonderful theatre music, the outcome – surely – of Birtwistle's time spent at the National Theatre. As so often in this work, traditional instrumental topics and roles (military trumpets, hunting horns, etc.) are deployed in new contexts and exciting ways to bring fresh expression to the drama. Ominous, swelling brass chords with growling tubas set the scene. An almost mocking passage in contrary motion leads to a call on trumpet and drums and a portentous falling figure on the tubas. Squealing woodwind and anxious horns presage Orpheus' destruction by violent thunderbolt strikes, the sound of which echoes away in five cadential gong strokes.

Exodos

In a Greek tragedy, the exodos is the final scene that follows the last stasimon or choral ode. Appropriately, then, the final section of *The Mask of Orpheus* emerges from the Immortal Dance of the Chorus at the end of the fourth exchange of sequence 4 (occurrence 15). The Exodos presents a dying away. It returns to the void where the work began. 'The Exodos is an extension of the structure of tides into a general decay. This is affected by a series of echoes that become fainter and fainter and more and more separated in time' (libretto, p. 61). It parallels the Parados and, as such, suggests the possibility of a cyclic structure to the work as a whole. In the background electronic auras, alongside the dying echoes of the tides, we can make out the sound of bees, and perhaps of cicadas in the (Virgilian) Mediterranean heat, as life once more emerges from death. Aristaeus 'makes peace with the wood nymphs and propitiates Orpheus so that he is once again allowed to cultivate bees, vines and olives' (libretto, p. 61).

In the foreground the only musical events that take place have all been heard before: these are the final statements of each of the six responses, each statement occurring at an increasingly greater temporal interval and separated by just the indistinct sounds of the auras. Nothing is new. Among the first words of Orpheus at the start of Act I had been 'I remember'; now at the end of Act III he has nothing *but* his musical memories, repeated *al niente*. This passage seems to express both a nihilism and a pessimism in keeping with the melancholic thread that has woven its way through the entire work. This is reinforced by the continual presence in the Exodos of the pitch class E (in the electronic Aura of the Tides), the only element of musical continuity. It acts as a pedal, gently ebbing and flowing like the tides themselves, always the same yet always different, eternally present. By the very end of the act, even that E becomes less and less distinct until finally we enter a realm of complete nothingness. It is not desolate, as the end of Act II was; it is just an empty landscape.

The Exodos extends over about seven minutes. It forms a courageous musical ending to this vast work, powerful in its understatement. In terms of the drama it symbolizes effectively the silencing of Orpheus by Apollo, a return to the dominion of Apollo, where the work began, and the emergence of the timeless Orphic myth (Orphism) out of the death of Orpheus. It also symbolizes the possibility of a certain kind of renewal in that, beyond the individual and collective tragedies of humankind, the seasons will still continue to turn and the tides will still continue to flow. But, also, the dissolution we experience at the end of *The Mask of Orpheus*, as at the end of so many works by Birtwistle, speaks of wider issues relating to modernity and identity. The presentation of the Orpheus story here articulates a profound melancholy, a deep pessimism, a sense of the failure of modern culture, as well as a yearning for return and renewal. For me, all this is caught poignantly in the closing moments of the work. Identity is dissolved. Words vanish. Only music can try to express the inexpressible, to utter the ineffable. In the final chapter I attempt to make sense of this and to interpret more widely the achievement of *The Mask of Orpheus*.

Chapter 5
Interpreting Orpheus

... these are no longer the myths of the Greeks. By now, they are ours, and we have made them into the myths we need, the stories through which we seek to understand ourselves. ... And though they lead only to an acknowledgement of the bitterness of the human predicament, rather than to any kind of solution, that in itself offers some kind of dignity in the face of doom. (Neil MacGregor[1])

... every age must re-examine them [myths] because of our desperate need to understand. (Peter Hall[2])

What, then, is *The Mask of Orpheus* about? What is the value today of retelling a story about a grieving lover who, if he ever actually existed, lived three millennia ago? How do we interpret Birtwistle and Zinovieff's achievement for the late twentieth century and beyond? Why does *The Mask of Orpheus* speak so powerfully of the *present* to all who have come into contact with it?

The Mask of Orpheus is a work very much of its own time. The years 1945–73 have been seen by many commentators as a 'golden age', a period of unprecedented economic growth and prosperity in the capitalist West, driven by rapidly advancing technologies. These were years of increasing democratization in which, through the expansion of education, the working and lower-middle classes were brought closer to the centres of social and political power. Such liberation has come to be symbolized particularly by the iconic decade known as the Sixties. But the oil crisis of 1973 signalled that '[a]n era was at an end. The decades since 1973 were to be, once again, an age of crisis.'[3] The commencement of work on *The Mask of Orpheus* coincided almost precisely with the start of the economic decline of the West, and the instability and loss of confidence that ensued. Of course, it would be foolish indeed to try to claim that the creators of *Orpheus* were consciously trying to 'write their times' into the work; nonetheless, with the benefit of a number of decades' perspective, I think it is possible to see just how acutely *Orpheus* articulates the anxieties of a newly emerging post-industrial, post-imperial, post-modern age.

---

[1]   Neil MacGregor, 'Singing to generations yet to come', in Mark Pappenheim (ed.), *BBC Proms Guide 2003* (London: British Broadcasting Corportation, 2003), 5–6.

[2]   Peter Hall, *Exposed by the Mask: Form and Language in Drama* (London: Oberon, 2000), 23.

[3]   Eric Hobsbawm, *Age of Extremes: the Short Twentieth Century, 1914–1991* (London: Abacus, 1995), 286.

Of Modernism and Postmodernism

The Mask of Orpheus stands as a late flowering of a high modernism. Its modernist traits manifest themselves at many different levels. A fundamental characteristic is its disruption of narrative (textual, dramatic, musical) with the consequent alienation of the listener and spectator: old certainties lose their controlling power; 'the centre cannot hold'. One outcome of this is a certain self-reflexivity, a focus inwards on structure rather than outwards on to representation. *Orpheus* (like *Nenia* before it) is to an extent about itself, about its own materials, particularly song, and less about, say, character. In this regard, it has much in common not only with a landmark modernist work such as Stravinsky's *Oedipus rex*, but also with key post-war statements, whose subject matter is also primarily song, voice and performance: Berberian's *Stripsody*, Berio's *Sequenza No. 3*, Boulez's *Le marteau sans maître* (an important formative work for Birtwistle) and Cage's *Aria*. The work's structuralism also locates it within the aesthetic purview of post-war serialist thought: the myriad number charts in Birtwistle's sketches, for example, and the overt concern of both composer and librettist with the minutiae of structure – planned to the second – present the work as a constructed artefact.

A related facet is the work's fascination with technology. This is obviously present in the virtuosic, up-to-date electronic components, but a play is also made of the technology of theatre and performance. In the drawings in the libretto we see a crude technology of puppetry and stage machinery, whose workings are foregrounded, not hidden. Technology stands symbolically at the heart of the opera in the form of the imaginary structure of the Arches. This could be a nostalgic representation of antique technological prowess, such as a glorious Roman aqueduct; equally it could symbolize the declining industrial era in a late-capitalist world ('Many arches are cracked or broken' – libretto frontispiece). For the modernist such technology represents simultaneously a utopian hope of progress and a dystopian violence to the subject.

This violence is a sign of the work's own century. Especially in Act II, *The Mask of Orpheus* focuses on the primitive savagery of the original myth, articulated via a visceral (mechanical) rhythmic virtuosity. Percussion dominates; expressive, romantic strings are entirely absent. Everywhere the violent, modernist 'urge to fragmentation'[4] is clearly evident. The fracturing of voices and narratives echoes the violence perpetrated against twentieth-century humanity and reflects a post-Freudian thinking about dreams, identity and even madness. Yet there also is a deep resistance to this powerful centrifugal force which is equally characteristic of modernism, a yearning for the opposite, for a line, for Ariadne's thread of melody, which attempts to hold things together even in the certain knowledge that – like Orpheus' quest for Eurydice – it will fail. Even though Orpheus' head was severed from his body, it

---

[4]   James McFarlane, 'The mind of modernism', in Malcolm Bradbury and James McFarlane (eds), *Modernism 1890–1930* (Harmondsworth: Penguin, 1976), 88.

still continued to sing. An avant-garde stance does not preclude retaining links with tradition: although Orpheus is cut off from the past, his remembrance of that past persists. (Indeed, his memory is all that he has.) A hesitant narrative emerges through the work's many disruptions; traditional forms and operatic types are continually evoked; the sketches reveal an obsessive quest after compositional order that acts as a countervailing force to the discontinuities of text and drama. Modernism explores the interface between a fractured tradition and a speculative progress.

Yet *The Mask of Orpheus* also suggests the possibility of interpretation in terms that move beyond modernity. The multiple identities of the principal characters, who, being both mythical and masked, are 'mere' representations; the simultaneous retelling of many versions of the myth where no one story takes priority; the concern with the re-presentation of extant materials rather than with the crafting of new ones; the absence of a linear narrative or of a single, narrative vantage-point; the absence, indeed, of any objective sense of reality; the deferral of linguistic meaning (most notably in the invention of Orphic); the celebration of technology for its own sake rather than as a symbol of progress; the collapsing, by the end, of past and future into some kind of ahistorical present – all these facets point towards a postmodern frame of reference. In part, this locates *Orpheus* in its time (Jean-François Lyotard's seminal *The Postmodern Condition*, for example, with its questioning of grand narratives, appeared in 1979); in part, it helps to contextualize one of the work's important themes of the constructed and contingent nature of events and identities. This is not to contradict the work modernist concerns, enumerated above; rather, it highlights the fact that, at the end of the twentieth century, modernism had become decentred and disempowered as a cultural project, that modernism persisted as just one possibility among many. Were it not for the fact that it imposes an inappropriately linear narrative on the work, we might even think of *The Mask of Orpheus* as charting a move away from the modern (Acts I and II) towards the postmodern (Act III), from the formalist towards the contextual, from identity (however fractured) towards representation. Orpheus' progress mirrors that of twentieth-century man.

Of Lateness

Modernism is a symptom of the decline of modernity. Modernist art speaks of the break-up, of the losses of the late-modern era, as much as it looks to the future. Via nostalgia the modernist dwells on this loss; in so doing she or he keeps alive its image as a critique of the present. Adorno recognized this in late Beethoven.[5] After Adorno, Edward Said has spoken of Beethoven's late compositions as being about 'lost totality', and has stated that the figure of Beethoven 'seems to inhabit the late

---

[5] Theodor W. Adorno, *Beethoven: the Philosophy of Music*, ed. Rolf Tiedeman, tr. Edmund Jephcott (Cambridge: Polity, 1998), esp. chaps 9–11.

works as a lamenting personality'.[6] A late style, Said argues, is variously characterized by apartness, exile, anachronism, alienation, a melancholic world-weariness, intransigence, difficulty, unresolved contradiction. In the hands of Birtwistle and Zinovieff the lamenting Orpheus personifies the late-modern condition.

Of Myth and Ritual

> In the first half of this century it was possible for artists like Stravinsky, Eliot and Strauss to deal with myth on terms of familiarity. Birtwistle, on the other hand, shows us something alien, even barbaric, but terribly important. Or the comparison might be made with other times in operatic history when a new version of the Orpheus legend was called up to answer a new vision not only of opera but also of the nature of the self: Birtwistle's work is nothing less. [7]

Myth has been important for modernists because it engages, *inter alia*, with memory and symbol, with psychology and identity. The need for myth has grown in inverse proportion to the decline in the status of religion. In an age of brutality, myth helps us to understand. Orpheus especially – man and god, victim and artist – speaks to the twentieth century through his laments. Music ritualizes these laments; in *The Mask of Orpheus*, music functions as a mask in universalizing Orpheus' laments. Birtwistle's music, built in large part by means of varied repetition, represents ritual. But by Act III the music has *become* ritual. Via the electronic projection and movement of sound throughout the performing space, the audience is not just a witness to but also a participant in the ritual. As Catherine Bell writes, ritual is 'the means by which collective beliefs and ideas are simultaneously generated, experienced and affirmed as real by the community. Hence, ritual is the means by which individual perception and behavior are socially appropriated or conditioned.'[8] And for Claude Lévi-Strauss, music and myth parallel each other in that both demand to be apprehended 'as a totality': 'the basic meaning of the myth is not conveyed by the sequence of events but … by bundles of events even though these events appear at different moments in the story'.[9] In *The Mask of Orpheus* it is through music, not narrative, that the myth of Orpheus is ritually refashioned for the late twentieth century.

---

[6]   Edward W. Said, *On Late Style: Music and Literature against the Grain* (London: Bloomsbury, 2006), 13, 11.

[7]   Paul Griffiths, review of premiere of *The Mask of Orpheus* in *The Times* (23 May 1986); repr. in Griffiths, *The Substance of Things Heard: Writings about Music* (Rochester, NY: University of Rochester Press, 2005), 325.

[8]   Catherine Bell, *Ritual Theory, Ritual Practice* (New York: Oxford University Press, 1992), 20.

[9]   Claude Lévi-Strauss, *Myth and Meaning* (London: Routledge, 1978), 40.

Of Masks and Identity

The modernist subject is one in crisis. The violence meted out to the subject in the twentieth century has, at times, appeared to place its very existence under threat. This loss of a sense of self, this fracturing of identity, has become the subject matter of much modernist art. Examples from early in the century abound: the primitive barbarism of Picasso's *Les demoiselles d'Avignon* and Stravinsky's *The Rite of Spring* are exemplars. Adorno's account of the latter, for instance, in terms of dehumanization and the 'liquidation of the victim', is indicative of a wider understanding of the violence to the individual represented in modernist art.[10] The machine was one symbol of this dehumanization; another was the mask. Drawing on a range of ancient, folk and ethnic sources, the mask in much early twentieth-century art symbolized, variously, a universalism, collectivism and dehumanization. An important document is the journal *The Mask* (whose first issue appeared in March 1908), established by Edward Gordon Craig, whose ideas on puppets and masks as the means by which to achieve a non-naturalistic theatre were extremely influential. Craig dubbed his new masked performer the 'Über-marionette' (after Nietzsche), who 'will not compete with life – rather will go beyond it'. Each 'Über-marionette' employed 'multiple masks, reinforcing its symbolic function and further destroying both any sense of the actor's own subjectivity and any suggestion of realism'.[11] Glenn Watkins sums up the significance of the mask for early modernists:

> The mask was to assume an extraordinary role in the theatre of numerous countries during the 1920s and, beyond the African connection, was legitimized through its recall of the tradition of Greek theatre, No drama, and the early plays of the Expressionists. Meyerhold, Craig, Appia, Lermontov, Kaiser, O'Neill, Eliot, Cocteau, and a host of dramatists, who sensed the power of the mask's attendant anonymity and universality, participated in its revival. With them, Léger acknowledged the potential of the mask to transcend the individual and to suggest human universals. Masks were also capable of striking a sense of terror and awe ....[12]

This is played out in *The Mask of Orpheus*. The mask present in the very title indicates the allegorical nature of the work as a whole. (There are echoes, too, of the Elizabethan and Jacobean masque, a courtly entertainment combining dance, speech and song in the context of a central allegorical idea.) As Peter Hall has observed, the

---

[10]   See Theodor W. Adorno, *Philosophy of New Music*, tr. Robert Hullot-Kentor (Minneapolis: University of Minnesota Press, 2006).

[11]   W. Anthony Sheppard, *Revealing Masks: Exotic Influence and Ritualized Performance in Modernist Music Theater* (Berkeley: University of California Press, 2001), 30.

[12]   Glenn Watkins, *Pyramids at the Louvre: Music, Culture, and Collage from Stravinsky to the Postmodernists* (Cambridge, MA: Belknap, 1994), 120.

'Greek stage itself … is a mask',[13] in that the main action takes place off stage. The same can be said of *Orpheus* in that little takes place on the stage, and what we see is often unconnected with the story being told. The majority of events are recalled in memory or dream. The libretto proposes actions, décor and *dramatis personae* that are symbolic: 'A number of stage instructions are given which, while seeming very precise, are allegorical' (libretto, p. 2). All this reinforces the formal, mythical, non-narrative nature of the work: in other words, its meaning lies beyond the story that is being (re)told. It focuses our attention on the centrality of the music.

The wearing of masks by the principal stage characters is crucial. The masks formalize; they universalize; they direct our attention away from individual character towards wider (collective) issues. This is not to say that the work is without expression, but the masks inevitably generate a sense of alienation or estrangement. This is necessary in a work dealing with such deep emotions. Their literal depiction would be, literally, unbearable. As Peter Hall – a crucial influence on Birtwistle – puts it, the use of masks 'is in every case an attempt to know the unknowable, to experience the unspeakable and to enact the repulsive'.[14] In this context music, too, appears to function like a mask. The 'terror and awe' of the climax of Act II could only be represented via a mask. This is the moment when Orpheus' sense of self reaches its crisis point. The death of Orpheus, the violent annihilation of a particular subject, is made universal by the wearing of a mask. But the mask also dehumanizes. We witness the death with horrified fascination. The mask reveals the proximity of the human and the sub-human.

Of Loss, Mourning and Melancholy

The Mask of Orpheus is about the pathology of mourning. There are no external events; the drama takes place in the mind of one modern person. That person is given the name Orpheus, that is, he adopts the mask of Orpheus, but it is not actually about a historical figure with that name. It is a study in the tragic, psychological consequences of loss (a key characteristic of melancholia first identified by Freud). By the time we reach the end of Act III we realize that it is an allegory on loss – the losses both personal and collective of the twentieth century.

What is the object of loss? Firstly, of course, Eurydice. Orpheus' grief echoes down the ages. What makes his sorrow all the more painful is the self-knowledge that it is his own weakness in loving her too much that has resulted in her loss. If only he had not looked back … In his second Song of Failure, sung at the end of Act II, Orpheus recognizes the failure of his heroic journey, and the failure of his own will. Orpheus' compulsive repetition of the desire to retrieve his lover was well understood by Freud: 'where the predisposition to obsessive neurosis is present, the consequence

---

13   Hall, *Exposed by the Mask*, 24.
14   Ibid., 25.

of ambivalence gives mourning a pathological shape and forces it in the form of self-reproaches for having been oneself responsible for the loss of the love-object, of having wanted that loss'.[15] The repeating structures of *Orpheus* reflect this.

It is insightful to interpret Orpheus' Act II journey in terms of the five stages of personal grief.[16] The act begins with a reminder of Eurydice's death in the Time Shift. Orpheus' first reaction is one of *denial*, a refusal to accept the fact of her death, and he thus embarks (or so he dreams) on his quest to retrieve her. The dominant emotion of the early arches is *anger*, as Orpheus vents his fury both on those around him and on himself. In the course of his journey, by means of his music and words, Orpheus *bargains* with those who stand in his way, even with the awesome trio of Hades, Persephone and Hecate (not realizing that they are only projections of himself and Eurydice). Eventually, in the fear, terror, sadness and misery of *depression*, he is confronted with the reality of his situation, that he cannot retrieve Eurydice from the dead, that he has only been dreaming. This leads, finally, to a realization and (partial) *acceptance*, a letting-go of his emotional attachment. The open fifths speak of his desolation and despondency. He sings his Song of Failure and then hangs himself. As far back as about the second century BC, Aristotle (or one of his followers) had noted the 'prevalence [among melancholics] of suicide by hanging amongst the young'.[17] And the handling of loss in *The Mask of Orpheus* finds striking parallels in the contemporary work of Julia Kristeva, who, following Freud, comments that the sadness of mourning and the stupor of melancholy share 'intolerance for object loss and the signifier's failure to insure a compensating way out of the states of withdrawal in which the subject takes refuge to the point of inaction … or even suicide'.[18]

But Act II also has collective resonances. Written during the First World War, Freud's 'Timely reflections on war and death' had considered the disillusion engendered by war, when civilization collapses to reveal 'only the most primitive, the oldest and most brutal psychical attitudes'.[19] These savage, primeval forces are revealed at the climax of Act II. It is, then, of the collapse of civilized man that *The Mask of Orpheus* also speaks, and it is this failure of modern culture that Orpheus laments. Tradition recedes; the past is seen as if through a fractured lens – aria can

---

[15]   Sigmund Freud, 'Mourning and melancholia' [written 1915, published 1917], in *On Murder, Mourning and Melancholia*, tr. Shaun Whiteside (London: Penguin, 2005), 211.

[16]   As first defined by Elisabeth Kübler-Ross, *On Death and Dying* (New York: Macmillan, 1969).

[17]   Aristotle [or a follower of Aristotle], *Problems* [*c.*2nd century BC], repr. in Jennifer Radden (ed.), *The Nature of Melancholy: from Aristotle to Kristeva* (New York: Oxford University Press, 2000), 57

[18]   Julia Kristeva, 'A counterdepressant', from *Black Sun: Depression and Melancholy* [1987], repr. in Radden (ed.), *The Nature of Melancholy*, 337.

[19]   Sigmund Freud, 'Timely reflections on war and death' [1915], in *On Murder, Mourning and Melancholia*, 182.

only enact memory. The consequence is a profoundly pessimistic melancholy, which infuses the entire work. Indeed, melancholy is revealed as the dominant temperament of the twentieth century. It is only through lament that we can begin to come to terms with the horrors of that century. Birtwistle confesses to having a 'melancholy state of mind'.[20] And melancholia is a strain that runs right through his music, from his earliest to his most recent works. Birtwistle's music occupies a world of shadows, a place in which the composer is able to comment on the tragic losses of late-modern culture. Like Orpheus, he chooses to linger on what has been lost rather than to take solace in an imagined future: *in darkness let me dwell.*

Of Nostalgia, Memory and Alienation

At the heart of the Orpheus story is an act of looking back, a decidedly modern action. Nostalgia – a term coined in the late seventeenth century from the Greek *nostos*, meaning 'return home', and *algia*, 'longing' – is 'a longing for a home that no longer exists or has never existed'. The sentiment of nostalgia, writes Svetlana Boym, 'the mourning of displacement and temporal irreversibility, is at the very core of the modern condition'.[21] Orpheus longs to return to Eurydice, to reverse time; his laments speak of his recognition of his displacement from the past, his recognition that the wholeness he desires can never be achieved. His nostalgia takes refuge in memory: 'I remember', he sings repeatedly. The nostalgic Orpheus is displaced, dislocated. This is also the predicament of late-modern man, for whom Orpheus acts as spokesman. Nostalgia finds its mode of expression, once again, in melancholy.

'Modern nostalgia is a mourning for the impossibility of mythical return, for the loss of an enchanted world', writes Boym.[22] For Orpheus, this enchanted world is that place of idealized love before the death of Eurydice or of innocent youth as an Argonaut. It is deeply ironic that this nostalgic need to look back was precipitated by another act of looking back. Yet the longed-for Arcadian landscape, the 'realm of perfect bliss and beauty, a dream of ineffable happiness', is only a chimera. Arcady is tempered with an air of 'sweetly sad' melancholy.[23] *Et in Arcadia ego*: death is even in Arcadia. Dislocated, alienated, late-modern man looks back to a prelapsarian moment of wholeness, of stasis, knowing both that return is impossible and that he is himself responsible for the loss of innocence. These ideas are poignantly captured in the Act I Duet of Love, which presents us with a melancholic pastoral landscape in which the past – in the form of aria, melody – fragments, in which even

---

[20]   David Beard, 'Beauty and the beast: a conversation with Sir Harrison Birtwistle', *Musical Times*, 1902 (Spring 2008), 17.

[21]   Svetlana Boym, *The Future of Nostalgia* (New York: Basic Books, 2001), pp. xiii, xvi.

[22]   Ibid., 8.

[23]   Erwin Panofsky, '*Et in Arcadia ego*: Poussin and the elegiac tradition', in *Meaning and the Visual Arts* (Harmondsworth: Peregrine, 1970), 342.

the recollection of love is coloured by the knowledge that it has already been lost. Nostalgia is the yearning for what cannot be. All that is left is memory. Yet memory distorts. The alienation of the modern subject is complete. The ultimate consequence is silence, with which *The Mask of Orpheus* ends.

Of Time

> Time present and time past
> Are both perhaps present in time future
> And time future contained in time past.
> If all time is eternally present
> All time is unredeemable. ...
>
> At the still point of the turning world. Neither flesh nor fleshless;
> Neither from nor towards ... [24]

T.S. Eliot eloquently captures a fundamental modernist attitude, one that represents the collapse of the old certainty of 'time's arrow'. The modernist, like Orpheus, looks both forwards and backwards, yet is locked in some kind of eternal present. Time appears to turn back on itself, to repeat itself, to stand still. Time can be expressed only through memory. Time and temporality are, according to Fredric Jameson, nothing less than 'the great high modernist thematics, the elegiac mysteries of *durée* and memory'; their waning, he argues, is symptomatic of postmodernism which is 'dominated by categories of space rather than by categories of time'.[25]

'I remember.' *The Mask of Orpheus* is full of echoes, distortions, fragments, dreams, time shifts and memories. Nothing is heard for the first time. Occasionally a melody appears to assert itself unequivocally in the present, but this too, we come to realize, is only a memory. This is the central tragedy of Orpheus and of modernism.

At the end of *The Mask of Orpheus* we reach the still point of the turning world. There is neither 'from' nor 'towards'. Behind and beyond the mask of Orpheus lies eternal stasis. Clock time – the mechanical, the technological, modernity itself – is transcended and we experience a realm of 'pure' time or duration, Bergson's *durée*. Eventually myth, memory, identity, all decay. Unlike the end of Act II, the end of Act III does not offer a vision of despair, even in the face of the crises of modernity. In the seasons and the tides, the world continues to turn; one life is extinguished but the cycle of life continues. A mysterious *élan vital* persists, heard in the sound of buzzing bees.

---

[24] T.S. Eliot, 'Burnt Norton' [1935], from *Four Quartets*, in T.S. Eliot, *Collected Poems 1909–1962* (London: Faber& Faber, pbk ed., 1974), 189, 191.

[25] Fredric Jameson, *Postmodernism, or, the Cultural Logic of Late Capitalism* (London: Verso, 1991), 16.

Chapter 6
Looking Back
Interviews with Peter Zinovieff
and Harrison Birtwistle

Peter Zinovieff

[Jonathan Cross] *When did you first meet Harry Birtwistle?*[1]

[Peter Zinovieff] Late '60s. 1968, was it? He came to me because he wanted to use electronics. I think the BBC had sent him to see me in Putney, and he was living in Twickenham. Later, he had a fire in his house, so he and his family came to live in my house for I think five months. Our children became like cousins. That was a very important sealing of our relationship. At that time I also had a house in Raasay and we used to spend lots of time up there, all the holidays. Later Harry went to live on Raasay in a house he'd bought from me.

So you collaborated in the '60s and early '70s on various electronic pieces at your Putney studio, and on Nenia: the Death of Orpheus. *At what stage did it become clear to you that you both wanted to work together on this big Orpheus piece?*

I can never quite remember. Originally *Orpheus* wasn't going to be *Orpheus*. It was first commissioned by Covent Garden as *Faust*. It was both our idea. I wrote a big libretto for *Faust*. It's in three parts and it's got three sub-divisions. It was a major effort to do it. But after it was finished we both decided that Orpheus would make a better legend.

Why?

It was more mythological. With Faust there were so many different stories. They were too near, too close, too ridiculous – steam engines and so on.

So it was really an idea looking for a subject matter?

---

[1]   This conversation with Peter Zinovieff took place on 24 October 2008 at his home in Cambridge.

Yes. *Faust* was the same sort of thing as *Orpheus*. But the *Faust* text was completely mad! My daughter Sofka[2] is called Eurydice so I was always rather keen on Orpheus. And also on Greece. I'd worked as a geologist in Cyprus instead of doing national service.

When did you first encounter Ovid?

I've known it since always. They're such good stories.

Do you read Greek and Latin?

Badly. You had to have Latin to get into Oxford in those days. I don't read Ancient Greek. But I know a bit of modern Greek.

What were your other sources?

I concentrated mainly on Ovid. As it wasn't meant to be exact, I'm sure I invented bits too, although perhaps that wasn't necessary. They are extraordinary stories, about how Orpheus died, about his skull being washed up.

And before Orpheus *you had written the text for* Nenia ...

... that was just a wild sort of poem. It came out of the blue really. It didn't have anything to do with *Orpheus*. It wasn't a study for that work.

Had you done anything like it before?

I wrote quite a lot of texts for Tristram Cary.[3] They weren't usually just plain texts: there was always another element – 'inside' and 'outside' texts, simultaneous things going on. When I was younger I used to write a huge amount – poetry, unfinished stories. I think my imagination was very fertile in text.

So what were your principal literary sources? What were you reading at the time?

---

[2]   Sofka Zinovieff (b. 1961) grew up 'in a house by the river Thames in Putney, where her father, Peter Zinovieff, had an electronic music studio. ... Several months a year were spent on the Isle of Raasay in the Inner Hebrides, which remains an influence and inspiration. ... Sofka moved to Greece in 2001 and lives by the sea outside Athens .... Her book *Eurydice Street: a Place in Athens* was published in 2004' (http://sofkazinovieff.com/biography.html; accessed 30 October 2008).

[3]   English composer (1925–2008), pioneer of electronic music in the UK, who established the first studio at the Royal College of Music in 1968. A co-founder of EMS with Zinovieff in 1969, he helped design and market the VCS3 synthesizer.

I used to love fishing. In Raasay there are a lot of wonderful lochs. Scottish trout fishing is a highly active sport, but whenever there was a pause I used to read the *Four Quartets* of Eliot. I've got a battered copy. For me the *Quartets* and fishing are always joined in my mind! Eliot is very important for me. I love Eliot. I think I've got all his books.

Eliot was much more important 40 years ago – he was much closer then. Young people now don't read Eliot in the awestruck way we did. There was no other poet who could put incomprehensible things in such a wonderful, acceptable form. I didn't mind it seeming meaningless when I first read it!

When you finally got to work on the Orpheus *text, how did that relationship work?*

It wasn't collaborative at all. I wrote the text. Harry loves being told what to do, even if he doesn't do it! So when it says '2 seconds of silence', that's not Harry saying I want two seconds of silence, it's me saying you have two seconds of silence here. It gave him a discipline. He followed the timings of Act II absolutely – he was in Raasay doing that. The tide structure of Act III, which I think is brilliant, is clear, but has never been shown. It's always been cut. It's very difficult to explain to people the tides, especially those who don't realize what tides do, that they get higher and lower.

How did your work in electronic music and with EMS feed into the early stages of the Orpheus *project?*

In the early stages it was, of course, an integral part, but in the end Harry went to IRCAM. EMS was basically a research lab. No composer who worked there paid to do so. The way in which we made money was to design and sell synthesizers, and any profit went into the studio. We got tricked into bad business in America and the whole thing gradually collapsed. The National Theatre took it over, but everything got put into the basement, where it wasn't looked after. So Harry had no choice but to go to IRCAM.

Now I think of it, I do believe it could have worked. We made some marvellous, primitive, complicated material with the computer, and sometimes the fluke of it gave absolutely wonderful sounds. Without very much intervention from me, just setting up the parameters in the right way, you could get these amazingly complicated sounds, which could not be written down.

I do remember going to look round Covent Garden to see where loudspeakers would go, which seemed rather forward when the piece hadn't been written.

Where did the idea for the Orphic language come from?

I don't know, but it was such fun, inventing a language! It does work. It does sound foreign, doesn't it? It certainly doesn't sound like a pretend English.

Looking back on The Mask of Orpheus *now, how do you see it?*

I don't think if I did it now I could allow myself the freedom to be so wild. My arrogance then was extraordinary, that I thought I had permission to do something so daring.

Harry wrote me a really nice letter once saying he was sure it was the best thing he would ever do. I think it is a very important piece of his.

Harrison Birtwistle

[Jonathan Cross] *How does* The Mask of Orpheus *now appear to you after all this time?*[4]

[Harrison Birtwistle] It's funny music, isn't it? [*Looking at score*] It's so Cubist, using blocks of music.

Does it now seem like music from elsewhere?

From another planet. I've just done another Orpheus piece, about Eurydice.[5] It's nothing like this!

How does your new piece treat the Orpheus story?

There's a moment in *The Mask of Orpheus* that has not been realized in production. The fundamental idea is that in the underworld the characters are all so-called puppets, which is a metaphor for some other sort of dramatic representation. They're not human any more. The gods are even bigger puppets and they only scream and shout and say incoherent things. Eurydice changes: she undergoes a metamorphosis into a puppet. When Orpheus goes down to look for her, he finds her as this puppet. I always had the idea that, as they travel back together, she would be slowly transformed into a child. It's a moment that I thought would be interesting to make into a piece in its own right – just that moment.

My new piece begins not very long before the moment when Orpheus turns, so the climax comes at the beginning, within three minutes. And then it's about Eurydice's journey back. Orpheus returns to the land of the living, singing off stage, while she travels deeper and deeper, in one direction only. There's another element too, where she becomes a chorus figure and speaks about herself as the character.

---

4   This conversation with Harrison Birtwistle took place on 28 November 2008 at his home in Mere, Wiltshire.

5   *The Corridor*, a 'scena' to a libretto by David Harsent, for soprano, tenor and six instruments, premiered at the Aldeburgh Festival in June 2009.

She's looking at herself. This is set apart by a different style of vocal delivery – speech that's notated. Eurydice appears behind the on-stage instrumentalists as if she is actually talking to these players, who answer her. I call them 'shades'. They become like characters and are a part of the piece, but they remain a very shadowy presence. It's a ritual.

I imagine something quite specific visually. In the theatre there's no such thing as close-up as there is in the cinema. *The Corridor* is an attempt to make a sort of chamber theatre, which has the same relationship to opera as a string quartet has to the orchestra. You can deal with a different order of detail because it's so much more intimate than grand opera.

It's very different from *The Mask of Orpheus*. *Orpheus* is quite radical, isn't it?

What do you mean by that?

It was a dramatic statement. I was aiming for a kind of Japanese theatre. *Orpheus* is a highly formalized piece, like Noh drama. I remember seeing Noh a long time ago in London when they had something called, I think, the World Theatre. It's impossible to deal with as a Westerner: it's so foreign. It lacks all the obvious exuberance of other world theatre, like that of Africa or South America. It's high culture; it's something very rarefied. It's a kind of religion. I think Noh theatre influenced *Orpheus* more than I realized. *Orpheus* is quite abstract: there are no tunes.

Well, I disagree! There are some beautiful melodies in places, such as the love duet in Act I.

But they're not there consciously. You can write tunes despite yourself. I have this obsession now with endless melody. That's what I'm doing in *The Corridor*.

How much input did you have into the first production in 1986?

None. It was very brave of David Freeman to take it on. It seemed imponderable to most people. When you look at the libretto you don't know where to start. You should start with the music; later, if you want the subtext, then you go to the libretto. In some ways the text doesn't matter. They are poems of the music. It's called a mask: it's something you understand as a sort of dumb show, because it uses a myth we should all be familiar with. It enabled me to deal with the essential elements of the narrative as if they were music. Consequently there are all these blocks, and it doesn't matter what order they come in.

Orpheus is a totally impractical piece. It makes no concession to theatrical practicality. It just says, 'do what you can with it'; it's much more open to interpretation than the surface formalism suggests. When you read the text, it seems absolutely precise, but how it should be realized is something quite different, I think.

How did you deal with the text, when it's not clear how it relates to the story being told?

Well, that's it: it doesn't relate to the story. I don't think that matters. You could put another text into it … which is how it began, as *Faust*. I didn't get anywhere with that. I never set any of it. I found *Orpheus* more potent. It's also a myth about the power of music, a story told about music in music. And it's also about something that's given and something that's taken away. I think that's interesting, and that's why I keep coming back to it. You only need one myth in a lifetime – the others are all sideshows!

Well, some of those 'sideshows' also appear in this piece as the Passing Clouds …

Yes, that's a way of slashing it, of breaking it up, so that it becomes about something else through interruption.

How did these electronic components come about? You made the tapes with Barry Anderson in Paris. Did you have a clear idea of what you wanted from the start?

It was very difficult to get into a position where the electronic contribution was primitive enough. I didn't want something that sounded like 'hi-tech' music. It needed to function as an entity in itself but it also needed to belong within the sound-world of the piece. There are also other elements called 'veils', auras, but they're just cosmetic, an enrichment, because there are no strings. These auras should be all around you in the theatre.

Why are there no strings?

I just wanted plucked instruments. In any case, the strings take up too much room for what they contribute! It's not in the nature of the piece, where the rhythmic, percussive elements predominate. What would the strings bring to this? They're too lyrical.

    I wrote a cello piece a few years ago [*Lied*]. I didn't try to do it in a romantic way, but also I didn't know how to escape the romantic associations of the instrument. How do you get away from the way the instrument speaks? In the end, I don't think you should try. But you shouldn't indulge yourself either. In *Lied* I explored a dialogue between elements.

How are the six Passing Clouds and Allegorical Flowers structured?

They were all fully notated, rhythmically. I don't know where the scores are now. Barry and I worked on them together. It took a long time. They're impossible rhythms for a human, but for a machine they're easy.

Those pieces sound to me as if they're all versions of the same thing.

They are. There are three lyrical ones and three violent ones. I'd like to improve them: I don't think they're fast enough. You could easily make them faster today without changing the pitch. I'd speed the violent ones up to give them more nervous energy.

And what about the language spoken by Apollo and Orpheus?

We were searching for a way of making a primitive voice and we stumbled across the technicians making the CHANT program at IRCAM. It struck me that that was exactly what we wanted. There was a direct analogy between Orpheus trying to speak, trying to be coherent, and these people at IRCAM actually trying to make this voice. We were only able to use about six words, primitive utterances like 'RUFI'.

The beginning of *Orpheus* should be like somebody being born and learning to speak. In the last Act I imagine Orpheus struggling to speak. It should be a real virtuoso effort, like the Minotaur in my last opera, straining to be coherent. The ending could be wonderful, but it's never been done, with the head floating away, singing, representing an idea of the eternal.

So, who is Orpheus?

Me! Orpheus is a melancholic, and so am I. Also I think there's something eternal about him. The story is as relevant now as it ever was.

Can you remember when you first encountered Orpheus?

In the *Georgics*. They had a resonance.

And you had the idea of doing a TV Orpheus *with Peter Hall?*

That's when the whole idea started. Cyril Bennett at London Weekend Television asked if I wanted to write an opera for TV. Peter Hall and I were going to make it as a film. Then he went to Covent Garden and suggested I did the piece for the Royal Opera. Then he left Covent Garden, and we were going to do it for Glyndebourne, but it turned out that Glyndebourne wasn't big enough, and so the piece moved to ENO. There was never enough money. If it hadn't been for Jocelyn Herbert saying that she would do the piece under any circumstances, even if there was no money at all, then I don't think it would have happened. That's the journey of the piece. I gave up writing in the middle of it. I didn't want a white elephant. Only when they said they'd definitely do it did I start writing again.

What was it like working with Peter Zinovieff?

The text was entirely his. It's a piece of 'computer-ese', really, in the formal way that it's cut up. I think the structures of the arches and the tides is a brilliant idea, but I also think the first act would have been better if it had had a similar structuring device. The arithmetical aspect of the structures attracted me, because they seem random, outside my control, something given. You make a machine and you have to go along with it … and I did.

For me what is so wonderful about Act II is its continuity that cuts across the individual arches. While respecting the verse structure of the Song of Magic, there is an incredible inevitability about the way the music unfolds across the entire act.

Yes. You keep adding ingredients and you wonder how you can possibly make it more intense. It's overwhelming at one point, isn't it?

You used to talk about such situations in terms of cantus and continuum.

It's the same idea. You see Orpheus the Man singing, and at the same time you see him as the Hero moving into the underworld. It's a potent idea.

How did your experience at the National – and particularly your work with Peter Hall on the Oresteia *– change the way you thought about the relationship between music and theatre in* Orpheus?

I think I felt a very long way away from the world of *Orpheus* that I had already created [in Acts I and II], and the world of the National Theatre. There seemed no connection with what I did at the National.

And what was it like, returning to Orpheus *after a long gap?*

I remember going back into it. It was like discovering the Dead Sea Scrolls and trying to decipher them. It wasn't simply a question of picking up where you left off. It was a terrible business, I remember. It was a real struggle.

Orpheus is the kind of piece you do early in your career. That's why I think it's a very radical piece.

Do you see it as a very necessary stage in your own development?

Yes.

And are you still proud of it?

Well, I don't think my dream has been realized. That's what I feel. I'm still waiting.

Appendix A

The Passing Clouds of Abandon and the Allegorical Flowers of Reason

First Passing Cloud of Abandon (Act I, scene 1): The Story of Dionysus[1]

The body of Dionysus was torn to shreds by the Titans. The pieces were boiled in a cauldron and turned into a pomegranate tree. Nevertheless Rhea, his grandmother, was able to reconstitute him.

Second Passing Cloud of Abandon (Act I, scene 2): The Story of Lycurgas

Dionysus was nearly caught and killed by Lycurgas. Rhea drove Lycurgas mad. So much so that he chopped down and killed his own son, thinking that he was pruning a vine. The whole land grew barren in horror at his crime. His people led Lycurgas to Mt. Pangaeum where wild horses pulled his body apart.

First Allegorical Flower of Reason (Act I, scene 2): The Anemone

Despite Venus' warning, her beloved Adonis hunted a boar and was grievously wounded in the genitals. Venus vainly tried to save him. In sorrow she turned his blood into an anemone. The flower lasts a short time and its petals fall off easily in the wind that gave it its name.

Second Allegorical Flower of Reason (Act II, scene 3): The Hyacinth

As Apollo and the youth Hyacinth competed at the discus, Hyacinth was killed by the returning discus that Apollo had thrown. Despite all the God could do the boy died. Apollo changed him into the hyacinth with the mournful Greek characters 'AI-AI' marked on it to this day.

---

[1] Texts reproduced directly from Zinovieff, libretto, p. 47.

Third Allegorical Flower of Reason (Act III, scene 2): The Lotus

Beautiful Dryope was feeding her infant at her breast by the edge of a pool. She picked some flowers and saw, to her horror, blood fall from them. She had not known that Lotus, a nymph, had changed herself into the flowers to escape from Priapus' lust. Dryope prayed to the water nymphs and tried to leave but she was slowly transformed into a lotus tree. Her husband and father protected the tree from animals and allowed her son to play under the shade of what had been his mother.

Third Passing Cloud of Abandon (Act III, scene 3): The Story of Pentheus

Pentheus disliked the dissolute appearance of Dionysus. Dionysus sent him mad so that while he thought that he was tying up Dionysus, he was actually tying up a bullock. The Maenads tore the bullock to pieces and as Pentheus tried to stop them they tore him to pieces too. It was his own mother who wrenched off his head.

Appendix B
Musical Cuts

The only complete performances of the work to date have all entailed substantial cuts to Acts I and III. (The careful proportions and musical continuity of Act II demand its being presented complete.) These cuts are also to be found on the CD recording of the work. They are detailed here.

The necessity for these cuts emerged at a relatively late stage in the preparation of the first production. The work went into rehearsal with three 'learning sessions' for the chorus in late February 1986. The first full orchestra and chorus rehearsal took place on 13 March, and the first production rehearsal on 17 March. An internal ENO memorandum of 21 February 1986 gave the first warning that the running time might exceed four hours. A letter from the managing director, Peter Jonas, to Birtwistle dated 3 March made clear that 'it must not be longer than 4 hours. ... We must take this deadly seriously.' The net cost of the production was exceptionally high, and the managing director was acutely aware of the need to contain and, where possible, reduce costs. If it overran the four-hour limit, then union rules dictated heavy additional payments to performers and stage crew, and it was imperative that this situation was avoided. Cuts were therefore demanded. Although the composer still regrets the effect this had on the overall proportions of the work, at the time he recognized he had little choice. A company memo from Peter Jonas of 10 March 1986 reported that 'Harry welcomes any cuts that are deemed necessary during rehearsals.'[1]

Act I

Scene 1: just before fig. 30–just before fig. 39, pp. 29–41

Cut directly from the end of the first Conversation of Silence (The Spontaneous Remark) ('I will!') to the end of the first Silence (Silence in Vow) ('I will!'), thereby omitting the first and second extensions of the Love Duet, the second exchange and the first Complicated Question.

---

[1]   All documents in ENO Archive.

Scene 2: figs 64–5, p. 70 and figs 69–70, p. 75

A small number of bars of instrumental music and a signal of Apollo are twice omitted during Aristaeus' recitative.

Scene 3: figs 85–104, pp. 90–108

Cut from the start of the second Immortal Dance (Funeral Dance) (verse 1) to the start of the third exchange, thereby omitting much of the Funeral Dance, the second Complicated Question, the first two statements of the first Hysterical Aria, the fourth and fifth extensions of the first Love Duet and the first Spoken Argument.

Act III

Scenes 1/2: after fig. 13–fig. 43, pp. 268–300

A very substantial cut from the start of the Fishing Net response at the very end of scene 1 to the Oar response that precedes the third Dream (The Fulfilment), thereby omitting in entirety the first two statements of sequence 3 and the first two exchanges (sequence 4). As a consequence, the third Allegorical Flower is shifted from before fig. 28 (p. 283) to before fig. 48 (p. 306).

Scene 2: figs 48–52, pp. 306–12

Cut from the start of the Fishing Net response to the beginning of Orpheus' third Song of Magic, thereby omitting the first presentation of the Cry of Memory (sequence 1).

Scene 3: before and after fig. 77, pp. 339–40

A small cut, omitting an electronic signal and the Bird Skull response.

Scene 3: figs 108–10, pp. 369–73

A small cut from the end of the final Passing Cloud to the response (Fossil Shell) that precedes the final exchange, thereby omitting periods of stasis when only the Aura is sounding, a statement of the Rockfall response and a fragment of the Love Duet.

Appendix C
The Mask of Orpheus:
World Premiere Production

English National Opera (London Coliseum), 21 May 1986

Orpheus	The Man	Philip Langridge *tenor*
	The Hero	Graham Walters *mime*
	The Myth/Hades	Nigel Robson *tenor*
Euridice	The Woman	Jean Rigby *mezzo-soprano*
	The Heroine	Zena Dilke *mime*
	The Myth/Persephone	Ethna Robinson *mezzo-soprano*
Aristaeus	The Man	Tom McDonnell *baritone*
	The Hero	Robert Williams *mime*
	The Myth/Charon	Rodney Macann *bass baritone*
The Oracle of the Dead/Hecate		Marie Angel *soprano*
The Troupe of Ceremony/ Judges of the Dead	The Caller	Richard Angas *bass*
	First Priest	Mark Curtis *tenor*
	Second Priest	John Kitchiner *baritone*
	Third Priest	Richard Suart *baritone*
The Three Women/Furies	First Woman	Janis Kelly *soprano*
	Second Woman	Kate McCarney *mezzo-soprano*
	Third Woman	Tamsin Dives *mezzo-soprano*
The Troupe of the Passing Clouds		Ian Cameron, Linda Coggin, Michael Knapp, Mollie Guilfoyle, Peter Neathey, Marcus Pearman, Kirsten Soar *mimes*
Conductors		Elgar Howarth, Paul Daniel
Electronic Material and Sound Diffusion		Barry Anderson
Director		David Freeman
Designer		Jocelyn Herbert
Lighting		Andy Phillips
Sound Engineer		Philip Clifford

Bibliography

Abbate, Carolyn, *In Search of Opera* (Princeton: Princeton University Press, 2001)

Adlington, Robert, *The Music of Harrison Birtwistle* (Cambridge: Cambridge University Press, 2000)

Adorno, Theodor W., *Philosophy of Modern Music* [1948], tr. A.G. Mitchell and W.G. Blomster (London: Sheed and Ward, 1973). New translation as *Philosophy of New Music*, tr. Robert Hullot-Kentor (Minneapolis: University of Minnesota Press, 2006)

_____, *Quasi una Fantasia: Essays on Modern Music*, tr. Rodney Livingstone (London: Verso, 1992)

_____, *Beethoven: the Philosophy of Music*, ed. Rolf Tiedeman, tr. Edmund Jephcott (Cambridge: Polity, 1998)

Albright, Daniel, *Stravinsky: the Music Box and the Nightingale* (New York: Gordon and Breach, 1989)

_____, *Untwisting the Serpent: Modernism in Music, Literature, and Other Arts* (Chicago: University of Chicago Press, 2000)

Apollonius Rhodius, *The Argonautica*, tr. R.C. Seaton (London: Heinemann, 1912)

Aristotle [or a follower of Aristotle], *Problems* [*c*.2nd century BC], repr. in Jennifer Radden (ed.), *The Nature of Melancholy: from Aristotle to Kristeva* (New York: Oxford University Press, 2000), 55–60

Babbitt, Milton et al., 'Brave new worlds', *Musical Times*, 1816 (June 1994), 330–37 (Birtwistle, 334–6)

Beard, David, 'An analysis and sketch study of the early instrumental music of Sir Harrison Birtwistle (*c*.1957–77)', DPhil dissertation, University of Oxford, 2000

_____, 'Beauty and the beast: a conversation with Sir Harrison Birtwistle', *Musical Times*, 1902 (Spring 2008), 9–25

Bell, Catherine, *Ritual Theory, Ritual Practice* (New York: Oxford University Press, 1992)

Bell, Michael, 'The metaphysics of Modernism', in Michael Levinson (ed.), *The Cambridge Companion to Modernism* (Cambridge: Cambridge University Press, 1999), 9–32

Berger, Karol, 'Time's arrow and the advent of musical modernity', in Karol Berger and Anthony Newcomb (eds), *Music and the Aesthetics of Modernity: Essays* (Cambridge, MA: Harvard University Press, 2005), 3–22

_____, *Bach's Cycle, Mozart's Arrow: an Essay on the Origins of Musical Modernity* (Berkeley: University of California Press, 2007)

Berio, Luciano, Harrison Birtwistle et al, 'Whither opera? The composers speak out', *Opera*, 51/2 (February 2000), 164–73

[Birtwistle, Harrison,] *The Harrison Birtwistle Site*, http://www.braunarts.com/birtwistle/harry2.html (accessed 30 September 2008)

Boulez, Pierre, 'Stravinsky remains', in *Stocktakings from an Apprenticeship*, tr. Stephen Walsh (Oxford: Clarendon Press, 1991), 55–110

Boym, Svetlana, *The Future of Nostalgia* (New York: Basic Books, 2001)

Brown, Howard Mayer, 'Opera (i), II: origins', *Grove Music Online*, http://www.oxfordmusiconline.com/subscriber/article/grove/music/40726pg2 (accessed 30 September 2008)

Cave, Terence, *Recognitions: a Study in Poetics* (Oxford: Clarendon Press, 1988)

Clements, Andrew, '*The Mask of Orpheus*', *Opera*, 37/7 (July 1986), 851–7

Cone, Edward T., 'Stravinsky: the progress of a method', *Perspectives of New Music*, 1/1 (1962), 18–26

Courtney, Cathy (ed.), *Jocelyn Herbert: a Theatre Workbook* (London: Art Books International, 1993)

Cross, Jonathan, 'Lines and circles: on Birtwistle's *Punch and Judy* and *Secret Theatre*', *Music Analysis*, 13/2–3 (1994), 203–25

_____, *The Stravinsky Legacy* (Cambridge: Cambridge University Press, 1998)

_____, *Harrison Birtwistle: Man, Mind, Music* (London: Faber and Faber, 2000)

_____, 'The piano music of Harrison Birtwistle', liner notes for *The Axe Manual: Complete Piano Works* (London: Metronome Recordings, 2004, MET CD 1074), 3–14

Dearden, Ian, 'The electronic music of *The Mask of Orpheus*', liner note for *The Mask of Orpheus* (London: NMC Recordings, 1997, NMC D050), 15–16

Dolar, Mladen, 'If music be the food of love', in Slavoj Žižec and Mladen Dolar, *Opera's Second Death* (New York: Routledge, 2002), 1–102

Driver, Paul, 'Sir Harrison Birtwistle – ein Porträt / Sir Harrison Birtwistle – a Portrait', in Basil Rogger (ed.), *Roche Commissions: Sir Harrison Birtwistle* (Lucerne: Roche, 2004), 10–24. Repr. as 'Harrison Birtwistle', in *Theseus Games: a Celebration of Harrison Birtwistle*, programme book, ed. Lucy Breaks, for the Birtwistle Festival at the South Bank Centre, London (Oct–Nov 2004), 3–5

Fowler, Don, 'Pyramus, Thisbe, King Kong: Ovid and the presence of poetry', in *Roman Constructions: Readings in Postmodern Latin* (Oxford: Oxford University Press, 2000), 156–67

Freud, Sigmund, *On Murder, Mourning and Melancholia* [1917], tr. Shaun Whiteside (London: Penguin, 2005)

Friedman, J.B., *Orpheus in the Middle Ages* (Cambridge, MA: Harvard University Press, 1970)

Grass, Günther, 'On stasis in progress: variations on Albrecht Dürer's Melencolia I', in *From the Diary of a Snail*, tr. Ralph Manheim (London: Minerva, 1997 [first published in German in 1972; first English translation published 1974]), 286–310

Graves, Robert, *Greek Gods and Heroes* (New York: Dell Laurel-Leaf, 1960)

_____, *The Greek Myths* (London: Penguin, 1992 [1960])

Griffiths, Dai, 'On grammar schoolboy music', in Derek B. Scott (ed.), *Music, Culture, and Society: a Reader* (Oxford: Oxford University Press, 2000), 143–5

Griffiths, Paul, *New Sounds, New Personalities: British Composers of the 1980s* (London: Faber and Faber, 1985)

_____, *The Substance of Things Heard: Writings about Music* (Rochester, NY: University of Rochester Press, 2005)

Guthrie, W.K.C., *Orpheus and Greek Religion: a Study of the Orphic Movement* (Princeton: Princeton University Press, 1952)

Hall, Michael, *Harrison Birtwistle* (London: Robson, 1984)

_____, 'Composer and producer speak', in the programme book for the premiere performances of *The Mask of Orpheus*, ed. Nicholas John (May 1986) [no page numbers]

_____, 'The sanctity of the context: Birtwistle's recent music', *Musical Times*, 129/1 (January 1988), 14–16

_____, *Harrison Birtwistle in Recent Years* (London: Robson, 1998)

Hall, Peter, *Peter Hall's Diaries: the Story of a Dramatic Battle*, ed. John Goodwin (London: Oberon, 2000 [1983])

_____, *Making an Exhibition of Myself* (London, Oberon, 2000 [1993])

_____, *Exposed by the Mask: Form and Language in Drama* (London: Oberon, 2000)

Henze, Hans Werner, *Music and Politics: Collected Writings 1953–81*, tr. Peter Labanyi (London: Faber and Faber, 1982)

_____, *Bohemian Fifths: an Autobiography*, tr. Stewart Spencer (London: Faber and Faber, 1998)

Hoban, Russell, *The Moment under the Moment* (London: Picador, 1993)

Hobsbawm, Eric, *The Age of Extremes: the Short Twentieth Century, 1914–1991* (London: Abacus, 1995)

Howarth, Elgar, '*The Mask of Orpheus*', *Opera*, 37/5 (May 1986), 492–5

Jameson, Fredric, *Postmodernism, or, the Cultural Logic of Late Capitalism* (London: Verso, 1991)

Jankélévitch, Vladimir, *Music and the Ineffable*, tr. Carolyn Abbate (Princeton: Princeton University Press, 2003)

Kapp, Reinhard, 'Chronologisches Verzeichnis (in progress) der auf Orpheus (und/oder Eurydike) bezogenen oder zu beziehenden Opern, Kantaten, Instrumentalmusiken, literarischen Texte, Theaterstücke, Filme und historiographischen Arbeiten', www.musikgeschichte.at/kapp-orpheus.pdf (last updated 27 May 2007)

Kristeva, Julia, 'A counterdepressant', from *Black Sun: Depression and Melancholy* [1987], repr. in Jennifer Radden (ed.), *The Nature of Melancholy: from Aristotle to Kristeva* (New York: Oxford University Press, 2000), 335–43

Kübler-Ross, Elisabeth, *On Death and Dying* (New York: Macmillan, 1969)

Lévi-Strauss, Claude, *Myth and Meaning* (London: Routledge, 1978)

Lorraine, Ross [in conversation with Harrison Birtwistle], 'Territorial Rites 1', *Musical Times*, 1856 (October 1997), 4–8

_____, 'Territorial Rites 2', *Musical Times*, 1857 (November 1997), 12–16

MacGregor, Neil, 'Singing to generations yet to come', in Mark Pappenheim (ed.), *BBC Proms Guide 2003* (London: British Broadcasting Corporation, 2003), 5–8

McFarlane, James, 'The mind of modernism', in Malcolm Bradbury and James McFarlane (eds), *Modernism 1890–1930* (Harmondsworth: Penguin, 1976), 71–93

Mellers, Wilfrid, *The Masks of Orpheus: Seven Stages in the Story of European Music* (Manchester: Manchester University Press, 1987)

Messiaen, Olivier, *Traité de rythme, de couleur, et d'ornithologie (1949–1992)*, 7 vols (Paris: Leduc, 1994–)

Morgan, Tom, 'Birtwistle's *The Mask of Orpheus*', in Michael Finnissy and Roger Wright (eds), *New Music '87* (Oxford: Oxford University Press, 1987), 76–8

Osborne, Nigel, 'Orpheus in Paris', in programme book for premiere performances of *The Mask of Orpheus*, ed. Nicholas John (May 1986) [no page numbers]

Ovid [Publius Ovidius Naso], *Metamorphoses*, tr. A.D. Melville (Oxford: Oxford University Press, 1986)

Panofsky, Erwin, *Meaning and the Visual Arts* (Harmondsworth: Peregrine, 1970)

Petersen, Peter, 'Das Orpheus-Projekt von Hans Werner Henze und Edward Bond', in Claudia Maurer Zenk (ed.), *Der Orpheus-Mythos von der Antike bis zur Gegenwart* (Frankfurt am Main: Peter Lang, 2004), 133–67

Plato, *The Republic*, tr. Desmond Lee (Harmondsworth: Penguin, rev. ed. 1974)

Porter, Andrew, 'Another Orpheus sings', *The New Yorker* (23 June 1986), 84–8

Rilke, Rainer Maria, *Sonnets to Orpheus with Letters to a Young Poet*, tr. Stephen Cohn (Manchester: Carcanet, 2000)

Said, Edward W., *On Late Style: Music and Literature against the Grain* (London: Bloomsbury, 2006)

Sheppard, W. Anthony, *Revealing Masks: Exotic Influences and Ritualized Performance in Modernist Music Theater* (Berkeley: University of California Press, 2001)

Sternfeld, F.W., *The Birth of Opera* (Oxford: Clarendon Press, 1993)

Straus, Joseph, *Stravinsky's Late Music* (Cambridge: Cambridge University Press, 2001)

Stravinsky, Igor and Robert Craft, *Themes and Conclusions* (London: Faber and Faber, 1972)

_____, *Dialogues* (London: Faber and Faber, 1982)

Strunck, Oliver, *Source Readings in Music History* (New York: Norton, 1950)

Taylor, Michael, 'Narrative and musical structures in Harrison Birtwistle's *The Mask of Orpheus* and *Yan Tan Tethera*', in Hermann Danuser and Matthias Kassel (eds), *Musiktheater heute* (Mainz: Schott, 2003), 173–93

Tippett, Michael, *Those Twentieth Century Blues: an Autobiography* (London: Hutchinson, 1991)

Tooley, John, *In House: Covent Garden. 50 Years of Opera and Ballet* (London: Faber & Faber, 1999)

Virgil [Publius Virgilius Maro], *The Georgics*, tr. L. P. Wilkinson (London: Penguin, 1982)

Watkins, Glenn, *Pyramids at the Louvre: Music, Culture, and Collage from Stravinsky to the Postmodernists* (Cambridge, MA: Belknap, 1994)

Whittall, Arnold, '*Orpheus* – and after', *Musical Times*, 1865 (Winter 1998), 55–8

_____, 'The mechanisms of lament: Harrison Birtwistle's "Pulse Shadows" ', *Music and Letters*, 80/1 (1999), 86–102

_____, *Exploring Twentieth-Century Music: Tradition and Innovation* (Cambridge: Cambridge University Press, 2003)

_____, 'Henze's haunted sensibility', *Musical Times*, 1895 (Summer 2006), 5–15

Wintle, Christopher, 'A fine & private place', *Musical Times*, 1845 (November 1996), 5–8

Wright, Patrick, 'On melancholy and the humour of the night/Über die Melancholie und die Wesensart der Nacht', in Basil Rogger (ed.), *Roche Commissions: Sir Harrison Birtwistle* (Lucerne: Roche, 2004), 68–85. Repr. as 'On melancholy and the humour of the night', in *Theseus Games: a Celebration of Harrison Birtwistle*, programme book, ed. Lucy Breaks, for the Birtwistle Festival at the South Bank Centre, London (Oct–Nov 2004), 23–5

Zenck, Claudia Maurer, 'Maler, Dichter, Komponist – *Orpheus und Eurydike* von Oskar Kokoshka und Ernst Krenek', in Claudia Maurer Zenck (ed.), *Der Orpheus-Mythos von der Antike bis zur Gegenwart* (Frankfurt am Main: Peter Lang, 2004), 247–72.

Zinovieff, Peter, 'Electronic music diary summer 1976', *Bulletin of the Computer Arts Society* (May 1977), reproduced at http://members.tripod.com/werdav/vocpzino.htm (accessed 30 September 2008)

Žižec, Slavoj and Mladen Dolar, *Opera's Second Death* (New York: Routledge, 2002)

Index

References to illustrations and music examples are in **bold**.

ORDER FORM

For your discounted 3 disc set of the *Gramophone* Award winning *Mask of Orpheus* please fill in the details below and send to: NMC Recordings Ltd, Somerset House, Third Floor, South Wing, Strand, London, WC2R 1LA, UK

'*Unquestionably the greatest achievement by a British composer in our time. Now, with the arrival of this magnificent recording, there is at last a chance to explore it carefully ... the performance is beyond praise*' The Guardian

Including Jon Garrison, Peter Bronder, Jean Rigby, Anne-Marie Owens, Alan Opie, Omar Ebrahim and Marie Angel. BBC Symphony Orchestra, BBC Singers, Andrew Davis & Martyn Brabbins *conductors*

Special price: £15.99 + Postage & Packing   (usual price: £25.99)
Postage UK: free
Postage EUROPE 'standard': add £2.75
Postage REST OF WORLD 'standard': add £3.25

Name:
Address:
Address:
Postcode:
Tel:
Email:

I would like to receive monthly NMC e-newsletters   Yes ☐ No ☐

I enclose a cheque for £   (don't forget to add P&P)

Please debit my Visa/Mastercard/Switch:
Card no.
Issue no. (Switch)
Amount to debit:
Expiry date:
Security code (last 3 digits on reverse)
Cardholder's name:
Cardholder's signature:
Date:

www.nmcrec.co.uk   nmc@nmcrec.co.uk